PhantomJS Cookbook

Over 70 recipes to help boost the productivity of your
applications using real-world testing with PhantomJS

Rob Friesel

[PACKT]
PUBLISHING

open source
community experience distilled

BIRMINGHAM - MUMBAI

PhantomJS Cookbook

First published: June 2014

Production Reference: 1050614

Published by Packt Publishing Ltd.
Livery Place
35 Livery Street
Birmingham B3 2PB, UK.

ISBN 978-1-78398-192-2

www.packtpub.com

Cover Image by Poonam Nayak (pooh.graphics@gmail.com)

Credits

Author

Rob Friesel

Reviewers

Jamie Mason

Phil Sales

Ian Walter

Stéphane Wirtel

Commissioning Editor

Julian Ursell

Acquisition Editor

Nikhil Karkal

Content Development Editor

Manasi Pandire

Technical Editor

Nikhil Potdukhe

Copy Editors

Janbal Dharmaraj

Sayanee Mukherjee

Laxmi Subramanian

Project Coordinator

Danuta Jones

Proofreaders

Paul Hindle

Joanna McMahon

Indexers

Hemangini Bari

Tejal Soni

Production Coordinators

Conidon Miranda

Nilesh R. Mohite

Cover Work

Nilesh R. Mohite

About the Author

Rob Friesel is a senior user interface developer and 10-year veteran at Dealer.com, where he develops UI frameworks and toolkits for their enterprise platform. He blogs about and presents on a variety of technologies, but his first love is the front-end. He has contributed as a credited reviewer to several books on JavaScript and one on Clojure. He tweets at @founddrama and blogs at http://blog.founddrama.net/.

This book would not have been possible without the support and encouragement of so many people. I can't possibly name them all, but there are few who come instantly to mind: the editorial team at Packt Publishing, everyone at Dealer.com for listening to me ramble about this stuff, Jonathan Phillips for being my first JavaScript mentor, Mike Fogus for showing the way, Amy (my wife and partner-in-crime) for giving me the space, and my sons Holden and Emery for every little worthwhile distraction.

About the Reviewers

Jamie Mason is a consultant JavaScript engineer from the UK. Previously a senior engineer at BSkyB—one of the UK's largest media organizations—he now helps companies of all shapes and sizes with their JavaScript architecture, front-end performance, and more. He is the developer of the popular image optimization tool ImageOptim-CLI, and he tweets about all things front-end at `@fold_left`.

Phil Sales is a software development manager who has worked in this role for more than 10 years. He started and managed development and testing teams for various companies, mostly in the banking domain. Most of his projects have been web application oriented, with a Java/J2EE flavor. His latest endeavor involves starting up a Manila office for a UK-based software vendor, with development, testing, and support teams. He has previously reviewed the book *Getting Started with PhantomJS, Aries Beltran, Packt Publishing*.

I would like to thank Aries Beltran for getting me involved in reviewing books. I would also like to thank my wife, Reza and my two boys, Kevin and Sean, who I hope will learn how to code soon.

Ian Walter is a software developer and designer living in Boston, MA. He likes creating software solutions that balance functionality and design. He has worked on every step of the development process, from the design and mockup phase to the deployment and devops phase, but enjoys working on front-end development the most. He currently works as the Senior Full Stack Developer at `Flashnotes.com`, an online marketplace for students.

Stéphane Wirtel is a passionate developer interested in High Availability, Replication, and Distributed Systems. He is also a core developer of the OpenERP project for six years now, and a consultant for the High Availability of OpenERP and the SaaS architecture of OpenERP. He has been a Linux user for 15 years and has been working with Python for a decade. If your breakfast is composed of Redis, ZMQ, Riak, Flask, Salt, LLVM and Cpython, or Erlang and Golang, then you will want to discuss this with him.

Stéphane does the promotion of Python through the Python-FOSDEM event (`http://www.python-fosdem.org`) at Brussels. He is also a member of the Python Software Foundation and the Association Francophone of Python (AFPy). You can reach him via `http://wirtel.be` or via twitter `@matrixise`. The OpenERP company (`http://www.openerp.com`) is his current employer.

Stéphane is a technical reviewer of the books *Getting Started with PhantomJS, Aries Beltran, Packt Publishing* (`http://www.packtpub.com/getting-started-with-phantomjs/book`) and *Designing for Scalability with Erlang/OTP, Francesco Cesarini and Steve Vinoski, O'Reilly Media* (`http://shop.oreilly.com/product/0636920024149.do`).

I would like to thank my wife Anne, my daughter Margaux, my family, and my friends.

www.PacktPub.com

Support files, eBooks, discount offers, and more

You might want to visit www.PacktPub.com for support files and downloads related to your book.

Did you know that Packt offers eBook versions of every book published, with PDF and ePub files available? You can upgrade to the eBook version at www.PacktPub.com and as a print book customer, you are entitled to a discount on the eBook copy. Get in touch with us at service@packtpub.com for more details.

At www.PacktPub.com, you can also read a collection of free technical articles, sign up for a range of free newsletters and receive exclusive discounts and offers on Packt books and eBooks.

http://PacktLib.PacktPub.com

Do you need instant solutions to your IT questions? PacktLib is Packt's online digital book library. Here, you can access, read and search across Packt's entire library of books.

Why Subscribe?

- Fully searchable across every book published by Packt
- Copy and paste, print and bookmark content
- On demand and accessible via web browser

Free Access for Packt account holders

If you have an account with Packt at www.PacktPub.com, you can use this to access PacktLib today and view nine entirely free books. Simply use your login credentials for immediate access.

Table of Contents

Preface

With all the exciting things going on in the browser space, this is a fantastic time to be a front-end developer. The family of technologies that we call HTML5 is giving us new opportunities that were difficult or even impossible just a few years ago, and JavaScript has flourished alongside it as rich web applications have become the norm. Throughout this time, the WebKit project has emerged as the leader of this innovative streak. If you are unfamiliar with WebKit, it is an open source web browser engine with contributors from companies such as Apple, Google, and Nokia, to name a few. WebKit powers Safari, versions of Chrome, and PhantomJS.

The reason you are reading this book is because you have discovered PhantomJS and want to harness its full potential.

PhantomJS is one of the most important innovations in the front-end development tool chain in the last several years. It has proven to be the ideal environment for lightning-fast tests, both manual and automated. Since it is simply a specialized build of WebKit, front-end developers can have confidence that their tests are being executed in a real browser, not a simulated environment. As it is truly headless, it can be deployed anywhere without the hassle of configuring Xvfb. Perhaps best of all, PhantomJS is fully scriptable using JavaScript, a tool that every front-end developer already knows. All these elements combined have uniquely positioned PhantomJS as the preferred testing environment among front-end developers for quick feedback and continuous integration.

The *PhantomJS Cookbook* focuses on using PhantomJS as the preferred testing environment. This book provides practical recipes that demonstrate the fundamentals of this headless browser and also help you take advantage of it for a variety of testing tasks. In this book, you will learn how to integrate PhantomJS into your development workflow at all stages. You will learn how you can receive immediate feedback from your unit tests. You will learn how to create a functional test suite that is both fast and automatic. Also, you will learn how to add PhantomJS to your continuous integration system so that you can make end-to-end and front-end performance tests first-class citizens of your build.

What this book covers

Chapter 1, Getting Started with PhantomJS, introduces the PhantomJS browser and how to work with it from the shell. It covers installing PhantomJS and how to run it with different command-line arguments.

Chapter 2, PhantomJS Core Modules, discusses the core modules in PhantomJS, such as `phantom` and `system`, and covers how to use the `fs` module to work with the filesystem. The chapter also explains how to create your own modules and load them into your PhantomJS scripts.

Chapter 3, Working with webpage Objects, introduces webpage objects and includes sophisticated strategies for dealing with web page content. You will learn how to interact with the page, simulate events, and capture those interactions for successful tests.

Chapter 4, Unit Testing with PhantomJS, explores how to use PhantomJS as an environment for JavaScript unit tests. This chapter focuses on the Jasmine BDD testing framework, but will also introduce two other popular frameworks, Mocha and QUnit.

Chapter 5, Functional and End-to-end Testing with PhantomJS, demonstrates functional and end-to-end testing strategies with PhantomJS. The chapter surveys several different functional testing tools, including Selenium, Poltergeist (a driver for Capybara), and CasperJS.

Chapter 6, Network Monitoring and Performance Analysis, illustrates how to perform automated performance analysis with PhantomJS. The chapter explores topics such as how to generate a HAR file for waterfall analysis, and how to use libraries such as confess.js and YSlow for automated performance analysis.

Chapter 7, Generating Images and Documents with PhantomJS, shows how to generate images and PDFs with PhantomJS. The chapter provides an overview of PhantomJS' built-in image rendering features and explains how to apply them.

Chapter 8, Continuous Integration with PhantomJS, demonstrates PhantomJS as part of a continuous integration (CI) strategy. The chapter surveys CI, using Jenkins as its specimen, and shows how to fail builds on that system, concluding with a recipe for comprehensive CI example.

What you need for this book

By and large, the only things that you will need for the recipes in this cookbook are your normal web development toolkit and PhantomJS. For most recipes, you will not need anything more than a terminal and a text editor or IDE. Some recipes, such as those that discuss functional testing or continuous integration, will require other specific pieces of software to be installed (for example, Selenium, Capybara, Jenkins, and so on), but those requirements will be discussed in context with those recipes.

Also, many of the recipes in this book illustrate their principles by executing against a Node.js-based demonstration application. If you wish to follow along with the recipes exactly as is, you will need to have Node.js version 0.10.2 or greater installed on your system.

Who this book is for

The *PhantomJS Cookbook* is targeted at experienced web developers who are interested in using PhantomJS to add a comprehensive testing strategy to their development workflows. This book assumes that you already have knowledge of the foundational front-end development skills (such as JavaScript, HTML, and CSS) and some experience with testing fundamentals. Some familiarity with PhantomJS is beneficial but not strictly required. Lastly, some recipes may involve some other programming languages (for example, Java or Ruby) and these will be called out where necessary.

Conventions

In this book, you will find a number of styles of text that distinguish between different kinds of information. Here are some examples of these styles, and an explanation of their meaning.

Code words in text, database table names, folder names, filenames, file extensions, pathnames, dummy URLs, user input, and Twitter handles are shown as follows: "We can launch the PhantomJS REPL from the command line using the `phantomjs` command."

A block of code is set as follows:

```
var system = require('system');
system.args.forEach(function(arg, i) {
  console.log(i + ' = ' + arg);
});
phantom.exit();
```

When we wish to draw your attention to a particular part of a code block, the relevant lines or items are set in bold:

```
phantom.onError = function onErrorFn(msg, trace) {
  console.error('[PHANTOMJS ERROR] ' + msg);
  phantom.exit(1);
};
```

Any command-line input or output is written as follows:

```
phantomjs --cookies-file=cookie-jar access-secure-site.js
```

New terms and **important words** are shown in bold. Words that you see on the screen, in menus or dialog boxes for example, appear in the text like this: "Lastly, click on **Save** to persist the changes to this job."

> Warnings or important notes appear in a box like this.

> Tips and tricks appear like this.

Reader feedback

Feedback from our readers is always welcome. Let us know what you think about this book—what you liked or may have disliked. Reader feedback is important for us to develop titles that you really get the most out of.

To send us general feedback, simply send an e-mail to feedback@packtpub.com, and mention the book title via the subject of your message.

If there is a topic that you have expertise in and you are interested in either writing or contributing to a book, see our author guide on www.packtpub.com/authors.

Customer support

Now that you are the proud owner of a Packt book, we have a number of things to help you to get the most from your purchase.

Downloading the example code

You can download the example code files for all Packt books you have purchased from your account at http://www.packtpub.com. If you purchased this book elsewhere, you can visit http://www.packtpub.com/support and register to have the files e-mailed directly to you. The example code is also available on GitHub at https://github.com/founddrama/phantomjs-cookbook.

Errata

Although we have taken every care to ensure the accuracy of our content, mistakes do happen. If you find a mistake in one of our books—maybe a mistake in the text or the code—we would be grateful if you would report this to us. By doing so, you can save other readers from frustration and help us improve subsequent versions of this book. If you find any errata, please report them by visiting http://www.packtpub.com/submit-errata, selecting your book, clicking on the **errata submission form** link, and entering the details of your errata. Once your errata are verified, your submission will be accepted and the errata will be uploaded on our website, or added to any list of existing errata, under the Errata section of that title. Any existing errata can be viewed by selecting your title from http://www.packtpub.com/support.

Piracy

Piracy of copyright material on the Internet is an ongoing problem across all media. At Packt, we take the protection of our copyright and licenses very seriously. If you come across any illegal copies of our works, in any form, on the Internet, please provide us with the location address or website name immediately so that we can pursue a remedy.

Please contact us at copyright@packtpub.com with a link to the suspected pirated material.

We appreciate your help in protecting our authors, and our ability to bring you valuable content.

Questions

You can contact us at questions@packtpub.com if you are having a problem with any aspect of the book, and we will do our best to address it.

1
Getting Started with PhantomJS

In this chapter, we will cover the following recipes:

- ▶ Installing PhantomJS
- ▶ Launching the PhantomJS REPL
- ▶ Running a PhantomJS script
- ▶ Running a PhantomJS script with arguments
- ▶ Running PhantomJS with cookies
- ▶ Running PhantomJS with a disk cache
- ▶ Running PhantomJS with a JSON configuration file
- ▶ Debugging a PhantomJS script

Introduction

PhantomJS is the *headless WebKit* – a fully-fledged WebKit-based browser with absolutely no graphical user interface. Instead of a GUI, PhantomJS features a scripting API that allows us to do just about anything that we would do with a normal browser. Since its introduction in 2010, PhantomJS has grown to be an essential tool in the web development stack. It is ideal for fast unit test watches, end-to-end tests in continuous integration, screen captures, screen scraping, performance data collection, and more.

The recipes in this chapter focus on PhantomJS fundamentals. We will discuss how to install PhantomJS, how to work with its **Read-Evaluate-Print Loop** (**REPL**), how to employ its command-line options, and how to launch PhantomJS in a debug harness.

Installing PhantomJS

Let's begin the *PhantomJS Cookbook* with the recipe that is the prerequisite for all of the other recipes—downloading and installing PhantomJS so that it is available on our computers.

Prebuilt binaries of PhantomJS are available for most major platforms, and in the interest of expedience and simplicity, that is how we proceed. PhantomJS is designed to be a stand-alone application, and in most situations, no external dependencies are required.

Getting ready

To install PhantomJS, we will need access to the Internet and permission to install applications.

How to do it...

Perform the following steps to download and install PhantomJS:

1. Navigate to the PhantomJS download page at `http://phantomjs.org/download`.

2. Locate and download the prebuilt binary that is appropriate for our system. Prebuilt binaries exist for the following operating systems:

    - Windows (XP or later).
    - Mac OS X (10.6 or later).
    - Linux (for 32-bit or 64-bit systems). Current binaries are built on CentOS 5.8, and should run successfully on Ubuntu 10.04.4 (Lucid Lynx) or more modern systems.

3. Extract the prebuilt binary. For Windows and OS X systems, this will be a `.zip` archive; for Linux systems, this will be a `.tar.bz2` archive. For Windows machines, the binary should be `phantomjs.exe`; for OS X and Linux machines, the binary should be `bin/phantomjs`.

> We should place the binary somewhere on your system that makes sense to us.

4. Once extracted, make sure to add PhantomJS to the system's PATH.

> The PATH or *search path* is a variable on the command line that contains a list of directories searched by the shell to find an executable file when it is called. On POSIX-compatible systems (Linux and OS X), this list is delimited by colons (`:`), and on Windows, it is delimited by semicolons (`;`). For more information about the PATH variable, visit `http://en.wikipedia.org/wiki/PATH_(variable)`.
>
> For a tutorial that focuses on POSIX-compatible systems, visit `http://quickleft.com/blog/command-line-tutorials-path`.
>
> For documentation on the Windows PATH, visit `http://msdn.microsoft.com/en-us/library/w0yaz275(v=vs.80).aspx`.

5. After placing the PhantomJS binary on our PATH, we can verify that it was installed by typing the following in the command line:

```
phantomjs -v
```

The version of PhantomJS that we just installed should print out to the console.

> If we have trouble here, we should check out the troubleshooting guide on the PhantomJS project site at `http://phantomjs.org/troubleshooting.html`.

How it works...

In an effort to lower the barrier to entry and help drive adoption, the prebuilt binaries of PhantomJS are made available by community volunteers. This is, in part, an acknowledgment that building PhantomJS from the source code can be a complex and time-consuming task. To quote the build page on the PhantomJS site: "*With 4 parallel compile jobs on a modern machine, the entire process takes roughly 30 minutes.*" It is easy to imagine that this might scare off many developers who just want to try it out.

These prebuilt binaries should therefore make it easy to drop PhantomJS onto any system and have it running in minutes. These binaries are intended to be fully independent applications, with no external library dependencies such as Qt or WebKit. On some Linux systems, however, a little extra work may be required to ensure that the libraries necessary for proper font rendering (for example, `FreeType` and `Fontconfig`) are in place, along with the basic font files.

> Throughout this book, our code will assume that we are using Version 1.9 or higher of PhantomJS.

There's more...

In addition to the prebuilt binaries, Mac OS X users may also install PhantomJS using Homebrew. To do this, enter the following as the command line:

```
brew update && brew install phantomjs
```

Note that installing PhantomJS with Homebrew also means that we will be compiling it from source.

> Homebrew is an open source, community-run package manager for OS X built on top of Git and Ruby. To find out more information about Homebrew, check out its website at `http://brew.sh`.
>
> As a bonus, Homebrew also automatically adds PhantomJS to your PATH.

Installing from Source

In the event that one of the prebuilt binaries is not suitable for your specific situation, you may need to consider building PhantomJS from the source code. If this is the case, you will want to check out the build instructions that are listed at `http://phantomjs.org/build.html`; note that you will need the developer tools specific to your system (for example, Xcode on OS X and Microsoft Visual C++ on Windows) to be installed before you begin.

Launching the PhantomJS REPL

In this recipe, we will learn how to use the PhantomJS REPL. The PhantomJS REPL is an excellent tool for getting familiar with the runtime environment and for quickly hacking out an idea without needing to write a fully qualified script.

Getting ready

To run this recipe, we will need to have PhantomJS installed on our PATH. We will also need an open terminal window.

How to do it...

Perform the following steps to invoke and work in the PhantomJS REPL:

1. At the command-line prompt, type the following:

   ```
   phantomjs
   ```

2. When the PhantomJS REPL starts up, we should see its default command-line prompt:

   ```
   phantomjs>
   ```

3. At the PhantomJS prompt, we can enter any command from the PhantomJS API or any other valid JavaScript expressions and statements. The REPL will print the return value from the expression we entered, although we may need to wrap the expression in a `console.log` statement for a readable response, for example:

```
phantomjs> 1 + 1
{}
phantomjs> console.log(1 + 1)
2
undefined
phantomjs> for (var prop in window) console.log(prop)
document
window
// 475 more...
undefined
```

4. When we are finished in the REPL, type the following command to exit the REPL:

`phantom.exit()`

How it works...

The PhantomJS REPL, also called interactive mode, was introduced to PhantomJS starting with Version 1.5. The REPL is the default mode for PhantomJS when the application is invoked without any arguments.

REPL stands for Read-Evaluate-Print Loop. The commands we enter at the prompt are *read* by the interpreter, which *evaluates* them and *prints* the results, before finally *looping* back to the prompt for us to continue. Many programming environments feature REPLs (for example, Node.js provides another popular JavaScript REPL), and the debugger consoles in tools such as the Chrome Developer Tools and Firebug would also qualify as REPLs. REPLs are useful for quickly trying out ideas in the runtime environment.

In our example, we enter the PhantomJS REPL by invoking `phantomjs` from the command line without any arguments. Once we are in the REPL, we can type in whatever commands we need to explore our ideas, hitting *Enter* after each command. Note that we must enter a full and syntactically valid expression or statement before hitting *Enter*; if we do not, PhantomJS will report an error (for example, **Can't find variable: foo** or **Parse error**).

The PhantomJS REPL also features auto-completion. Hitting the *Tab* key in the REPL will autoexpand our options. We can even hit *Tab* multiple times to cycle through our available options; for example, try typing `p` and then hit *Tab* to see what options the REPL presents.

Finally, when we are finished, we use `phantom.exit()` to leave the REPL; we can also use the *Ctrl + C* or *Ctrl + D* key commands to exit the REPL.

Running a PhantomJS script

This recipe demonstrates how to run a script using the PhantomJS runtime.

Getting ready

To run this recipe, we will need PhantomJS installed on our PATH. We will also need a script to run with PhantomJS; the script in this recipe is available in the downloadable code repository as `recipe03.js` under `chapter01`. If we run the provided example script, we must change to the root directory for the book's sample code.

> **Downloading the example code**
>
> You can download the example code files for all Packt books you have purchased from your account at `http://www.packtpub.com`. If you purchased this book elsewhere, you can visit `http://www.packtpub.com/support` and register to have the files e-mailed directly to you. Alternatively, you can use the Git version control system to clone the repository. The repository is hosted on GitHub at `https://github.com/founddrama/phantomjs-cookbook`.

How to do it...

Given the following script:

```
console.log('A console statement from PhantomJS on ' +
  new Date().toDateString() + '!');

phantom.exit();
```

Type the following at the command line:

phantomjs chapter01/recipe03.js

> Throughout this book, we will be using POSIX-compatible filesystem paths for command-line examples. Windows users may find it helpful to change the forward slashes (/) to back slashes (\) in filesystem paths.

How it works...

Our preceding example script performs the following actions:

1. We print a message to the console (including a date string) using `console.log`.

2. The script exits the PhantomJS runtime using `phantom.exit`.

3. Since we did not provide an integer argument to `phantom.exit`, it returns an exit code of `0` (its default) to the shell.

As we learned in the *Launching the PhantomJS REPL* recipe, PhantomJS will enter the REPL when invoked without any arguments. However, the runtime environment will attempt to evaluate and execute the first unrecognized argument as though it were a JavaScript file, regardless of whether or not it ends in `.js`. Most of the time that we work with PhantomJS, we will interact with it using scripts such as these.

As long as PhantomJS can resolve the first unrecognized argument as a file and correctly parse its contents as syntactically valid JavaScript, it will attempt to execute the contents. However, what happens if those preconditions are not met?

If the argument cannot be resolved as a file on disk, or if the file has no contents, PhantomJS will print an error message to the console, for example:

```
phantomjs does-not-exist-or-empty
Can't open 'does-not-exist-or-empty'
```

If the argument exists but the file's contents cannot be parsed as a valid JavaScript, then PhantomJS will print an error message to the console and hang, for example:

```
phantomjs invalid.js
SyntaxError: Parse error
```

> In the event of such a `SyntaxError`, the PhantomJS process will not automatically terminate, and we must forcefully quit it (*Ctrl + C*).

Recall that PhantomJS is a headless web browser, and it helps to think of it as a version of Chrome or Safari that has no window. Just as we interact with our normal web browser by entering URLs into the location bar, clicking the back button, or clicking links on the page, so we will need to interact with PhantomJS. However, as it has no window and no UI components, we *must* interact with it through its programmable API. The PhantomJS API is written in JavaScript, and scripts targeting the PhantomJS runtime are also written in JavaScript; the API is documented online at `http://phantomjs.org/api/`.

There's more...

If you have been exposed to both PhantomJS and Node.js, you may be wondering about the differences between them, especially after witnessing demonstrations of their respective REPLs and script running abilities. When comparing the two, it is helpful to consider them using the phrase "based on" as your frame of reference. Node.js is *based on* Google Chrome's V8 JavaScript engine; PhantomJS is *based on* the WebKit layout engine. Node.js *is* a JavaScript runtime; PhantomJS *has* a JavaScript runtime. Where Node.js is an excellent platform for building JavaScript-based server applications, it does not have any native HTML rendering. This is the key differentiator when comparing it to PhantomJS. The mission of PhantomJS is not to provide a platform for building JavaScript applications, but instead to provide a fast and standards-compliant headless browser.

See also

▸   The *Running a PhantomJS script with arguments* recipe

Running a PhantomJS script with arguments

In this recipe, we will learn how to run a PhantomJS script with additional arguments that are passed into the script for evaluation. Note that these are arguments passed into the execution context and are *not* command-line arguments for the PhantomJS runtime itself.

Getting ready

To run this recipe, we will need a script to run with PhantomJS; the script in this recipe is available in the downloadable code repository as `recipe04.js` under `chapter01`. If we run the provided example script, we must change to the root directory for the book's sample code. Lastly, we will need the arguments we wish to pass into the script.

How to do it...

Given the following script:

```
if (phantom.args.length === 0) {
  console.log('No arguments were passed in.');
} else {
  phantom.args.forEach(function(arg, index) {
    console.log('[' + index + '] ' + arg);
  });
}

phantom.exit();
```

Enter the following command at the command line:

```
phantomjs chapter01/recipe04.js foo bar "boo baa"
```

We will see the following results printed in the terminal:

```
[0] foo
[1] bar
[2] boo baa
```

How it works...

Our preceding example script performs the following actions:

1. It checks the length of the `phantom.args` array and prints a message if that array is empty.
2. If the `phantom.args` array is not empty, we iterate over the items in the array, printing their index followed by the value of the argument itself.
3. Lastly, we exit from the PhantomJS runtime using `phantom.exit`.

As we discussed in the *Running a PhantomJS script* recipe, PhantomJS will attempt to evaluate and execute the first unrecognized argument as though it were a valid JavaScript file. But what does PhantomJS do with all of the arguments after that?

The answer is that they are collected into the `phantom.args` array as string values. Each argument after the script name goes into this array. Note that `phantom.args` does not include the script name itself. Instead, PhantomJS records that in the read-only `phantom.scriptName` property.

There's more...

It is worth noting that both `phantom.args` and `phantom.scriptName` are both marked as deprecated in the API documentation. As such, usage of both of these properties is discouraged. Although using them for quick one-off or exploratory scripts is fine, neither of these properties should go into any library that we intend to maintain or distribute.

Wherever possible, we should use the `system.args` array (from the `system` module) instead of `phantom.args` and `phantom.scriptName`.

> When in doubt, check the PhantomJS project website and its documentation at `http://phantomjs.org/api/`. It is actively maintained, and as such will contain up-to-date information about the preferred APIs.

See also

▸ The *Inspecting command-line arguments* recipe in *Chapter 2, PhantomJS Core Modules*

Running PhantomJS with cookies

In this recipe, we will learn how to use the `cookies-file` command-line switch to specify the location of the file for persistent cookies in PhantomJS.

Getting ready

To run this recipe, we will need a script to run with PhantomJS that accesses a site where cookies are read or written. We will need a filesystem path to specify it as the command-line argument, making sure that we have write permissions to that path.

The script in this recipe is available in the downloadable code repository as `recipe05.js` under `chapter01`. If we run the provided example script, we must change to the root directory for the book's sample code.

Lastly, the script in this recipe runs against the demo site that is included with the cookbook's sample code repository. To run that demo site, we must have Node.js installed. In a separate terminal, change to the `phantomjs-sandbox` directory (in the sample code's directory) and start the app with the following command:

```
node app.js
```

> Node.js is a JavaScript runtime environment based on Chrome's V8 engine. It has an event-driven programming model and non-blocking I/O and can be used for building fast networking applications, shell scripts, and everything in between. We can learn more about Node.js including how to install it at `http://nodejs.org/`.
>
> We will use this demo for many recipes throughout this cookbook. When we run the demo app for the first time, we need to download and install the Node.js modules that it depends on. To do this, we can change to the `phantomjs-sandbox` directory and run the following command:
>
> ```
> npm install
> ```

How to do it...

Given the following script:

```
var webpage = require('webpage').create();

webpage.open('http://localhost:3000/cookie-demo', function(status) {
```

```
    if (status === 'success') {
      phantom.cookies.forEach(function(cookie, i) {
        for (var key in cookie) {
          console.log('[cookie:' + i + '] ' + key + ' = ' +
            cookie[key]);
        }
      });

      phantom.exit();
    } else {
      console.error('Could not open the page! (Is it running?)');
      phantom.exit(1);
    }
});
```

Enter the following command at the command line:

```
phantomjs --cookies-file=cookie-jar.txt chapter01/recipe05.js
```

> PhantomJS will create the cookie-jar.txt file for us; there is
> no need to create it manually.

The script will print out the properties for each cookie in the response, as follows:

```
[cookie:0] domain = localhost
[cookie:0] expires = Sat, 07 Dec 2013 02:05:06 GMT
[cookie:0] expiry = 1386381906
[cookie:0] httponly = false
[cookie:0] name = dave
[cookie:0] path = /cookie-demo
[cookie:0] secure = false
[cookie:0] value = oatmeal-raisin
[cookie:1] domain = localhost
[cookie:1] expires = Sat, 07 Dec 2013 02:04:22 GMT
[cookie:1] expiry = 1386381862
[cookie:1] httponly = false
[cookie:1] name = rob
[cookie:1] path = /cookie-demo
[cookie:1] secure = false
[cookie:1] value = chocolate-chip
```

We can then open cookie-jar.txt in a text editor and examine its contents. The *cookie jar*
file should look something like the following:

```
[General]
cookies="@Variant(\0\0\0\x7f\0\0\0\x16QList<QNetworkCookie>\0\0\0\0\
x1\0\0\0\x2\0\0\0_dave=oatmeal-raisin; expires= Sat, 07 Dec 2013
  02:05:06 GMT; domain=localhost;
  path=/cookie-demo\0\0\0^rob=chocolate-chip; expires= Sat, 07 Dec
  2013 02:04:22 GMT; domain=localhost; path=/cookie-demo)"
```

How it works...

Our preceding example script performs the following actions:

1. It creates a `webpage` object and opens the target URL (`http://localhost:3000/cookie-demo`).

2. In the callback function, we check for `status` of `'success'`, printing an error message and exiting PhantomJS if that condition fails.

> Throughout this cookbook, we will use exit codes of `0` and `1` for *success* and *failure* respectively, because those are the exit codes traditionally used for those reasons on POSIX and Windows systems.

3. If we successfully open the URL, then we loop through each cookie in the `phantom.cookies` collection and print out information about each one.

4. Lastly, we exit from the PhantomJS runtime using `phantom.exit`.

When we start PhantomJS with the `cookies-file` argument, we are telling the runtime to read and write cookies from a specific location on the filesystem. What this allows us to do is to use cookies in PhantomJS like we would with any other browser. In other words, an HTTP response or client-side script can set cookies, and when we run our PhantomJS script against that URL again, we can trust that the cookies are still there in the file.

Notice that the cookie jar file itself is essentially a plain text file. The actual file extension does not matter; we used `.txt` in our example, but it could just as easily be `.cookies` or even no extension at all. When persisting the cookies, PhantomJS writes them to this file. If we examine the file, then we see that it is a serialized, text-based version of the `QNetworkCookie` class that PhantomJS uses behind the scenes. Although the on-disk version is not necessarily easy to read, we can easily make a copy and parse it or transform it into its constituent cookies. This can be useful for examining their contents after a script has completed (for example, to ensure that the expected values are being written to disk).

Additionally, with the cookies written to disk, they are available for future PhantomJS script runs against URLs that expect the same cookies. For example, this can be useful when running scripts against sites that require authentication where those authentication tokens are passed around as cookies.

See also

▶ The *Managing cookies with the phantom object* recipe in *Chapter 2, PhantomJS Core Modules*

Running PhantomJS with a disk cache

In this recipe, we will learn about running PhantomJS with an on-disk cache that is enabled using the `disk-cache` and `max-disk-cache-size` command-line arguments. We can use this to test how browsers cache our static assets.

Getting ready

To run this recipe, we will need a script to run with PhantomJS that accesses a website with cacheable assets. Optionally, we will also need a sense of how large we wish to set the on-disk cache (in kilobytes).

The script in this recipe is available in the downloadable code repository as `recipe06. js` under `chapter01`. If we run the provided example script, we must change to the root directory for the book's sample code.

Lastly, the script in this recipe runs against the demo site that is included with the cookbook's sample code repository. To run that demo site, we must have Node.js installed. In a separate terminal, change into the `phantomjs-sandbox` directory (in the sample code's directory) and start the app with the following command:

```
node app.js
```

How to do it...

Given the following script:

```
var page  = require('webpage').create(),
    count = 0,
    until = 2;

page.onResourceReceived = function(res) {
  if (res.stage === 'end') {
    console.log(JSON.stringify(res, undefined, 2));
  }
};

page.onLoadStarted = function() {
  count += 1;
  console.log('Run ' + count + ' of ' + until + '.');
};

page.onLoadFinished = function(status) {
  if (status === 'success') {
```

```
        if (count < until) {
          console.log('Go again.\n');
          page.reload();
        } else {
          console.log('All done.');
          phantom.exit();
        }
      } else {
        console.error('Could not open page! (Is it running?)');
        phantom.exit(1);
      }
    };

    page.open('http://localhost:3000/cache-demo');
```

Enter the following command at the command line:

```
phantomjs --disk-cache=true --max-disk-cache-size=4000
  chapter01/recipe06.js
```

The script will print out details about each resource in the response as JSON.

How it works...

Our preceding example script performs the following actions:

1. It creates a `webpage` object and sets two variables, `count` and `until`.

2. We assign an event handler function to the `webpage` object's `onResourceReceived` callback. This callback will print out every property of each resource received.

3. We assign an event handler function to the `webpage` object's `onLoadStarted` callback. This callback will increment `count` when the page load starts and print a message indicating which run it is.

4. We assign an event handler function to the `webpage` object's `onLoadFinished` callback. This callback checks the `status` of the response and takes action accordingly as follows:

    ❑ If `status` is not `'success'`, then we print an error message and exit from PhantomJS

    ❑ If the callback's `status` *is* `'success'`, then we check to see if `count` is less than `until`, and if it is, then we call `reload` on the `webpage` object; otherwise, we exit PhantomJS

5. Finally, we open the target URL (`http://localhost:3000/cache-demo`) using `webpage.open`.

There's more...

Even though the disk cache is off by default, PhantomJS still performs some in-memory caching. This detail becomes important in later explorations, as it produces some otherwise difficult to explain results. For example, in our preceding sample script, we used `webpage.reload` for our second request of the URL, and in that second request, we saw all of the images re-requested. However, if we had used a second call to `webpage.open` (instead of `webpage.reload`), then the `onResourceReceived` callback would have shown a second request to the URL but *none* of the images would have been re-requested. (As an interesting aside, we would also see that behavior if we set the `disk-cache` argument to `false`; the in-memory cache cannot be disabled.)

Another interesting observation is that PhantomJS always reports an HTTP response status of `200 Ok` for every successfully retrieved asset. If we look at the Node.js console output for the demo app while our sample script runs, we can see the discrepancy. Again, when our sample script runs, we can see that an HTTP status code of `200` is reported by PhantomJS for each of the images during both the first and second request/response cycles. However, the output from the Node.Js app looks something like this:

```
GET /cache-demo 200 1ms - 573b
GET /images/583519989_1116956980_b.jpg 200 4ms - 264.64kb
GET /images/152824439_ffcc1b2aa4_b.jpg 200 8ms - 615.21kb
GET /images/357292530_f225d7e306_b.jpg 200 6ms - 497.98kb
GET /images/391560246_f2ac936f6d_b.jpg 200 5ms - 446.68kb
GET /images/872027465_2519a358b9_b.jpg 200 5ms - 766.94kb
GET /cache-demo 200 1ms - 573b
GET /images/152824439_ffcc1b2aa4_b.jpg 304 3ms
GET /images/357292530_f225d7e306_b.jpg 304 3ms
GET /images/391560246_f2ac936f6d_b.jpg 304 2ms
GET /images/583519989_1116956980_b.jpg 304 3ms
GET /images/872027465_2519a358b9_b.jpg 304 3ms
```

We can see that the server responds with `304 Not Modified` for each of the image assets. This is exactly what we would expect for a second request to the same URL when the assets are served with `Cache-Control` headers that specify a `max-age`, and for assets that are also cached to disk.

disk-cache

We can enable the disk cache by setting the `disk-cache` argument to `true` or `yes`. By default, the disk cache is disabled, but we can also explicitly disable it by providing `false` or `no` to the command-line argument. When the disk cache is enabled, PhantomJS will cache assets to the on-disk cache, which it stores at the desktop services cache storage location. Caching these assets has the potential to speed up future script runs against URLs that share those assets.

max-disk-cache-size

Optionally, we may also wish to limit the size of the disk cache (for example, to simulate the small caches on some mobile devices). To limit the size of the disk cache, we use the `max-disk-cache-size` command-line argument and provide an integer that determines the size of the cache in kilobytes. By default (if you do not use the `max-disk-cache-size` argument), the cache size is unbounded. Most of the time, we will not need to use the `max-disk-cache-size` argument.

Cache locations

If we need to inspect the cached data that is persisted to disk, PhantomJS writes to the desktop services cache storage location for the platform it's running on. These locations are listed as follows:

Platform	Location
Windows	`%AppData%/Local/Ofi Labs/PhantomJS/cache/http`
Mac OS X	`~/Library/Caches/Ofi Labs/PhantomJS/data7`
Linux	`~/.qws/cache/Ofi Labs/PhantomJS`

> These locations may not exist until after we have run PhantomJS with the `disk-cache` argument enabled.

See also

▸ The *Opening a URL within PhantomJS* recipe in *Chapter 3, Working with webpage Objects*

Running PhantomJS with a JSON configuration file

In this recipe, we will learn how to store PhantomJS configuration options in a JSON document and load those options using the `config` command-line argument.

Getting ready

To run this recipe, we will need a JSON-formatted configuration file with our PhantomJS command-line options.

The script in this recipe is available in the downloadable code repository as `recipe07.js` under `chapter01`. If we run the provided example script, we must change to the root directory for the book's sample code. An example configuration file is also in this directory as `recipe07-config.json`.

Lastly, the script in this recipe runs against the demo site that is included with the cookbook's sample code repository. To run that demo site, we must have Node.js installed. In a separate terminal, change to the `phantomjs-sandbox` directory (in the sample code's directory) and start the app with the following command:

```
node app.js
```

How to do it...

Select our command-line configuration options (changing hyphenated property names into their camel-cased equivalents) and apply our values. Save these configuration settings to a JSON-formatted document. For example, the contents of `recipe07-config.json` under `chapter01`:

```
{
    "cookiesFile"      : "cookie-jar.txt",
    "ignoreSslErrors" : true
}
```

> For more information about JSON, including its formatting rules, visit `http://www.json.org`.

Given the script from the *Running PhantomJS with cookies* recipe earlier in this chapter, enter the following at the command line:

```
phantomjs --config=chapter01/recipe07-config.json
  chapter01/recipe07.js
```

How it works...

The configuration file is a JSON document where we can take our preferred command-line arguments and store them on disk. The keys in the JSON object have a one-to-one correspondence with the command-line arguments themselves – the hyphenated command-line argument names are converted to their camel-cased versions (for example, `cookies-file` becomes `cookiesFile`). The values in the JSON object follow easy conversion rules based on the most applicable JavaScript primitives: strings are strings, numbers are numbers, and `true/false` or `yes/no` become the corresponding `true` or `false` Boolean literals. Creating our own JSON-formatted configuration file requires only two things: a text editor and the knowledge of which command-line arguments we wish to capture in it.

> See `http://phantomjs.org/api/command-line.html` for the complete list of documented command-line options in the PhantomJS API.

> The `help` and `version` command-line arguments do not have corresponding versions in the JSON configuration file. Also, at the time of writing this book, there is a documented defect wherein the JSON key for the `load-images` argument is not recognized.

The example script in this recipe (`recipe07.js` under `chapter01`) is identical to the one that we used for our demonstration in the *Running PhantomJS with cookies* recipe; we are reusing it here for convenience. For a more thorough explanation of what it is doing, see the *How it works...* section under that recipe.

When launching PhantomJS with the `config` command-line argument, the PhantomJS runtime interprets the argument's value as a path on the filesystem and attempts to load and evaluate that file as a JSON document. If the file cannot be parsed as a JSON document, then PhantomJS prints a warning and ignores it. If the file is correctly parsed, then PhantomJS configures itself as if the arguments in the JSON document had been passed as normal command-line arguments.

This raises an interesting question: given equivalent arguments, which one takes precedence? The one specified in the JSON configuration file? Or the one specified on the command line? The answer is that it depends which one comes last. In other words, given `recipe07-config.json`, we can run:

```
phantomjs --cookies-file=jar-of-cookies.txt
  --config=chapter01/recipe07-config.json chapter01/recipe07.js
```

That creates `cookie-jar.txt`, as specified in `recipe07-config.json`. While the following command creates `jar-of-cookies.txt`, as specified on the command line:

```
phantomjs --config=chapter01/recipe07-config.json
  --cookies-file=jar-of-cookies.txt chapter01/recipe07.js
```

There's more...

Saving a PhantomJS configuration to a JSON document can help us in a couple of ways. First, by putting it into a file, we can put it under version control and track the changes to that configuration over time. Also, by putting the configuration into a file, it can more easily be shared across teams or jobs in continuous integration.

See also

- The *Running PhantomJS with cookies* recipe

Debugging a PhantomJS script

In this recipe, we will learn about remote debugging PhantomJS scripts using the `remote-debugger-port` and `remote-debugger-autorun` command-line arguments.

Getting ready

To run this recipe, we will need the following:

- PhantomJS installed on our `PATH`
- A script to run with PhantomJS, which we are interested in debugging
- Our computer's IP address
- An open port over which the debugger will communicate
- Another browser such as Google Chrome or Safari

The script in this recipe is available in the downloadable code repository as `recipe08.js` under `chapter01`. If we run the provided example script, we must change to the root directory of the book's sample code.

The script in this recipe runs against the demo site that is included with the cookbook's sample code repository. To run that demo site, we must have Node.js installed. In a separate terminal, change to the `phantomjs-sandbox` directory and start the app with the following command:

```
node app.js
```

How to do it...

Given the following script:

```
var page = require('webpage').create();

page.onResourceReceived = function(res) {
  if (res.stage === 'end') {
    console.log(JSON.stringify(res, undefined, 2));
  }
};

page.open('http://localhost:3000/cache-demo', function(status) {
  if (status === 'success') {
```

```
        console.log('All done.');
        phantom.exit();
    } else {
        console.error('Could not open page! (Is it running?)');
        phantom.exit(1);
    }
});
```

Enter the following at the command line:

**phantomjs --remote-debugger-port=9000 --remote-debugger-autorun=true
  chapter01/recipe08.js**

Note that with the `remote-debugger-autorun` argument set to `true`, the script will run immediately as it normally would, but it will also ignore calls to `phantom.exit` and suspend execution, printing out the following message:

Phantom::exit() called but not quitting in debug mode.

> If we want more control over when the script begins (for example, we want to set breakpoints first), then simply omit the `remote-debugger-autorun` argument. By omitting that argument, PhantomJS will start and will load the script, but will not execute it until you issue the `__run()` command in the debugger.

Now we can open our other browser (for example, Chrome) and enter our IP address and the port that we specified with `remote-debugger-port`. For example, if our computer's IP address is `10.0.1.8`, we would enter `http://10.0.1.8:9000/` into the location bar. Then, we should see something like the following screenshot:

The viewport will contain the PhantomJS browsing session's history as a list. As we are interested in accessing the debugger tools, we will click on the link that reads **about:blank**. This will take us to /webkit/inspector/inspector.html, and it should look something like the following screenshot:

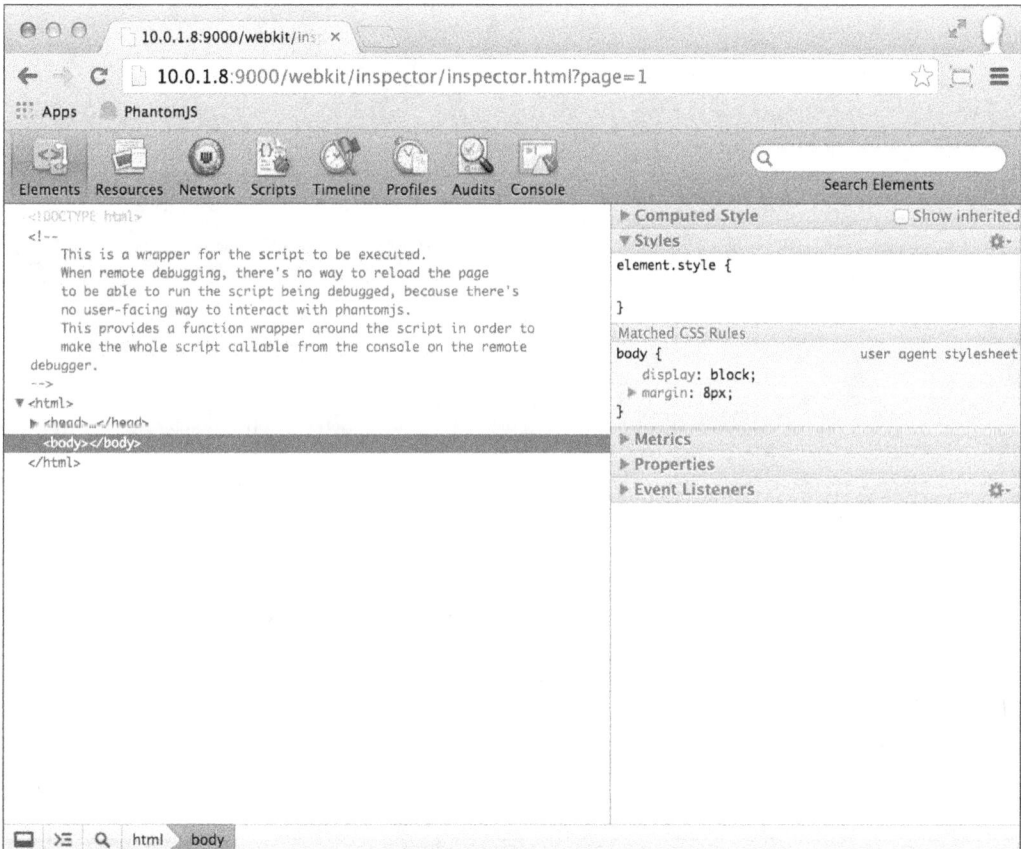

If we have worked in the Chrome or Safari developer tools before, the toolbar should be familiar. While debugging PhantomJS scripts, we will be particularly interested in the **Scripts** and **Console** tabs.

> For those unfamiliar with the WebKit Web Inspector, check out Majd Taby's thorough introduction, "The WebKit Inspector", at http://jtaby.com/blog/2012/04/23/modern-web-development-part-1.

Once we have the debugger open, click on the **Scripts** tab. In the **Scripts** tab, click on the drop-down menu (in the top toolbar, just below the tabs) and select **about:blank**. This will show us our script as seen in the following screenshot. Click on any line number in the left-side gutter to set a breakpoint.

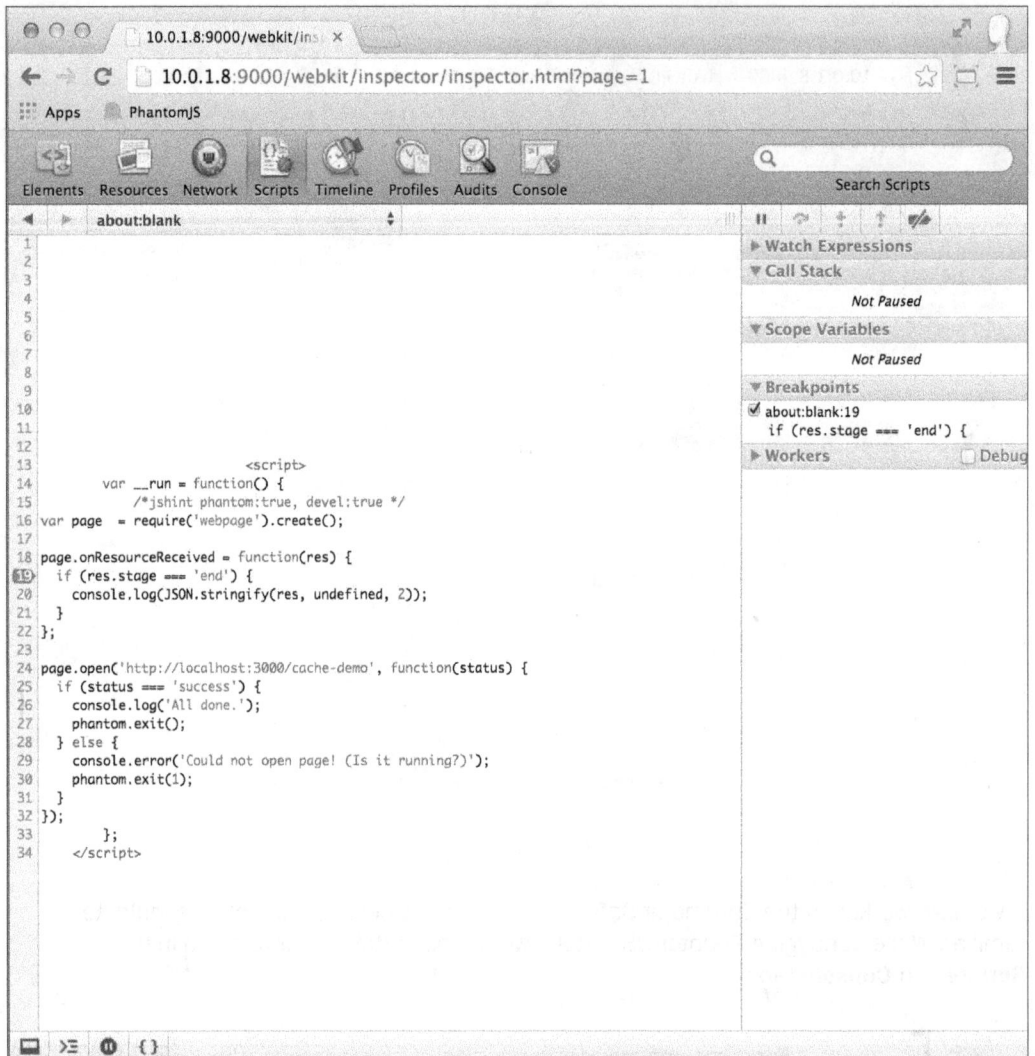

With our breakpoint set, click on the **Console** tab to toggle into the console. Since we used the `remote-debugger-autorun` argument, we will see our `console.log` and other such statements printed to the console from our first (automatic) run. Note the blue prompt at the bottom of the console as seen in the following screenshot; we can enter new expressions to be evaluated here at this prompt. To run our PhantomJS script again, we enter `__run()`.

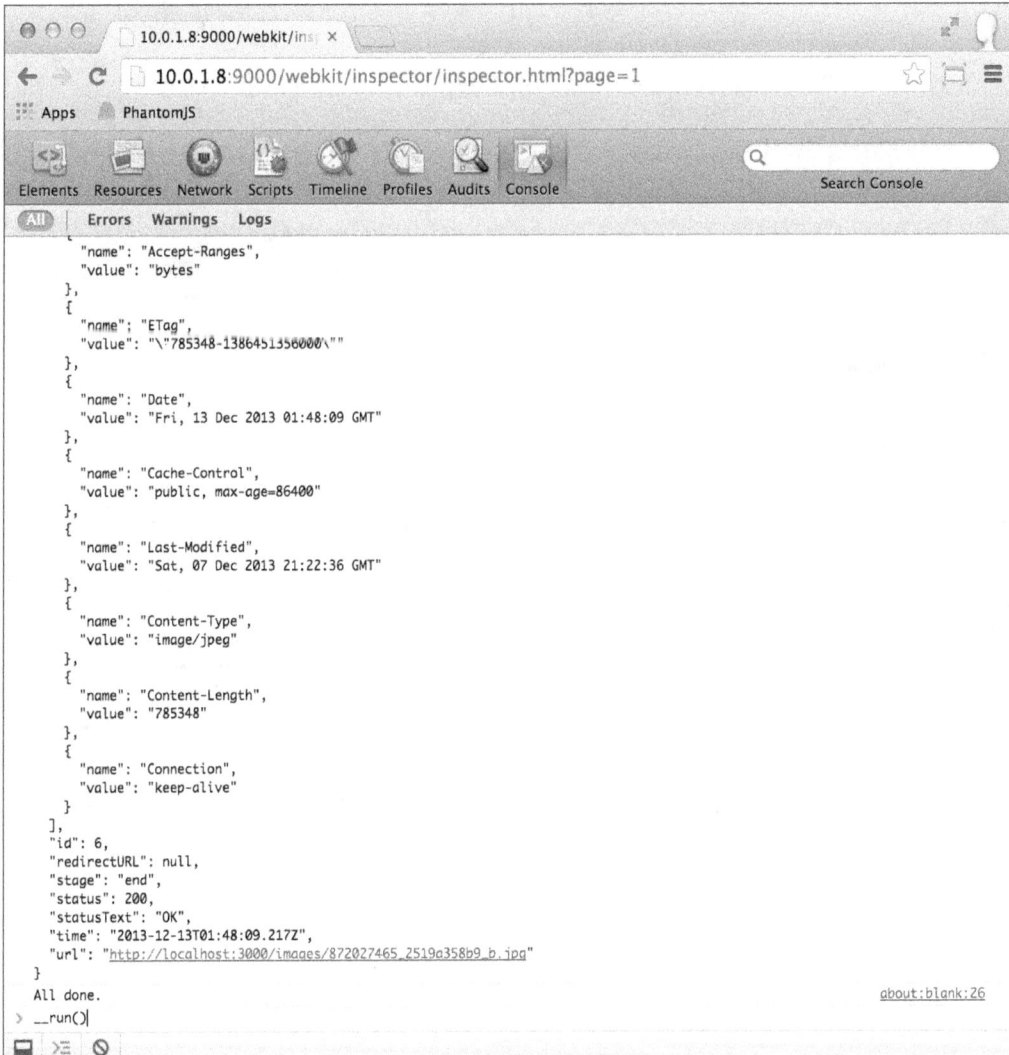

Entering `__run()` in the console will execute the script again. The script execution will pause on any breakpoints that we set and we will automatically be brought into the **Scripts** tab. In the **Scripts** tab, we can inspect our call stack, inspect local variables and objects at runtime, manipulate the runtime environment through the console, and more.

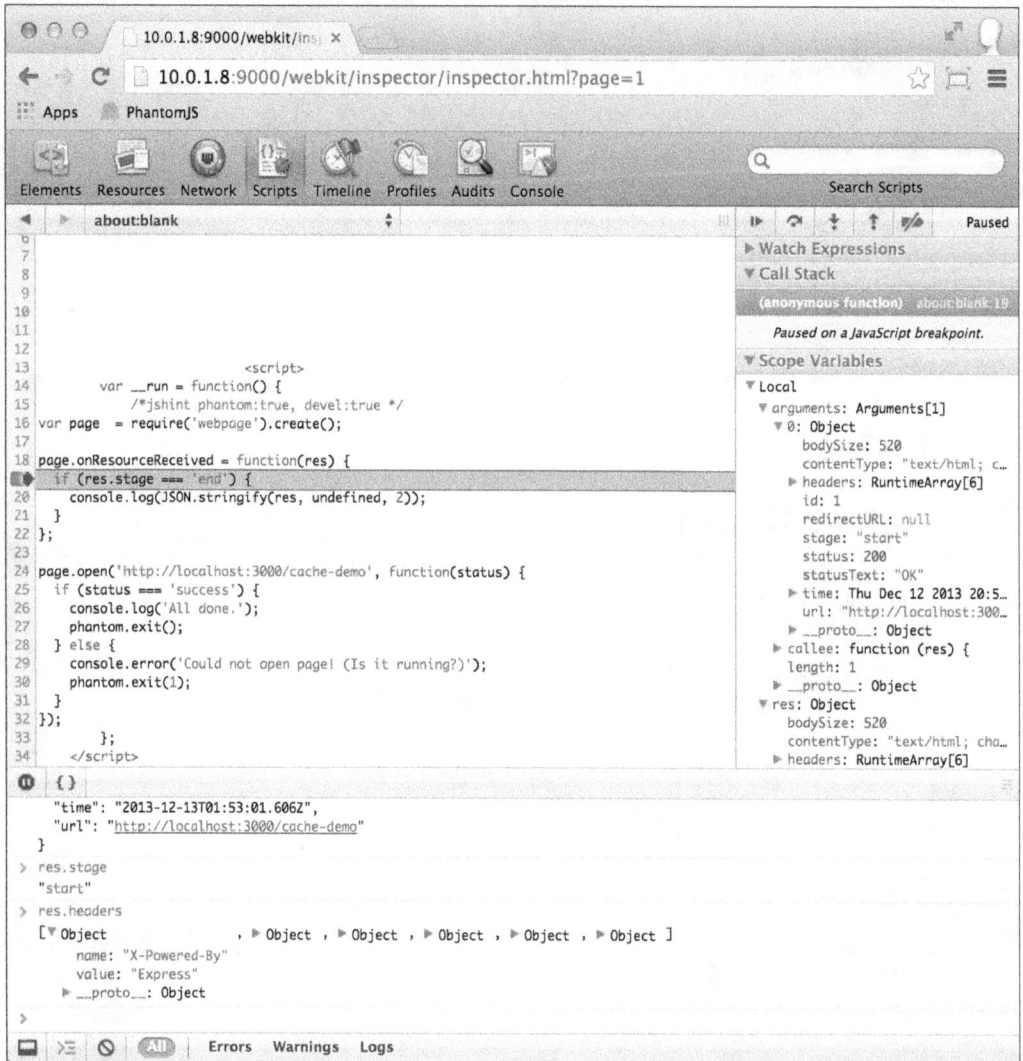

When we are done debugging our script, we can simply close the browser and then use *Ctrl + C* to quit the PhantomJS process in the terminal.

How it works...

Our preceding example script is a simple one. We proceed in the following manner:

1. We create a `webpage` object.

2. We assign an event handler function to the `webpage` object's `onResourceReceived` callback. This callback will print out each resource received using `JSON.stringify`.

3. Lastly, we open the target URL (`http://localhost:3000/cache-demo`) using `webpage.open`, calling `phantom.exit` in the callback.

There's more...

Effective debugging is an essential skill for every developer, and it is fantastic that PhantomJS has the WebKit remote debugging built-in as a first-class tool. While the debugger itself may be overkill for simple situations, sometimes `console.log` just isn't a powerful enough (or fast enough) tool. In those cases, it is comforting to know that you have these debug tools at your disposal.

One important thing to note about using the remote debugger with PhantomJS is that we will need to be aware of what context we are attempting to debug. Are we debugging the PhantomJS script itself? Or a script on the page that the PhantomJS script is accessing? Or some interaction between them? In the simple case (as previously demonstrated), the remote debug mode makes it almost trivial to inspect our PhantomJS script's execution at runtime. However, it does take some extra work if we need to also debug a script on the page that PhantomJS is accessing. In those cases, we may find it useful to use the `remote-debugger-autorun` argument; this will pre-populate the debugger's landing page with links to the inspector for the PhantomJS script's context and also the accessed web page's context. We can open these links each in a new tab, giving a separate debugger session for each context we need to work in.

remote-debugger-port

Of the two debugger-related command-line arguments, `remote-debugger-port` is the essential one. The `remote-debugger-port` argument serves two functions. The first, implicit function is to put PhantomJS into the debug harness. Its second, explicit function is to set the port that PhantomJS will use for the WebKit remote debugging protocol.

Having these remote debugging capabilities in PhantomJS is extremely handy if we need to inspect or otherwise troubleshoot some misbehaving or unpredictable code. But something else that is nice about how the debugging toolkit is implemented is that we don't need anything else *except* another browser with a GUI. We do not need to install any special extensions in Chrome or Safari for the debugger to work. All we need to do is specify the port on the command line and point the browser at our computer's IP and *voila*—the full power of a GUI debugger for our otherwise headless web browser.

Although we can use any browser as the target viewport for the remote debugger, our best results will be in Safari or Chrome. Safari is currently the dominant WebKit-based browser; Chrome uses the Blink rendering engine, but retains many of the features from its WebKit heritage. The remote debugger will function in other browsers (for example, Firefox or Opera) but certain things may not render properly, making it much more difficult to use.

remote-debugger-autorun

The `remote-debugger-autorun` command-line argument is optional and if specified as `true`, the script passed to PhantomJS will be run immediately in the debug harness. While this may be a convenient feature, it is seldom what we want.

Under normal debugging, we would already have some idea of where our code is defective (for example, from the errors or stack traces that we already have). With that knowledge, we would want to start our PhantomJS script in the debug harness, then navigate to the **Scripts** tab and set our breakpoints, and *then* execute the script.

If we have not set the script to run automatically, then how do we execute it? If we look again at our script as it appears in the **about:blank** selection under the **Scripts** tab, we will notice that it has been wrapped in a function and assigned to the variable named __run. To execute our script, we enter __run() into the debugger console and hit enter to call the function.

2
PhantomJS
Core Modules

In this chapter, we will cover:

- ▶ Inspecting the version at runtime
- ▶ Managing cookies with the phantom object
- ▶ Specifying a path for external scripts
- ▶ Setting up a global PhantomJS error handler
- ▶ Controlling the exit status of a PhantomJS script
- ▶ Inspecting command-line arguments
- ▶ Inspecting system environment variables
- ▶ Saving a file from a PhantomJS script
- ▶ Reading a file from PhantomJS
- ▶ Creating a custom module for PhantomJS
- ▶ Loading custom modules in PhantomJS

Introduction

PhantomJS exposes several core APIs to work with the headless browser and with the operating system that hosts the runtime. For example, we can get information about PhantomJS, inspect our host environment for values assigned to variables, and read from or write to the filesystem with the help of these APIs.

The recipes in this chapter will focus on those APIs that are considered part of the PhantomJS core. Specifically, we will introduce and discuss the global `phantom` object, the `system` and `fs` modules, and how to create and load our own CommonJS-compatible modules.

Inspecting the version at runtime

This recipe will introduce the global `phantom` object in PhantomJS and discuss how we can inspect the version at runtime using the `version` property.

Getting ready

To run this recipe, we will need a script that accesses `phantom.version`. The script in this recipe is available in the downloadable code repository as `recipe01.js` under `chapter02`. If we run the provided example script, we must change to the root directory for the book's sample code.

How to do it...

Consider the following script:

```
console.log('PhantomJS');
console.log('  - major version: ' + phantom.version.major);
console.log('  - minor version: ' + phantom.version.minor);
console.log('  - patch version: ' + phantom.version.patch);
phantom.exit();
```

Given the preceding script, enter the following at the command line:

phantomjs chapter02/recipe01.js

Our output should look like the following:

PhantomJS
- **major version: 1**
- **minor version: 9**
- **patch version: 2**

How it works...

Our script operates by accessing the `version` object on the global `phantom` object and writing its properties (`major`, `minor`, and `patch`) to the console. The build of PhantomJS will have this metadata built in and exposed through `phantom.version` as read-only information.

Although our example is a trivial one, knowing the specific PhantomJS version at runtime can be helpful for building flexible scripts/libraries. For example, knowing the version at runtime can help us target preferred APIs while still falling back on older or deprecated ones in the event that those APIs are not available.

Managing cookies with the phantom object

In this recipe, we will discuss how to work with cookies in PhantomJS. The `phantom` object exposes two properties (`cookies` and `cookiesEnabled`) and three methods (`addCookie`, `clearCookie`, and `deleteCookie`) that we can use to inspect and manipulate cookies at runtime.

Getting ready

To run this recipe, we may wish to run PhantomJS with persistent cookies using the `cookies-file` command-line argument.

The script in this recipe is available in the downloadable code repository as `recipe02.js` under `chapter02`. If we run the provided example script, we must change to the root directory for the book's sample code.

Lastly, the script in this recipe runs against the demo site that is included with the cookbook's sample code repository. To run the demo site, we must have Node.js installed. In a separate terminal, change to the `phantomjs-sandbox` directory (in the sample code's directory) and start the app with the following command:

```
node app.js
```

How to do it...

Consider the following script:

```
var page = require('webpage').create(),
    url  = 'http://localhost:3000/cookie-demo';

if (!phantom.cookiesEnabled) {
  console.log('Note: cookies not enabled.');
}

page.open(url, function(status) {
  if (status === 'success') {
    console.log('We start with these cookies:');
    phantom.cookies.forEach(function(c) {
      console.info(JSON.stringify(c, undefined, 2));
    });
```

```
            phantom.addCookie({
                name: 'jerry',
                value: 'black-and-white',
                domain: 'localhost'
            });

            console.log('Added the "jerry" cookie; how many now? ' +
                phantom.cookies.length);

            phantom.deleteCookie('jerry');
            console.log('Deleted the "jerry" cookie; how many now? ' +
                phantom.cookies.length);

            phantom.clearCookies();

            console.log('How many cookies after a clear? ' +
                phantom.cookies.length);

            phantom.exit();
        } else {
            console.error('Something is wrong!');
            phantom.exit(1);
        }
    });
```

Given the preceding script, enter the following at the command line:

```
phantomjs --cookies-file=cookie-jar.txt chapter02/recipe02.js
```

> PhantomJS will create `cookie-jar.txt` for us; there is no need to create it manually.

Our output should look like the following:

```
We start with these cookies:
{
    "domain": "localhost",
    "expires": "Thu, 19 Dec 2013 03:04:33 GMT",
    "expiry": 1387422273,
    "httponly": false,
    "name": "rob",
    "path": "/cookie-demo",
    "secure": false,
```

```
    "value": "chocolate-chip"
}
{
    "domain": "localhost",
    "expires": "Thu, 19 Dec 2013 03:04:33 GMT",
    "expiry": 1387422273,
    "httponly": false,
    "name": "dave",
    "path": "/cookie-demo",
    "secure": false,
    "value": "oatmeal-raisin"
}
Added the "jerry" cookie; how many now? 3
Deleted the "jerry" cookie; how many now? 2
How many cookies after a clear? 0
```

How it works...

PhantomJS' global `phantom` object exposes properties and methods to inspect and manipulate the runtime environment, including two properties and three methods for working with cookies. They are:

- `cookies`: This is an array holding the cookies
- `cookiesEnabled`: This is a Boolean indicating whether cookies are enabled
- `addCookie(cookieObject)`: This adds the defined cookie to the CookieJar
- `deleteCookie(cookieName)`: This removes the named cookie from the CookieJar
- `clearCookies()`: This is to remove all cookies from the CookieJar

> We can find the cookie-related properties and methods discussed in the PhantomJS API documentation for the `phantom` object at `http://phantomjs.org/api/phantom/`.

These methods are in addition to any inspection or manipulation of cookies that occur as a result of server- or client-side script operations. In other words, remote servers can still get/set cookies on the HTTP request or response, and JavaScript running on the page can do the same, but PhantomJS provides a way for us to perform additional operations on cookies.

In our preceding example script, we perform the following actions:

1. We create a `webpage` object.
2. We check `phantom.cookiesEnabled` and write a message if cookies are *not* enabled.

> Note that `phantom.cookiesEnabled` is *not* a read-only property. When accessed, it returns a Boolean indicating whether the CookieJar is enabled; it is enabled (returns `true`) by default. However, we can set this property to `false` if we wish to disable cookies.

3. We open the target URL (`http://localhost:3000/cookie-demo`); in the callback function, we check `status` and exit PhantomJS with a warning message if it is not successful.

4. If the request is successful, we iterate through the original cookies using the standard `forEach` function on the `phantom.cookies` array, printing each one to the console.

> Note that `phantom.cookies` contains all the cookies that the runtime environment has currently loaded, and this may include cookies from previous sessions. For example, if we already have cookies in our CookieJar file and move the first `phantom.cookies` access to *outside* of the `open` callback, we may see cookies from the last time we accessed this particular URL.

5. We add a cookie using `phantom.addCookie`, which takes a single argument: an object that describes the cookie's properties. Note that the cookie object *must* contain a name, a value, and a domain property, or the method call will fail and return `false`.

6. We delete the cookie we just added using `phantom.deleteCookie`, which takes a single argument: a string for the name of the cookie we wish to delete.

> If we do not know the name of the cookie, we need to iterate through the `phantom.cookies` array to identify the name of the cookie we wish to delete.

7. We delete *all* cookies by calling `phantom.clearCookies`. This is functionally equivalent to calling the clear cookies command from a menu or dialog in any other browser. Lastly, we exit the PhantomJS runtime.

See also

▸ The *Running PhantomJS with cookies* recipe in *Chapter 1, Getting Started with PhantomJS*

Specifying a path for external scripts

In this recipe, we will introduce the `libraryPath` property on the `phantom` object and discuss how to use it to control the source of scripts that are loaded in the runtime via `injectJs`.

Getting ready

To run this recipe, we will need at least one injectable script and the script that we want to run.

The script in this recipe is available in the downloadable code repository as `recipe03.js` under `chapter02`. If we run the provided example script, we must change to the root directory for the book's sample code.

How to do it...

Consider the following script:

```
console.log('Initial libraryPath: ' + phantom.libraryPath);

phantom.libraryPath = phantom.libraryPath.replace(/chapter02$/,
  'lib');

console.log('Updated libraryPath: ' + phantom.libraryPath);

var isInjected = phantom.injectJs('hemingway.js');

if (isInjected) {
  console.log('Script was successfully injected.');
  console.log('Give me some Fibonacci numbers! ' +
    fibonacci(Math.round(Math.random() * 10) + 1));

  phantom.exit();
} else {
  console.log('Failed to inject script.');
  phantom.exit(1);
}
```

Given the preceding code block, enter the following at the command line:

phantomjs chapter02/recipe03.js

Our output should look like the following:

```
Initial libraryPath: /Users/robf/phantomjs-cookbook/chapter02
Updated libraryPath: /Users/robf/phantomjs-cookbook/lib
Script was successfully injected.
Give me some Fibonacci numbers! 0,1,1,2,3,5,8,13,21,34
```

How it works...

The `injectJs` method on the `phantom` object can take a script from the filesystem and inject it into the current execution context. It works by loading the specified file (relative to the current `libraryPath`), interpreting it, and applying the interpreted script (global variables and all) to the current context; this operates in much the same way as JavaScript is imported onto a web page via a `script` tag. We should use `injectJs` to import scripts that do *not* conform to the CommonJS module proposal.

> The CommonJS module proposal is a specification for loading code that minimizes pollution of the global scope or namespace in a JavaScript program by providing an `exports` object (within the module) where we can attach our public properties and methods, and a global `require` method that we can use to import those modules. For more information about the CommonJS module proposal, see `http://wiki.commonjs.org/wiki/Modules`.

Our preceding example script performs the following actions:

1. We write the current base path for library scripts to the console using the `phantom.libraryPath` property.

2. We update the default `libraryPath` (the script's working directory) to be our intended target directory. Then, we write that to the console as well.

3. We import a script using `phantom.injectJs`, passing (in our case) only the filename to the method. The method returns `true` if the script imports successfully and `false` if it does not; this Boolean value is assigned to our variable, `isInjected`.

4. If the script imports successfully, we call the `fibonacci` function that was imported from the script and write its results to the console. Then, we exit from PhantomJS. Otherwise, we exit PhantomJS with an error message.

There's more...

As mentioned in the preceding section, a call to `phantom.injectJs` is functionally equivalent to a `script` tag on a web page—code is read from the target, passed through the interpreter, and applied to the execution context. The `libraryPath` property plays an important role here because it provides the path on the filesystem that will be used to resolve any relative paths requested through `phantom.injectJs`.

Injectable scripts can be stored in any readable location on the filesystem. The key requirement of `injectJs` is that it can resolve the provided path and interpret the target as a syntactically correct JavaScript file.

phantom.libraryPath

The `libraryPath` property on the `phantom` object is a simple one—it is a string that holds the value for the absolute path that will be used to resolve scripts that are injected into the execution context. The property on the `phantom` object is read/write, so we can update it at any time during our script. However, it *must* be an absolute path. We can change `libraryPath` to be a relative path, but methods that depend on it (for example, `injectJs`) will fail. We can update `libraryPath` through a simple assignment, for example:

```
phantom.libraryPath = '/path/to/libraries';
```

phantom.injectJs

The `injectJs` method on the `phantom` object is one way that we can import external scripts into our current execution context. As mentioned in the discussion of our example script, calls to `phantom.injectJs` take a string as an argument, and that string should be a reference to a file on the filesystem, either as a filename, a relative path, or an absolute path. The script path argument is consumed as follows:

- If PhantomJS can interpret the path as absolute, it will attempt to retrieve the script from that location on the filesystem.

- If PhantomJS cannot interpret the path as absolute, it will attempt to resolve that script as relative to the specified `libraryPath`.

The `injectJs` method itself provides feedback about the loading operation in the form of its return value: `true` if the script was successfully injected, and `false` if it failed for any reason. If successfully injected, the interpreted contents of the script are applied to the *outer space* (and *not* within any `webpage` objects) of the PhantomJS execution context.

phantom.injectJs versus require

It is important to consider the contents of any script before importing it with `injectJs`. Just as scripts imported into a web page can easily "pollute" the global scope, so can scripts imported using `injectJs`. Put another way, if we have a variable named `foo` in our PhantomJS script, and then we use `injectJs` to import a script that *also* has a variable named `foo`, they will collide, and the most recently added value for `foo` will take precedence.

Compare `injectJs` with the global `require` function that assumes the target files to be CommonJS modules. Although scripts imported with `injectJs` have the potential to pollute the current execution context and clobber variables or function names, we have a lot more freedom to write these scripts in whatever style we choose. Contrast this with the `require` function, which expects to resolve an `exports` object with the exposed methods and properties. The `require` method is a safer solution, but it comes at the cost of flexibility, and it cannot take advantage of `phantom.libraryPath`; meanwhile, `injectJs` can consume scripts that otherwise target more platforms but carry more risks associated with the PhantomJS global scope. It's up to us to consider those trade-offs when designing our library scripts and how we will import them.

See also

▶ The *Reading a file from PhantomJS* recipe

▶ The *Loading custom modules in PhantomJS* recipe

Setting up a global PhantomJS error handler

This recipe introduces the onError callback and demonstrates how we can use it to catch and handle errors in the PhantomJS runtime. As this onError callback is attached to the phantom object, we can use it to handle errors that are not otherwise handled by try-catch statements in our PhantomJS scripts or by onError handlers attached to webpage objects.

Getting ready

To run this recipe, we will need a script that we believe has a tendency to fail.

The script in this recipe is available in the downloadable code repository as recipe04.js under chapter02. If we run the provided example script, we must change to the root directory for the book's sample code.

How to do it...

Consider the following script:

```
phantom.onError = function(message, trace) {
  console.error('[PHANTOMJS ERROR] ' + message);
  trace.forEach(function(t) {
    console.error('  >> [' + t.line + '] ' +
      (t.function ? '[' + t.function + '] ' : '') +
      t.file || t.sourceURL);
  });
  phantom.exit(1);
};

function doSomeErrorProneStuff() {
  throw new Error('Gremlins fed after midnight.');
}

doSomeErrorProneStuff();

console.log('Exiting cleanly.');
phantom.exit(0);
```

Given the preceding script, enter the following at the command line:

```
phantomjs chapter02/recipe04.js
```

Our output should look like the following:

```
[PHANTOMJS ERROR] Error: Gremlins fed after midnight.
  >> [13] [doSomeErrorProneStuff] chapter02/recipe04.js
  >> [16] chapter02/recipe04.js
```

How it works...

Our preceding example script performs the following actions:

1. We attach the error handler by assigning the error-handling function to `phantom.onError`. The `onError` function expects two parameters: `message`, which is the message on the thrown error and `trace`, which is an array representing the call stack leading to that unhandled error.

2. In our `onError` handler, we simply write the contents of the error message to the console and then write out the stack trace as well.

3. We enter the main part of our script, declare our error-prone function (`doSomeErrorProneStuff`), and immediately call that function. Note that `doSomeErrorProneStuff` only throws an error that is unhandled, thus dumping us into the `onError` handler.

4. Lastly, we write out a message to the console and then exit with a `0` status. However, this code is effectively unreachable because of the error thrown by `doSomeErrorProneStuff`.

Note that once we enter the `onError` handler, we are not returned to our previous execution context. Depending on the specifications of our script, we will need to consider how to proceed—is it sufficient just to console out the error message and stack trace? Or do we need to reattempt an operation (for example, rerun a request with different arguments or a longer timeout, and so on)? By applying a function to `phantom.onError`, we create a global error handler that will catch all otherwise unhandled exceptions.

There's more...

As previously mentioned, when assigned, `phantom.onError` effectively creates a global error handler in the PhantomJS runtime. It is worth noting here that simply setting up a function on `phantom.onError` is not a substitute for safe code. Our scripts should still perform the appropriate checks (for example, for types and non-null values, and so on) and use the `if` or `try-catch` statements for flow control, wherever they make sense. However, there will be occasions where it makes sense to set up error handlers with `onError`; for example, when we cannot know all the places where an error might occur and we must ensure that our script exits, even if it exits with an error code.

onError parameters

As previously mentioned, the `onError` callback function takes two parameters: `message` and `trace`. The `message` parameter is simple enough—it is the error message string from the unhandled error.

The other parameter, `trace`, is an array of objects representing the call stack leading up to the unhandled error. The individual objects in the `trace` array have the following properties:

- ▶ `file`: This is a relative path to the source file for the code that was being executed in that stack frame; `file` is mutually exclusive with the `sourceURL` property

- ▶ `sourceURL`: This is the URL for the source file for the code that was being executed in that stack frame; `sourceURL` is mutually exclusive with the `file` property

- ▶ `line`: This is an integer corresponding with the line number in the source code for the code that was being executed in that stack frame

- ▶ `function`: This is the name (if any) of the function being executed in that stack frame; if the function has no name, this will be an empty string

> We saw the properties of the `trace` objects in use in the `onError` callback function in our example script earlier in this recipe.

See also

- ▶ The *Recording debugger messages* recipe in *Chapter 3, Working with webpage Objects*

Controlling the exit status of a PhantomJS script

Although we have seen and used `phantom.exit` in all of our previous examples, we will now discuss it explicitly and learn in detail how it is used. In this recipe, we will learn how to control the exit status of the PhantomJS application.

Getting ready

To run this recipe, we require a script where we need to control the exit status.

The script in this recipe is available in the downloadable code repository as `recipe05.js` under `chapter02`. If we run the provided example script, we must change to the root directory for the book's sample code.

How to do it...

Consider the following script:

```
console.log('Running the PhantomJS exit demo...');

if (Math.floor(Math.random() * 10) % 2 === 0) {
  console.log('Exiting cleanly from PhantomJS!');
  phantom.exit();
} else {
  console.log('Exiting with an error status.');
  phantom.exit(1);
}
```

Given the preceding script, enter the following at the command line:

phantomjs chapter02/recipe05.js

If the script makes a clean exit, our output should look like the following:

Running the PhantomJS exit demo...
Exiting cleanly from PhantomJS!

If the script exits with an error, our output should look like the following:

Running the PhantomJS exit demo...
Exiting with an error status.

We can also verify this from the command line on Linux and OS X as follows:

echo $?

On Windows, we can verify it as follows:

echo %ERRORLEVEL%

We will see a 0 or a 1, depending on whether the script exited successfully or with an error, respectively.

How it works...

Though a trivial example, our example script works as follows:

1. We print our introductory message and then test whether a random number is even or odd using a % 2 calculation.
2. If we have an even number, we make a clean exit from PhantomJS by calling `phantom.exit`.
3. If we have an odd number, we exit from PhantomJS with an error by calling `phantom.exit` and passing it a non-zero integer.

The `phantom.exit` method is our only way to gracefully exit a script in PhantomJS. It takes an optional integer as its only parameter, and this integer is the exit status that will be returned to the shell session that initiated PhantomJS. If we do not pass any argument to `phantom.exit`, then it will assume we are exiting successfully and will return a 0.

There's more...

Controlling the PhantomJS exit status is an important component of integrating the application into many workflows. By exposing the ability to control the overall program exit status through the `phantom.exit` API, our JavaScript scripts become first-class citizens on the command line.

Type coercion with phantom.exit

Another interesting point to note about `phantom.exit` is that although its sole parameter expects an integer, it exhibits some "typical JavaScript" coercive behavior with non-integer arguments. For example, it effectively performs `Math.round` on floats, as follows:

```
phantom.exit(1.1);
// exits as 1
phantom.exit(1.9);
// exits as 2
```

Passing a string to `phantom.exit` will effectively cast the value to a number using the `Number` constructor on that argument before falling back to its previously stated rounding rules, as shown in the following code snippet:

```
phantom.exit('1');
// exits as 1
phantom.exit('1.5');
// exits as 2
phantom.exit('one');
// exits as 0
```

Note that strings that cannot be parsed into numbers are discarded, and the call to `phantom.exit` is treated as though no arguments were passed.

As a final curiosity, the casting behavior with `phantom.exit` extends to Boolean values as well. Consistent with JavaScript's rules for "truthy" and "falsy" values, `Number` casts `true` and `false` to 1 and 0, respectively. Though this makes sense in JavaScript's larger context, it may also seem somewhat counterintuitive when used with `phantom.exit` as follows:

```
phantom.exit(true);
// exits as 1 -- interpreted as an error
phantom.exit(false);
// exits as 0 -- interpreted as a success
```

Generally speaking, although we *can* pass these non-integer values to `phantom.exit`, we should *only* pass integers or call the method with no arguments.

Inspecting command-line arguments

In this recipe, we introduce the `system` module and discuss how to inspect arguments that are passed to the PhantomJS runtime environment from the command line. The `system` module is the bridge between PhantomJS, its host operating system, and the process it runs in.

Getting ready

To run this recipe, we will need a script that accepts arguments from the command line.

The script in this recipe is available in the downloadable code repository as `recipe06.js` under `chapter02`. If we run the provided example script, we must change to the root directory for the book's sample code.

How to do it...

Consider the following script:

```
var system = require('system'),
    args   = system.args;

console.log('script name is: ' + args[0]);

if (args.length > 1) {
  var restArgs = args.slice(1);
  restArgs.forEach(function(arg, i) {
    console.log('[' + (i + 1) + '] ' + arg);
  });
} else {
  console.log('No arguments were passed.');
}

phantom.exit();
```

Given the preceding script, enter the following at the command line:

```
phantomjs chapter02/recipe06.js first second "third and fourth"
```

Our output should look like the following:

```
script name is: chapter02/recipe06.js
[1] first
[2] second
[3] third and fourth
```

How it works...

Our example script works as follows:

1. We require the `system` module. This is the module that contains the `args` array of command-line arguments.

2. We assign the array of command-line arguments (`system.args`) to a variable, `args`.

3. We print out the name of the script from `args[0]`. The script name is always the first item in the arguments array.

4. We take the rest of the arguments (using `slice`) and iterate through them, printing out each one. If we failed to pass any other arguments, we simply print out a message saying so.

5. We exit from PhantomJS.

The `system` module is our "window to the world," giving us a handful of properties that allow us to see beyond PhantomJS and into the host operating system and its environment. In this recipe, we are specifically interested in the `args` array, which holds the command-line arguments otherwise passed to PhantomJS. As previously noted, the first item in the `args` array is always the script name (as specified on the command line); the remaining items are the strings that are parsed from the space-separated command-line arguments. It is important to note that every element in the `args` array is treated as a string; if we need to deal with other types, we will need to use the appropriate JavaScript parsing function (for example, `parseInt`, `parseFloat`, and `JSON.parse`).

There's more...

The `system.args` array replaces the `phantom.scriptName` and `phantom.args` properties that we saw in the *Running a PhantomJS script with arguments* recipe in *Chapter 1, Getting Started with PhantomJS*. As we noted previously, `phantom.scriptName` and `phantom.args` are both deprecated, and we should prefer `system.args` for our scripts.

Establishing a command-line convention

Note that PhantomJS allows us to pass command-line arguments to our scripts, but it is not opinionated about the format that those arguments take. Scripts that target PhantomJS and make sufficiently prolific use of command-line arguments for runtime configuration should adopt a consistent command-line argument pattern. Although unenforced, PhantomJS establishes its convention through its own command-line API named parameters, with keys prefixed by two dashes (--) and values separated by an equal to sign (=). For example:

```
phantomjs script.js --first=1 --second=true
```

If we frequently find ourselves in a situation where we need to parse these command-line arguments, we can write a tiny utility script to help us create these runtime configuration objects from the command-line arguments. For example:

```
function parseValue(v) {
  if (typeof v === 'undefined') {
    return true;
  } else {
    try {
      return JSON.parse(v);
    } catch (e) {
      return v;
    }
  }
}

function parseArguments(args) {
  return args.reduce(function(prev, current) {
      current = current.split('=');
      current[0] = current[0].replace(/^--/, '');

      prev[current[0]] = parseValue(current[1]);

      return prev;
    }, {});
}

// for example, use it like:
var args = require('system').args.slice(1);
parseArguments(args);
```

Such a utility script could be brought into other scripts through `phantom.injectJs` or by using `require` (with some slight changes).

See also

▸ The *Running a PhantomJS script with arguments* recipe in *Chapter 1, Getting Started with PhantomJS*

▸ The *Specifying a path for external scripts* recipe

▸ The *Loading custom modules in PhantomJS* recipe

Inspecting system environment variables

This recipe expands on the `system` module, demonstrating how to use its `env` property to obtain the values of variables set in the host environment.

Getting ready

To run this recipe, we will need a script that expects to retrieve values from variables set in the host environment; we should set those variables ahead of time for the sake of demonstration.

The script in this recipe is available in the downloadable code repository as `recipe07.js` under `chapter02`. If we run the provided example script, we must change to the root directory for the book's sample code.

How to do it...

Prepare the host environment by setting the `BOOK_TITLE` variable:

Platform	Set variable by
Windows	`SET BOOK_TITLE=PhantomJS Cookbook`
Mac OS X	`export BOOK_TITLE="PhantomJS Cookbook"`
Linux	`export BOOK_TITLE="PhantomJS Cookbook"`

Consider the following script:

```
var env  = require('system').env,
    prop = 'BOOK_TITLE';

var keys = Object.keys(env).filter(function(k) {
  return k === prop;
});

if (keys.length === 1) {
  console.log(keys[0] + ' = ' + env[keys[0]]);
} else {
```

```
    console.log('Could not find a property in env called ' + prop);
}
```

```
phantom.exit();
```

Given the preceding script, enter the following command at the command line:

phantomjs chapter02/recipe07.js

Our output should look like the following:

BOOK_TITLE = PhantomJS Cookbook

How it works...

Our example script works as follows:

1. We take the `system` module and grab the `env` property from it, assigning it to our own `env` variable.
2. We use `Object.keys` to get *just* the keys from `env`; we then pass these keys through the `filter` method, looking for one that matches the property we are looking for, that is, `BOOK_TITLE`.
3. If we find a property called `BOOK_TITLE` in `env`, we print out the value of the property. Otherwise, we print a message saying that we could find no such property.
4. We exit from PhantomJS.

The `env` property on the `system` module is a "plain" JavaScript object (key/value pairs) representing the environment variables and their values, as provided by the host operating system. The value of `env` is equivalent to what we would get on the command line for `printenv` (in Linux or OS X) or `SET` (in Windows). It can be useful for getting the value of system-wide properties or settings; however, `env` is read-only, and PhantomJS cannot add or change any of its properties.

There's more...

As noted previously, the `system` module is our window to the rest of the world in our host. We have seen how it can reveal arguments from the command line and spy on environmental variables, but `system` also exposes several other properties:

▶   The `os` property displays information about the host operating system. For example, consider the following in the REPL:

```
phantomjs> require('system').os
{
    "architecture": "32bit",
```

```
"name": "mac",
"version": "10.8 (Mountain Lion)"
}
```

► The `platform` property displays the name of the platform (`phantomjs`); it is read-only. For example, consider the following in the REPL:

```
phantomjs> require('system').platform
"phantomjs"
```

► The `pid` property is another read-only property, and it displays the process ID for the current PhantomJS runtime. For example, consider the following in the REPL:

```
phantomjs> console.log(require('system').pid)
11586
undefined
```

► The `system` module exposes three other undocumented objects: `stderr`, `stdin`, and `stdout`. All three of these objects have the following methods:

- ❑ `destroyed(QObject*)`
- ❑ `destroyed()`
- ❑ `deleteLater()`
- ❑ `read(QVariant)`
- ❑ `read()`
- ❑ `write(QString)`
- ❑ `seek(qint64)`
- ❑ `readLine()`
- ❑ `writeLine(QString)`
- ❑ `atEnd()`
- ❑ `flush()`
- ❑ `close()`

► With these methods, PhantomJS offers access to the standard streams for reading from and writing to our scripts interactively using the CommonJS IO/A proposal. However, although these objects and their methods were introduced in PhantomJS 1.9, they are undocumented, and we should approach them with caution.

> For more information on the CommonJS IO/A proposal, see http://wiki.commonjs.org/wiki/IO/A.

Saving a file from a PhantomJS script

Now we will introduce the `fs` module which provides an API for working with the filesystem from a PhantomJS script. In this recipe, we will demonstrate how to save a file from PhantomJS and use the `separator` property for generating filesystem-safe paths, checking whether the target directory exists, creating it if it does not, checking write permissions if it does, and then persisting the contents to the filesystem.

Getting ready

To run this recipe, we will need a script that expects to write a file to the filesystem. In order to write that file, we need write permissions in the destination directory.

The script in this recipe is available in the downloadable code repository as `recipe08.js` under `chapter02`. If we run the provided example script, we must change to the root directory for the book's sample code.

How to do it...

Consider the following script:

```
var fs        = require('fs'),
    targetDir = 'foo-log';

if (!fs.exists(targetDir)) {
  console.log('Creating directory ' + targetDir);
  fs.makeDirectory(targetDir);
}

if (!fs.isWritable(targetDir)) {
  console.error(targetDir + ' is not writable!');
  phantom.exit(1);
}

console.log('Writing file...');
var currentTime = new Date().getTime();
fs.write(targetDir + fs.separator + currentTime + '.txt',
  'Current time is ' + currentTime, 'w');

phantom.exit();
```

Given the preceding script, enter the following at the command line:

```
phantomjs chapter02/recipe08.js
```

We can verify that it worked by checking the filesystem, seeing that a new directory was created with the name foo-log, and checking that it contains one file with a timestamp as its name.

How it works...

Our example script works as follows:

1. We take the fs module and assign it to a variable with the same name. We also assign the name of our target directory to the variable targetDir.

2. We check whether our target directory exists using fs.exists. If the target directory does not exist, then we create it using fs.makeDirectory.

3. We check whether the target directory is writable using fs.isWritable. If it is not writable, we print an error to the console and exit PhantomJS.

4. Knowing that our target directory exists and is writable, we get the current time from a new Date object and store it in the currentTime variable. We use currentTime as part of the name of our file (adding .txt to the end); we also use currentTime as part of the string that is written to that file. We persist this to the filesystem using fs.write. In our call to fs.write, we construct the path using fs.separator, which ensures that it uses the correct separator for our filesystem.

> Note that fs.separator holds a / for POSIX-compatible systems (Linux and OS X) or a \ for Windows. If our scripts need to be portable across platforms, we must use fs.separator to ensure compatibility.

5. We exit from PhantomJS.

> For the API documentation on the fs (filesystem) module, see http://phantomjs.org/api/fs/.

The fs module is the API provided by PhantomJS for interacting with the host filesystem. It is modeled on the CommonJS Filesystem proposal; it features a robust set of properties and methods for reading from and writing to files and for working with directory trees.

> For more information on the CommonJS Filesystem proposal, see http://wiki.commonjs.org/wiki/Filesystem.

Note that we use defensive code when dealing with the filesystem. As noted before, we take care to check existence and permission at every step. Does our target directory exist? Can we write to it? Our example isn't even as defensive as it *could* be. It pays to be cautious when performing I/O—there's no telling what may go wrong along the way.

There's more...

Most of the methods that we call in our example return Booleans. As noted before, code that deals with the filesystem should be defensive, and as such, we find ourselves making extensive use of existential- and permissions-related methods.

exists

The `exists` method takes a single argument, `path`, which is a string specifying the relative or absolute path of the directory or file to check. The `exists` method returns `true` if the reference exists and `false` if it does not.

makeDirectory

The `makeDirectory` method takes a single argument, `path`, which is a string specifying the relative or absolute path of the directory to create. The `makeDirectory` method returns `true` if the directory is created successfully and `false` if it fails for any reason. Note that `makeDirectory` will not overwrite a directory that already exists, and it will return `false`.

isWritable

The `isWritable` method takes a single argument, `path`, which is a string specifying the relative or absolute path of the directory or file to check. `isWritable` returns `true` if the reference is writable and `false` if it is not.

write

The `write` method takes three arguments:

▶ `path`: This is the relative or absolute path, as a string, of the file to be written

▶ `content`: This is the content to be written to the filesystem, whether it is text or binary data

▶ `mode`: This is the write "mode" to use; it takes one of the following as a string: w (write), a (append), or wb (write binary)

Given these three arguments, `fs.write` will write the contents to the filesystem (assuming that the target directory exists and that we have write permissions); the method itself is `void` and returns `undefined`.

> In addition to the `write` method for writing files, the `fs` module also exposes `stream` objects that have `write` and `writeLine` methods. We will learn more about `steam` objects in the *Reading a file from PhantomJS* recipe later in this chapter.

See also

▶ The *Reading a file from PhantomJS* recipe

Reading a file from PhantomJS

In this recipe, we will expand on the `fs` module and demonstrate how to read from a file in PhantomJS. We will cover the `open` method and discuss the `stream` object that it returns.

Getting ready

To run this recipe, we will need a script that expects to read a file from the filesystem and a target file from which to read.

The script in this recipe is available in the downloadable code repository as `recipe09.js` under `chapter02`. If we run the provided example script, we must change to the root directory for the book's sample code.

How to do it...

Consider the following script:

```
phantom.onError = function(message, trace) {
  console.error('[Something went wrong!] - ' + message);
  phantom.exit(1);
};

var fs    = require('fs'),
    _name = 'reamde.txt',
    path  = require('system').args[0].split(fs.separator),
    file;

path = path.slice(0, path.length - 1).join(fs.separator);

fs.changeWorkingDirectory(path);

file = fs.open(_name, 'r');

console.log('[Reading ' + _name + '...]');
while (!file.atEnd()) {
  console.log(file.readLine());
}
```

```
console.log('[Closing ' + _name + '.]');
file.close();

phantom.exit();
```

Enter the following at the command line:

phantomjs chapter02/recipe09.js

Our output should look like the following:

```
[Reading reamde.txt...]
The Big U
Zodiac
Snow Crash
The Diamond Age: or A Young Lady's Illustrated Primer
Cryptonomicon
Quicksilver
The Confusion
The System of the World
Anathem
Reamde
[Closing reamde.txt.]
```

How it works...

Our example script works as follows:

1. We attach a global error handler using `phantom.onError`. As we are dealing with I/O on the filesystem, it pays to be defensive.

2. We require the `fs` module and assign it to a variable with the same name. We also assign the name of our target file to the _name variable. Then, we grab the path of the currently executing script, split it on the host operating system's path separator, and hold it as an array in the `path` variable.

3. We discard the filename from `path` and rejoin the path parts using the host operating system's path separator. Then, we change our working directory using `fs.changeWorkingDirectory`.

4. We create a handle to our target file using `fs.open`, which returns a `stream` object that we assign to the `file` variable.

5. We loop through the file in a `while` statement, using `file.atEnd` to check our progress through the lines of the file. In the body of the `while` statement, we use `file.readLine` to get the contents of the current line in the file and write them to the console.

6. We terminate our stream operation using `file.close`.

7. We exit from PhantomJS.

As we discussed in the *Saving a file from a PhantomJS script* recipe earlier in this chapter, we should be defensive when dealing with I/O operations. However, instead of the finely-grained checks we performed in that recipe, we charge ahead optimistically through our script and rely on our global error handler to bail us out in the event of a failure.

There's more...

Although we expanded somewhat on the `fs` module, the underlying lesson in this recipe is around the `stream` objects and how to work with them.

changeWorkingDirectory

The `changeWorkingDirectory` method (on the `fs` module) allows us to change the current working directory of the script's execution context. By default, our current working directory is the working directory from which the script was launched, and not necessarily the directory where the script "lives" on the filesystem. The `changeWorkingDirectory` method takes a single argument, `path`, which is a string specifying the relative or absolute path of the directory we want to change to. The `changeWorkingDirectory` method returns `true` if the directory change is successful and `false` if it is not.

open

The `open` method (on the `fs` module) is the critical component of this recipe; it gives us our handle to our target file, and it returns the `stream` object that we will work with while iterating through the file's contents.

The `open` method takes two arguments, which are:

▸ `path`: This is the relative or absolute path, as a string, of the file to be opened

▸ `mode`: This is the mode we will use when opening `stream` for this file; it takes one of the following as a string: `r` (read), `w` (write), `a` (append), `rb` (read binary), or `wb` (write binary)

Again, `open` returns a `stream` object.

stream objects

In PhantomJS, a `stream` object is a handle to a file on the filesystem. With that handle, we can inspect and manipulate the file. Note that `stream` objects impact our overhead for system resources (for example, by opening sockets), and we must be diligent about closing our streams as we finish with each object.

In our example, we perform some relatively trivial operations with our stream; for instance, checking if we are at the end and reading the line. Nevertheless, the example provides a solid foundation for how to think about and work with `stream` objects.

atEnd

The `atEnd` method on a `stream` object takes no arguments, and it returns `true` or `false` depending on whether we have reached the end of that file or not. Using `atEnd` is an excellent choice for iterating through the lines of a file when we have opened it in read mode.

readLine

The `readLine` method on a `stream` object returns the current line of content as a string. Note that we cannot query the stream for the current line or the total lines; these are bits of internal state that are not exposed on the API surface area.

close

The `close` method on a `stream` object completes our operations with it, and it is then ready to be garbage collected; `close` is a void method and returns `undefined`. Note that we cannot access the `stream` object after calling `close`.

Other stream methods

In addition to the previously described stream methods, `stream` objects have several other methods:

- `read`: This returns the entire content of `stream` as a string
- `write` and `writeLine`: These take a single string as an argument and write it to `stream`; specifically *how* the string is written will depend on the mode `stream` was opened in
- `seek`: This takes an integer as an argument and "seeks" that position in `stream`, effectively moving the read caret to that position; positions in `stream` are 0 indexed, and in this way we can think of them as arrays
- `flush`: This takes no arguments and immediately flushes all pending input or output on `stream`

See also

- The *Setting up a global PhantomJS error handler* recipe
- The *Inspecting command-line arguments* recipe
- The *Saving a file from a PhantomJS script* recipe

Creating a custom module for PhantomJS

In this recipe, we will learn how to create a custom module for PhantomJS that can be imported into our script using the `require` function.

Getting ready

For this recipe, we will only need a text editor. Some knowledge of CommonJS modules is useful but not strictly necessary.

How to do it...

In our text editor, we write the script that will be our module. As PhantomJS adheres to the CommonJS module system, the contents of this file will *not* pollute the global execution context after being imported; the only aspects of the script that are exposed will be those items attached to the `exports` object, and even then it must be assigned to a variable after the `require` expression.

For example, we could create our module in the following way:

```
function parseValue(v) {
  if (typeof v === 'undefined') {
    return true;
  } else {
    try {
      return JSON.parse(v);
    } catch (e) {
      return v;
    }
  }
}

function parseArguments(args) {
  return args.reduce(function(prev, current) {
      current = current.split('=');
      current[0] = current[0].replace(/^--/, '');

      prev[current[0]] = parseValue(current[1]);

      return prev;
    }, {});
}

exports.parseArgs = parseArguments;
```

This would create a module with a single exposed method (`parseArgs`, in our example).

> The preceding script is available in the downloadable code repository as `arg-parser.js` under `lib`. For more information about CommonJS modules, see `http://wiki.commonjs.org/wiki/Modules/1.1.1`.

How it works...

As previously mentioned, PhantomJS adheres to the CommonJS modules proposal, and as such, we can create modules targeting the PhantomJS platform by following these conventions. The key points to keep in mind while creating a module are as follows:

- The file constitutes the module. It may refer to other files and other modules, but the file referenced by the `require` expression will be that file.
- The file's contents do not pollute the global context. Variables and functions remain private to the module, unless explicitly exposed; this gives us a lot of freedom in how we design and implement our module.
- Only the `exports` object is exposed. The only aspects of our module that are exposed to its downstream consumers are those properties and methods that are assigned to slots on the `exports` object. This `exports` object is what is returned from a `require` expression after it has evaluated the module.

See also

- The *Loading custom modules in PhantomJS* recipe

Loading custom modules in PhantomJS

In this recipe, we will learn how to load custom modules in our PhantomJS scripts using the `require` function. PhantomJS has several built-in modules, but we can also write our own (see the *Creating a custom module for PhantomJS* recipe earlier in this chapter) and import them in this way.

Getting ready

To run this recipe, we will need a custom module that we want to import using the `require` function; we can use the `arg-parser.js` module that we wrote in the *Creating a custom module for PhantomJS* recipe earlier in this chapter.

The script in this recipe is available in the downloadable code repository as `recipe11.js` under `chapter02`. If we run the provided example script, we must change to the root directory for the book's sample code.

How to do it...

Assuming that we are using our `arg-parser.js` script from the previous recipe, consider the following script:

```
var argParser = require('../lib/arg-parser'),
    args      = require('system').args.slice(1);

args = argParser.parseArgs(args);

Object.keys(args).forEach(function(k) {
  console.log(k + ' = ' + args[k] +
    ' (' + (typeof args[k]) + ')');
});

phantom.exit();
```

Given the preceding script, enter the following at the command line:

phantomjs chapter02/recipe11.js --one=1 --two="uno dos" --three

Our output should look like the following:

one = 1 (number)

two = uno dos (string)

three = true (boolean)

How it works...

Our example script works as follows:

1. We import our custom module using the `require` function. Note that we use a relative path to that module, and that path is *relative to the path of the executing script* and *not* relative to the current working directory (as reported by `fs.workingDirectory`).

2. We obtain the script arguments by requiring the `system` module and referencing the `args` array. We then immediately `slice` the `args` array so that we have all of the arguments *except* the first one (the script name).

3. We parse the arguments by calling the `parseArgs` method that is exposed by our module.

4. We iterate through the arguments and output the keys, their associated values, and their types, as parsed by `parseArgs`.

5. We exit from PhantomJS.

> For a discussion of the trade-offs between importing modules with `require` versus importing scripts with `phantom.injectJs`, see the *Specifying a path for external scripts* recipe in this chapter.

See also

- ▸ The *Specifying a path for external scripts* recipe
- ▸ The *Inspecting command-line arguments* recipe
- ▸ The *Creating a custom module for PhantomJS* recipe

3
Working with webpage Objects

In this chapter, we will cover:

- ▸ Creating a web page instance in PhantomJS with the webpage module
- ▸ Opening a URL within PhantomJS
- ▸ Generating a POST request from PhantomJS
- ▸ Inspecting page content from a PhantomJS script
- ▸ Including external JavaScript on the page
- ▸ Recording debugger messages
- ▸ Simulating mouse clicks in PhantomJS
- ▸ Simulating keyboard input in PhantomJS
- ▸ Simulating scrolling in PhantomJS
- ▸ Simulating mouse hovers in PhantomJS
- ▸ Blocking CSS from downloading
- ▸ Causing images to fail randomly
- ▸ Submitting Ajax requests from PhantomJS
- ▸ Working with WebSockets in PhantomJS

Introduction

In addition to the core APIs discussed in the previous chapter, PhantomJS provides one other critically important module as part of its standard library: the `webpage` module.

The `webpage` module exposes methods for creating instances of `webpage` objects (which are functionally equivalent to browser windows); these instances then have a suite of methods and properties that we can use to inspect and interact with the web pages.

The recipes in this chapter take a deep dive into the `webpage` module and include strategies for dealing with web page content. In particular, the recipes introduce us to techniques for interacting with web pages and how to capture those interactions for successful tests.

Creating a web page instance in PhantomJS with the webpage module

This recipe introduces the `webpage` module and demonstrates how to create an instance of a `webpage` object.

Getting ready

To run this recipe, we will simply create an instance of a `webpage` object; we can do this in the REPL.

> See the *Launching the PhantomJS REPL* recipe in *Chapter 1, Getting Started with PhantomJS*, for more information about the REPL.

How to do it...

After entering the PhantomJS REPL, perform the following steps:

1. Import the `webpage` module and assign it to a variable with that name, using the following command:

    ```
    phantomjs> var webpage = require('webpage');
    undefined
    ```

2. Create an instance of a `webpage` object from the module, using the following command:

    ```
    phantomjs> var thePage = webpage.create();
    undefined
    ```

3. Loop through the properties on the `webpage` instance and print them out, using the following command:

    ```
    phantomjs> for (var p in thePage) console.log(p);
    objectName
    ```

```
title
frameTitle
content
frameContent
# and 88 more
undefined
```

4. Destroy the `webpage` instance and exit PhantomJS, using the following command:

```
phantomjs> thePage.close();
undefined
phantomjs> phantom.exit();
```

How it works...

The `webpage` module exposes only one function, `create`, which is a factory function for creating instances of `webpage` objects.

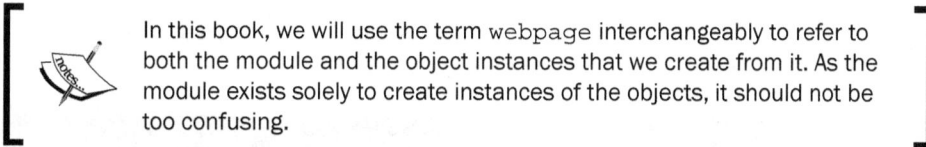

> In this book, we will use the term `webpage` interchangeably to refer to both the module and the object instances that we create from it. As the module exists solely to create instances of the objects, it should not be too confusing.

In our preceding example, we imported the `webpage` module using the `require` statement, and then we immediately created an instance of a `webpage` object using the module's `create` function.

We can think of individual `webpage` instances as if they were browser windows or tabs. These `webpage` objects can be assigned URLs (not unlike typing a URL into the address bar), can open those URLs, have a history (and can navigate forward and backward through it), and can have frames, errors, console messages, and just about every other thing that a customary browser window can have.

Our example demonstrates some of these properties and methods by iterating through the object and printing them out to the console.

Lastly, we mark the `webpage` object as finished and ready for garbage collection by calling its `close` method.

There's more...

The `webpage` module's `create` method takes a single undocumented argument: `opts`. The `opts` argument is an object of options and properties that would be assigned to the resulting `webpage` instance. Though this seems useful, most of the properties on a `webpage` object are simply ways of exposing internal state, and as such are internally managed; that being said, we *can* assign properties like event listeners (such as the ones we will discuss later in this chapter) to `webpage` objects in this way.

The WebPage constructor

Another way of creating `webpage` objects in a PhantomJS script is to use the (now deprecated) `WebPage` constructor. For example, instead of using the `webpage` module, as we did in our preceding example, we could do the following:

```
var thePage = new WebPage();
```

This code is functionally equivalent to:

```
var thePage = require('webpage').create();
```

We are likely to encounter the `WebPage` constructor in older PhantomJS scripts; though it is useful to recognize it, we should not use it for anything new.

Opening a URL within PhantomJS

This recipe expands on the `webpage` object and introduces its `open` method. Here, we will focus on the basic version of `open`, which takes a URL and a simple callback function.

Getting ready

To run this recipe, we will need a script that accesses a web page. For this example to complete, an Internet connection is also required.

The script in this recipe is available in the downloadable code repository as `recipe02.js` under `chapter03`. If we run the provided example script, we must change into the root directory for the book's sample code.

How to do it...

Consider the following script:

```
var webpage = require('webpage').create();

webpage.open('http://blog.founddrama.net/', function(status) {
```

```
switch (status) {
  case 'success':
    console.log('webpage opened successfully');
    phantom.exit(0);
    break;
  case 'fail':
    console.error('webpage did not open successfully');
    phantom.exit(1);
    break;
  default:
    console.error('webpage opened with unknown status: ' +
      status);
    phantom.exit(1);
}
});
```

Enter the following on the command line:

phantomjs chapter03/recipe02.js

The script will output the appropriate message based on whether it successfully opened the destination URL or not.

How it works...

Our example script performs the following actions:

1. It creates a `webpage` instance and assigns it to a variable with the same name.
2. It calls `webpage.open` and passes it two arguments: a URL (`http://blog.founddrama.net/`) and a callback function.

The callback function takes a single argument (`status`) and outputs the corresponding message depending on whether `open` was successful or not. After writing that message to the console, we exit from PhantomJS.

A `webpage` object is not very interesting by itself; we need to call `open` on it to arrive at any content worth working with. In the form presented in this example, we are passing two arguments to `webpage.open`: the first is the URL of our intended destination and the second is our callback function—it's what we want to do after we have opened (or failed to open) the URL. The callback function is called with one argument, `status`, which can be either the string `success` or `fail`. Once the page is successfully opened, we can do any number of manipulations with it; or, we can treat the failure condition as an opportunity to retry.

Also, we must remember not to exit from PhantomJS prematurely. Calls to `webpage.open` do not block, but instead kick off an asynchronous operation (retrieving that web page). If we place our call to `phantom.exit` outside of the callback function of `webpage.open`, we can cause our script to exit before the web page request is fulfilled. Make sure to place those calls to `phantom.exit` inside of the callback function, or else find some other means to monitor for the appropriate termination conditions.

There's more...

The `open` method on the `webpage` object has an overloaded signature. We can use it in the following forms:

- ▶ `open(url)`: Taking in the URL only, this form eschews the callback function and assumes that we will process the opened page using an `onLoadFinished` event handler.

- ▶ `open(url, callback)`: This is the form that we used in our preceding example; it takes the URL as the first argument and the callback function as the second argument. Note that the URL is always the first argument, and the callback, if present at all, is always the last. When we are dealing with `open`, we will mostly be using this form.

- ▶ `open(url, method, callback)`: This form (and the one that follows) is used when we wish to open a URL using an HTTP method other than `GET`. In this form, the URL is the first argument. We then specify the HTTP method (as a string) as the second argument, and then provide our callback function. We will mostly use this form for `DELETE` requests.

- ▶ `open(url, method, data, callback)`: Similar to the form we just discussed, this form is also not for `GET` requests. Once again, the URL is the first argument, we then specify the HTTP method (as a string) and provide the data associated with our request; lastly, we specify our callback function. We will mostly use this form for `POST` and `PUT` requests.

Lastly, there is one more form, `open(url, method, data, headers, callback)`, which matches the form discussed in our last bullet, except that we can provide additional request headers as an argument before our callback function. However, as this form is undocumented, we should prefer the `customHeaders` property on our `webpage` objects, and consider using them before this form of `open`. Be aware, however, that custom HTTP headers set with the `customHeaders` property are applied to every request, and not just the current request.

back function provided to the various forms of `webpage.open` is functionally equivalent to any function that may be assigned as the `webpage.onLoadFinished` event handler. However, the two are not mutually exclusive, and can either be used in concert or can cancel each other out. Generally speaking, we should use one or the other, unless there is a good reason to use them together.

The `webpage.onLoadFinished` handler is particularly useful in places where we need to change the behavior of our "after loading" response at runtime, or where we need a consistent handler for every such load event on a particu

See also

▶ The *Generating a POST request from PhantomJS* recipe

▶ The *Recording debugger messages* recipe, later in this chapter, which talks about working with the `webpage` object event handlers, including `onLoadFinished` and `onLoadStarted`.

Generating a POST request from PhantomJS

This recipe expands further on the `webpage.open` method by demonstrating its additional parameters for specifying an HTTP method and data. The recipe's discussion will also reframe the `open` method by illustrating how to use it for interacting with RESTful interfaces.

Getting ready

To run this recipe, we need a script that will make an HTTP request with a method other than `GET`, and some knowledge of what the URL expects with respect to the HTTP verb and the payload data (if any).

The script in this recipe is available in the downloadable code repository as `recipe03.js` under `chapter03`. If we run the provided example script, we must change to the root directory for the book's sample code.

Lastly, the script in this recipe runs against the demo site that is included with the cookbook's sample code repository. To run that demo site, we must have Node.js installed. In a separate terminal, change to the `phantomjs-sandbox` directory (in the sample code's directory), and start the app with the following command:

```
node app.js
```

How to do it...

Consider the following script:

```
var webpage  = require('webpage').create(),
    url      = 'http://localhost:3000/post-demo',
    postData = JSON.stringify({
            "foo": "bar",
            "now": new Date().getTime()
        });

webpage.customHeaders = { "Content-Type":"application/json" };

webpage.onInitialized = function() {
  webpage.customHeaders = {};
};

webpage.open(url, 'POST', postData, function(status) {
  if (status === 'fail') {
    console.error('Something went wrong posting to ' + url);
    phantom.exit(1);
  }

  console.log('Successful post to ' + url);
  phantom.exit(0);
});
```

Given the preceding script, enter the following at the command line:

`phantomjs chapter03/recipe03.js`

The script should print out the following:

`Successful post to http://localhost:3000/post-demo`

If we go back to the terminal where the demo app is running, we should see something like the following in the console:

`{ foo: 'bar', now: 1389059859377 }`

`POST /post-demo 200 1ms - 42b`

How it works...

Our preceding example script performs the following actions:

1. It creates a `webpage` instance and assigns it to a variable with the same name. It also assigns our target URL to the `url` variable, and it assigns our payload data to the `postData` variable.

2. Since we serialize our POST data as JSON, the script sets the Content-Type header to application/json using the webpage.customHeaders property.

3. Since customHeaders are sent with every request, and because we only want to send them with our first (POST) request, it uses the webpage.onInitialized event handler to clear out customHeaders. This event handler will be called after the web page is created but before the URL is loaded.

4. It calls the four-argument form of webpage.open to perform the POST operation. The arguments are as follows:

   ❑ The URL

   ❑ The HTTP method (for example, 'POST')

   ❑ The payload data (for example, serialized JSON or an x-www-form-urlencoded string)

   ❑ The callback function

In our callback function, we print a message about the success (or failure) of our POST, and then exit from PhantomJS.

> It is important to know what data format our target URL expects and craft our payload appropriately. Our example uses JSON because it is easier to read when compared to form data (a content type of application/x-www-form-urlencoded).

There's more...

What separates the code in this recipe from the simpler version of webpage.open that we saw in the *Opening a URL within PhantomJS* recipe in this chapter are the arguments in the second and third positions. To be specific, we are explicitly specifying which HTTP method (or verb) we want to use for our request with the second argument; if this request expects us to include data, we can pass it along as the next argument. In other words, although the default mode for webpage.open is to perform a GET request, we are free to specify any of the HTTP methods here.

In effect, this makes PhantomJS a REST client.

If you are asking "so what?", then consider it this way—by providing a way for PhantomJS to perform a POST through webpage.open, we can test the forms on our websites, but by permitting us to specify an HTTP method, it enables us to test our REST APIs as well. This increases PhantomJS' value as a tool for integration and functional testing.

This is not to suggest that PhantomJS is necessarily the best solution for testing your REST APIs. Clearly, we need to consider our project's requirements and the other factors specific to the situation—there may be other tools better suited to the job. On the other hand, it may be totally reasonable and prudent to test both the web application and the underlying REST API with PhantomJS, if for no other reason than we can test them both with the same tool. Again, we must perform the due diligence for our specific circumstance, but it's helpful to know that PhantomJS is an option.

Inspecting page content from a PhantomJS script

This recipe introduces `webpage.evaluate`, which provides us with a hook into the context and content of the web page we have requested, including ways to inspect and manipulate the DOM. The cornerstone for many of the recipes that lie ahead will be `webpage.evaluate`.

Getting ready

To run this recipe, we will need a script that loads a web page, and we will need a callback function to `webpage.open` that expects to work with the content of the HTTP response.

The script in this recipe is available in the downloadable code repository as `recipe04.js` under `chapter03`. If we run the provided example script, we must change to the root directory for the book's sample code. Lastly, for this example to work, we will need an Internet connection.

How to do it...

Consider the following script:

```
var webpage = require('webpage').create();

webpage.open('http://blog.founddrama.net/', function(status) {
  if (status === 'fail') {
    console.error('Failed to open requested page.');
    phantom.exit(1);
  }

  var titles = webpage.evaluate(function(selector) {
    var titles  = [],
        forEach = Array.prototype.forEach,
        nodes   = document.querySelectorAll(selector);

    forEach.call(nodes, function(el) {
      titles.push(el.innerText);
    });
```

```
    return titles;
}, '.post h2');

titles.forEach(function(t) {
  console.log(t);
});

phantom.exit();
});
```

Given the preceding script, enter the following at the command line:

```
phantomjs chapter03/recipe04.js
```

The script should print out the titles of the most recent posts on the blog.

How it works...

Our preceding example script performs the following actions:

1. It creates a `webpage` instance and assigns it to a variable with the same name.
2. It calls `webpage.open` on our target URL (`http://blog.founddrama.net/`) and passes it a callback function.
3. The callback function first inspects the `status` argument, and then it exits PhantomJS if it equals `fail`.
4. It retrieves the titles of the blog posts and assigns them to the `titles` variable by executing `webpage.evaluate`; it takes a callback function and an arbitrary number of other arguments that will be forwarded to the callback. In this case, our second argument is a selector string (`.post h2`).
5. The callback function to `webpage.evaluate` is executed in the context of the retrieved web page. In this example, we call `document.querySelectorAll` using the selector that was passed in as the second argument to `webpage.evaluate`. We then iterate through the `NodeList`, extracting the `innerText` of each element, and finally returning the `titles` array.

> Note that the callback function to `webpage.evaluate` is sandboxed; it has access to the DOM and to any JavaScript loaded on that web page, but it cannot "see out" into the PhantomJS execution context. We are limited with respect to what we can send back and forth between the inner (web page) and outer (PhantomJS) contexts, and what we send *must* be sent deliberately, through function arguments or return values. Generally speaking, we can only send primitive values (Booleans, numbers, and strings) or "JSON-ifiable" values (arrays and objects)—no functions, DOM nodes, or references.

6. After `webpage.evaluate` returns, the `titles` array will hold the values of the titles from the blog posts on the page. We can loop through the values using `forEach`, and print each one to the console.

7. Lastly, we exit from PhantomJS.

The two most important things to remember about `webpage.evaluate` are: it is perhaps *the* most critical tool in PhantomJS for inspecting web page contents, and its callback functions are sandboxed.

With respect to the first point, `webpage.evaluate` is an essential tool for inspecting the contents of the HTTP response. As noted previously though, the execution context for the callback function *is* that of the web page, and as such it has access to all of the same things that the web page has access to—the native DOM and BOM APIs, and any JavaScript loaded on that page. This is important because it means that not only can we inspect the web page's contents (as we did in our example), but we can also manipulate that page using our familiar JavaScript-based tools.

With respect to the sandboxed nature of the `webpage.evaluate` context—it is imperative to remember that we must be very deliberate and specific with how we try to move data between the two execution contexts (the inner context of the web page and the outer context of PhantomJS). As previously noted, if we can serialize the value as JSON, then it can cross the boundary between the two contexts; we cannot pass around complex objects such as DOM nodes or functions. Additionally, it is important to remember that the inner web page context cannot look *up* into the PhantomJS context. This may violate some of our expectations about how JavaScript works; it is not unreasonable to look at the preceding example and expect to refactor it to look more like this:

```
var titles = [];

webpage.evaluate(function(selector) {
    var forEach = Array.prototype.forEach,
        nodes   = document.querySelectorAll(selector);

    forEach.call(nodes, function(el) {
        titles.push(el.innerText);
    });
}, '.post h2');
```

After all, that's how scopes and closures work in JavaScript, right?

Except that in this case, we cannot consider the callback function of `webpage.evaluate` to be a *child scope* of the main script. Instead, we must look at it as more of a parallel scope to the one that otherwise contains it.

There's more...

In addition to `evaluate`, the PhantomJS `webpage` API also provides `evaluateAsync`. The `evaluateAsync` method is a void method, and it returns immediately. As such, it does not block (as `evaluate` does), but it also does not return any value after its evaluation is complete. We can use some of the event handlers (for example, `webpage.onConsoleMessage`) to intercept values, but if we are concerned with extracting data from the web page contents, then we are better off sticking with `webpage.evaluate`.

Including external JavaScript on the page

In this recipe, we will learn how to incorporate external JavaScript onto a web page using the `includeJs` and `injectJs` methods for remote and local scripts respectively.

Getting ready

To run this recipe, we will need a script that loads a web page, and also scripts that will be loaded by that script to use within the web page context.

The script in this recipe is available in the downloadable code repository as `recipe05.js` under `chapter03`. If we run the provided example script, we must change into the root directory for the book's sample code. Also, for this example to work, we will need an Internet connection.

Lastly, the script in this recipe runs against the demo site that is included with the cookbook's sample code repository. To run that demo site, we must have Node.js installed. In a separate terminal, change into the `phantomjs-sandbox` directory (in the sample code's directory), and start the app with the following command:

```
node app.js
```

How to do it...

Consider the following script:

```
var webpage = require('webpage').create(),
    script  = '../lib/hemingway.js',
    jquery  = 'http://ajax.googleapis.com/ajax/libs/jquery/2.0.3/
jquery.min.js';

webpage.open('http://localhost:3000/', function(status) {
  if (status === 'fail') {
    console.error('Failed to open web page.');
    phantom.exit(1);
  }
```

```
        if (webpage.injectJs(script)) {
          webpage.includeJs(jquery, function() {
            var fibs = webpage.evaluate(function() {
              var $ct  = $('<div></div>').appendTo('body'),
                  seed = Math.ceil(Math.random() * 10),
                  fibs = [];

              fibonacci(seed).forEach(function(n) {
                $ct.append('<div class="fib">' + n + '</div>');
              });


              $('.fib').each(function(i, el) {
                fibs.push(el.innerText);
              });

              return fibs;
            });

            console.log('Fibonacci numbers inserted included:');
            fibs.forEach(function(n) {
              console.log('  \u20D7 ' + n);
            });

            phantom.exit();
          });
        } else {
          console.error('Something went wrong trying to inject ' +
            script);
          phantom.exit(1);
        }
      });
```

Given the preceding script, enter the following at the command line:

phantomjs chapter03/recipe05.js

The script should print out a message that includes a list of the Fibonacci numbers that were inserted on the page.

How it works...

Our preceding example script performs the following actions:

1. It creates a `webpage` instance and assigns it to a variable with the same name. It also specifies the path to our local and remote scripts, and assigns them to `script` and `jquery` respectively.

2. It calls `webpage.open` on our target URL (`http://localhost:3000/`) and passes it a callback function.

3. Our callback function first inspects the `status` argument, and exits PhantomJS if it equals `fail`.

4. It calls `webpage.injectJs`, passing `script` as its sole argument; note that `webpage.injectJs` returns `true` if it successfully loads the file from the filesystem and places the script into the web page's execution context. If `webpage.injectJs` returns `false`, it prints a message to the console and exits from PhantomJS.

5. It calls `webpage.includeJs`, passing `jquery` as the first argument (specifying the URL of the script to load) and a callback function as the second argument.

6. In our callback function for `webpage.includeJs`, we declare the `fibs` variable and assign to it whatever value is returned from a call to `webpage.evaluate`.

7. In our call to `webpage.evaluate`, we perform the following:

    1. We create a container div (`$ct`) using jQuery, which we imported to the web page using `webpage.includeJs`.

    2. We create `seed`, which holds the seed value for our call to `fibonacci`.

    3. We create a `fibs` array for this context to hold our return values.

    4. We call `fibonacci` with `seed` and iterate over the values, appending a div (with a class of `fib`) for each. Note that the `fibonacci` function was imported using `webpage.injectJs` from the `hemingway.js` library.

    5. We use jQuery to iterate over those divs, and extract the Fibonacci values from the `innerText` of each element.

8. We return the array of Fibonacci numbers.

9. With the Fibonacci numbers assigned to `fibs`, we iterate over the list and print them to the console.

10. Lastly, we exit from PhantomJS.

There's more...

The obvious difference between `includeJs` and `injectJs` is that the former loads a remote file (from a URL) and the latter loads a local file (from the filesystem). However, to fully understand what separates these two methods, we should take a closer look at them.

includeJs

The `includeJs` method imports a script into the context of the loaded web page, loading that resource from a URL; it effectively behaves just like any other dynamic script loading operation—by creating script tags at runtime and appending them to the body. The following two arguments are taken by `includeJs`:

- The URL of the remote script resource as a string.
- A callback function that is executed in the context of the web page. This callback function takes a single argument (the URL of the imported resource) and has no return value.

> Note that `includeJs` is a void function and has no return value. Another important thing to note about `includeJs` is that it is asynchronous; it will not block the main thread of execution in our PhantomJS scripts while we wait for the remote script to finish loading.
>
> However, a word of caution about `includeJs`—the method provides us no feedback about the success or failure of the resource we are trying to load. Contrast this with `webpage.evaluate`, which passes a status argument to its callback function to inform us whether the resource loaded successfully; `includeJs` provides no such feedback and its callback function may never execute if the script resource fails to load (for example, because of a 404 error). As such, it may be prudent to wrap calls to `includeJs` in some kind of timeout.

injectJs

The `injectJs` method on a `webpage` instance (not to be confused with `phantom.injectJs`) imports a script into the context of the loaded web page, loading the resource from a file. Effectively, `injectJs` works by:

- Loading the script from the filesystem
- Evaluating that script
- Adding the contents of that script to the execution context of the web page

The `injectJs` method takes a single argument, the location of the file to load; if the file's path is relative, and PhantomJS cannot locate it relative to the current directory, then `phantom.libraryPath` is used to resolve the path.

The `injectJs` method returns `true` if the script was loaded successfully, and it returns `false` if it was not.

Another thing to note about `injectJs` is that *unlike* `includeJs`, it is a synchronous method, and it *will* block the thread until it returns.

See also

▸ The *Specifying a path for external scripts* recipe in *Chapter 2, PhantomJS Core Modules*

▸ The *Creating a custom module for PhantomJS* recipe in *Chapter 2, PhantomJS Core Modules*

▸ The *Loading custom modules in PhantomJS* recipe in *Chapter 2, PhantomJS Core Modules*

▸ The *Inspecting page content from a PhantomJS script* recipe

Recording debugger messages

This recipe introduces the onConsoleMessage callback, discusses how to intercept debugger messages on the web page, and forwards them to the command-line output. The onConsoleMessage demonstration serves as an introduction to the other callbacks (for example, onAlert, onLoadFinished, onResourceReceived, and so on) that can be attached to webpage instances, while also providing a frame of reference for working with them.

Getting ready

To run this recipe, we will need a script that loads a web page, and then we will need JavaScript that executes in the context of that web page and writes messages to its console object.

The script in this recipe is available in the downloadable code repository as recipe06. js under chapter03. If we run the provided example script, we must change to the root directory for the book's sample code.

How to do it...

Consider the following script:

```
var webpage = require('webpage').create();

webpage.onConsoleMessage = function(message, lineNum, sourceId) {
  console.log('[phantomjs:page] ' + message);
};

webpage.evaluate(function(url) {
  console.log('Hello from inside of ' + url);
}, webpage.url);

phantom.exit();
```

Given the preceding script, enter the following on the command line:

phantomjs chapter03/recipe06.js

The script's console output should look like the following:

```
[phantomjs:page] Hello from inside of about:blank
```

How it works...

Our preceding example script performs the following actions:

1. It creates a `webpage` instance and assigns it to a variable with the same name.

2. It assigns a callback function to `webpage.onConsoleMessage`. This callback function simply takes the console message from the web page (the `message` argument) and writes it to the console from the PhantomJS context.

> The API for the `onConsoleMessage` callback function specifies three parameters: `message` (which we are using here), `lineNum` (the line number in the script that generated the console message), and `sourceId` (the source identifier or filename). However, although the API outlines all three of these parameters, only `message` is currently implemented as of version 1.9.2.

3. We call `webpage.evaluate` with a callback function, passing in the current URL of `webpage` as the argument; the callback function does only one thing, it writes a message to the web page's console.

4. Lastly, we exit from PhantomJS.

It is important to note here that the web page's `console` object is sandboxed, just like the rest of the JavaScript execution context on the web page. As such, the web page's `console` is completely separate from the PhantomJS `console`. However, the `onConsoleMessage` callback provides a bridge between the two worlds, and it allows us to forward the console messages from the web page out to our PhantomJS script.

There's more...

The `onConsoleMessage` callback is only one of 17 event-handler callbacks that can be attached to `webpage` objects. As we previously illustrated with our `onConsoleMessage` example, these callbacks can be used to pass information from the web page to the PhantomJS context, or to have PhantomJS respond to events that occur within the web page.

These callbacks include:

▶ `onAlert`: This handles calls to `alert` on the web page

▶ `onCallback`: This is an experimental feature, the callback is used for posting messages from the web page directly into the PhantomJS context

> Note that `onCallback` is likely to be replaced by some other message-based solution.

- `onClosing`: This handles the web page's close event, either from within the web page (`window.close`) or from PhantomJS itself (`webpage.close`)

- `onConfirm`: This handles calls to `confirm` on the web page; returning `true` from the callback is equivalent to clicking on **OK**, while returning `false` is equivalent to clicking on **Cancel**

- `onConsoleMessage`: Described earlier in this recipe, this callback handles calls to the various `console` methods

- `onError`: This handles JavaScript errors on the web page

- `onFilePicker`: This handles filesystem prompts (for example, clicks to an HTML `input` element with `type="file"` set)

- `onInitialized`: This is called *after* the web page is created but *before* the URL is loaded

- `onLoadFinished`: This is called after the web page finishes loading; the callback takes a single argument (`status`) and is analogous to the callback function used with `webpage.open`

- `onLoadStarted`: This is called when the web page starts loading

- `onNavigationRequested`: This is called when any navigation event occurs on the page; the callback's arguments describe the circumstances of the navigation event

- `onPageCreated`: This is called when a new child window is opened (for example, via `window.open`); this is only fired for direct descendants of the web page to which the callback is assigned

- `onPrompt`: This handles calls to `prompt` on the web page; it returns a string to use as the input for the `prompt` window

- `onResourceError`: This is called when there is an error loading a resource onto the web page

- `onResourceReceived`: This is called when the web page has received a resource; it is fired once the reception starts, and again when it completes

- `onResourceRequested`: This is called when the web page requests a resource; used in combination with `onResourceReceived`, it can be used to generate the data for the web page's resource waterfall (among other uses)

- `onUrlChanged`: This is called when the web page navigates away from the current URL

> The individual callbacks are well documented in the online API for the PhantomJS `webpage` object at `http://phantomjs.org/api/webpage/`.

The callbacks that can be assigned to the `webpage` object are an important part of scripting PhantomJS, and they provide critical bridges between what is happening "inside" the web page and "outside" in the script. Some of these callbacks (for example, `onAlert`, `onConfirm`, `onPrompt`, and so on) provide us with ways to interact with the parts of the web page which are otherwise not part of the DOM. Other callbacks (for example, `onResourceError`, `onResourceReceived`, `onResourceRequested`, and so on) provide us with ways of gaining insight into metadata about the web page, its resources, and its lifecycle.

See also

▶ The *Setting up a global PhantomJS error handler* recipe in *Chapter 2, PhantomJS Core Modules*

▶ The *Causing images to fail randomly* and *Blocking CSS from downloading* recipes

Simulating mouse clicks in PhantomJS

In this recipe, we will demonstrate how to perform mouse clicks in a PhantomJS script.

Getting ready

To run this recipe, we will need a script that loads a web page, and that page will need a target to click on.

The script in this recipe is available in the downloadable code repository as `recipe07.js` under `chapter03`. If we run the provided example script, we must change to the root directory for the book's sample code.

Lastly, the script in this recipe runs against the demo site that is included with the cookbook's sample code repository. To run that demo site, we must have Node.js installed. In a separate terminal, change to the `phantomjs-sandbox` directory (in the sample code's directory), and start the app with the following command:

```
node app.js
```

How to do it...

Consider the following script:

```
var webpage = require('webpage').create(),
    url     = 'http://localhost:3000/';

webpage.viewportSize = { width: 1280, height: 800 };
```

```
webpage.onUrlChanged = function(targetUrl) {
  console.log('Latest URL: ' + targetUrl);
};

webpage.onLoadFinished = function(status) {
  if (status === 'fail') {
    console.error('webpage did not open successfully');
    phantom.exit(1);
  }

  if (webpage.url !== url) {
    console.log('URL changed; exiting...');
    phantom.exit();
  }

  var coords = webpage.evaluate(function() {
    var firstLink = document.querySelector('a');

    return {
      x: firstLink.offsetLeft,
      y: firstLink.offsetTop
    };
  });

  webpage.sendEvent('click', coords.x + 1, coords.y + 1);
};

webpage.open(url);
```

Given the preceding script, enter the following on the command line:

phantomjs chapter03/recipe07.js

The script should print out the following:

Latest URL: http://localhost:3000/
Latest URL: http://localhost:3000/cache-demo
URL changed; exiting...

How it works...

Note the page seen in the following screenshot:

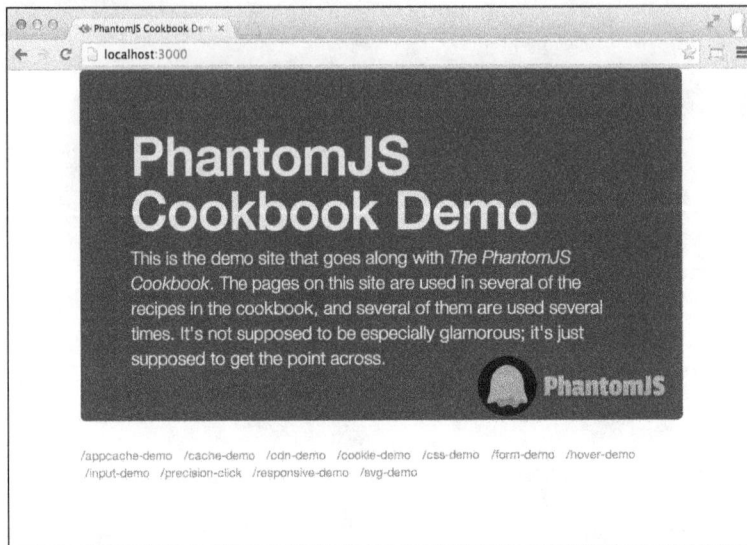

Our preceding example script performs the following actions:

1. It creates a `webpage` instance and assigns it to a variable with the same name; it also assigns our target URL to `url`.

2. It sets `webpage.viewportSize` as a way to control the size of the viewport on our virtual screen.

> While setting the size of the viewport *will* affect the position of the link on the page, and thus the coordinates that we retrieve during our inspection of the DOM, it is not strictly necessary to set it. However, it is a good habit to set the size of the viewport in our PhantomJS scripts, because it can make it easier to reason about our scripts and can better align the test environment to the ones we expect our code to run in.

3. We set the `onUrlChanged` callback function so that we can get feedback (in the form of `console` messages) when the URL on the `webpage` object is changing.

4. Since we expect to visit more than one URL, we skip the usual callback function to `webpage.open` and instead assign a handler to `onLoadFinished`.

5. In our `onLoadFinished` handler, we check the `status` argument first; if it equals `fail`, then we print a message and exit from PhantomJS.

6. Next, in our `onLoadFinished` handler, we check whether `webpage.url` (the current URL of the web page) matches `url`. If it does *not*, then we print a message and exit from PhantomJS.

7. To get the coordinates for our mouse click, we use `webpage.evaluate` and assign the result to the `coords` variable. In this case, we just click on the first link. As such, we use `document.querySelector('a')` to get a reference to the link, and then we return an object containing its `offsetLeft` and `offsetTop` properties.

8. We issue our click by calling `webpage.sendEvent` and passing it the string `click` as its first argument (to indicate which event to send), and then our `x` and `y` coordinates, as stored on the `coords` variable.

9. Lastly, we call `webpage.open` with our target URL, and we let the event handlers (as previously described) do the rest.

In a nutshell, our example script opens a web page, prints the URL, clicks on the first link, prints *that* URL, and exits.

There's more...

The signature for the `sendEvent` method is as follows:

```
sendEvent(mouseEventType, mouseX, mouseY, button)
```

Here, `mouseEventType` is required and the other three are optional.

The `sendEvent` method recognizes several available mouse events. These mouse events include:

- `mouseup`
- `mousedown`
- `click`
- `doubleclick`
- `mousemove`

All of these events have a one-to-one correspondence with the mouse events we are accustomed to dealing with in our normal web programming.

The coordinate arguments (`mouseX` and `mouseY`) are passed as integers.

The `button` argument takes a string that describes which button is being clicked on. The `sendEvent` method recognizes the following buttons:

- `left` (default)
- `right`
- `middle`

> [!NOTE]
> No button press is recognized when the event name is `mousemove`. We cannot simulate a drag-and-drop event.

Another curiosity to note about `sendEvent` is that it generates real mouse click events, and not simulated or synthetic DOM events. If PhantomJS is a headless browser, then we can think of mouse clicks of `sendEvent` as coming from an invisible or infinitely small mouse. This is helpful because these clicks will register with event handlers that might otherwise ignore certain synthetic DOM events.

See also

▸ The *Simulating keyboard input in PhantomJS* recipe

▸ The *Simulating scrolling in PhantomJS* recipe

▸ The *Simulating mouse hovers in PhantomJS* recipe

Simulating keyboard input in PhantomJS

In this recipe, we will demonstrate how to perform keyboard input in a PhantomJS script.

Getting ready

To run this recipe, we will need a script that loads a web page, and that page will need some element where we can perform text input.

The script in this recipe is available in the downloadable code repository as `recipe08.js` under `chapter03`. If we run the provided example script, we must change to the root directory for the book's sample code.

Lastly, the script in this recipe runs against the demo site that is included with the cookbook's sample code repository. To run that demo site, we must have Node.js installed. In a separate terminal, change to the `phantomjs-sandbox` directory (in the sample code's directory), and start the app with the following command:

node app.js

How to do it...

Consider the following script:

```
var webpage = require('webpage').create();

webpage.viewportSize = { width: 1280, height: 800 };
```

```
function getStageValue() {
  return webpage.evaluate(function() {
    return document.querySelector('#stage').innerText ||
        '<BLANK>';
  });
}

webpage.open('http://localhost:3000/input-demo', function(status) {
  if (status === 'fail') {
    console.error('webpage did not open successfully');
    phantom.exit(1);
  }

  console.log('Starting #stage text is: ' + getStageValue());

  webpage.evaluate(function() {
    document.querySelector('#demo').focus();
  });

  webpage.sendEvent('keypress', 'phantomjs');
  webpage.sendEvent('keypress', webpage.event.key.Enter);

  console.log('After input, #stage value is: ' + getStageValue());

  phantom.exit();
});
```

Given the preceding script, enter the following at the command line:

phantomjs chapter03/recipe08.js

The script should print out the following:

Starting #stage text is: <BLANK>
After input, #stage value is: phantomjs

How it works...

Note the page seen in the following screenshot:

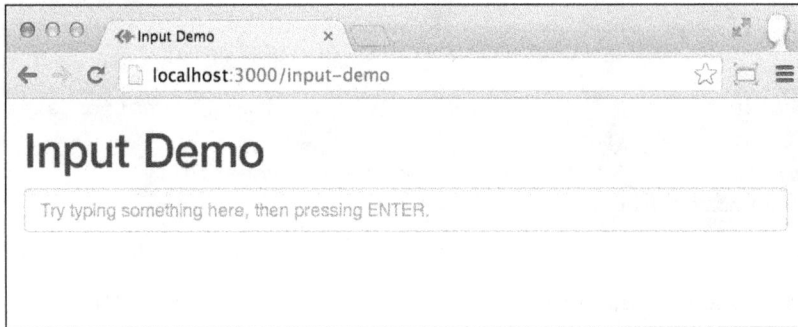

Our preceding example script performs the following actions:

1. It creates a `webpage` instance and assigns it to a variable with the same name.

2. It sets `webpage.viewportSize` as a way of controlling the size of the viewport on our virtual screen.

3. It creates the `getStageValue` function, which we will use to retrieve the inner text of the element with an ID of `stage`. If `stage` has no inner text, we will return the string `<BLANK>`.

4. We call `webpage.open` with our target URL (`http://localhost:3000/input-demo`) and callback function.

5. In our callback function, we check the `status` argument first; if it equals `fail`, then we print a message and exit from PhantomJS.

6. We call `getStageValue` and print the initial value of the `stage` element to `console`.

7. We call `webpage.evaluate`, and in the body of its callback function, we give focus to the input element we are interested in.

8. We make two consecutive calls to `webpage.sendEvent`. First, we send a `keypress` event with the string `phantomjs`, effectively typing in that string. Second, we send another `keypress` event, but this time our second argument is the character code for the `Enter` key, as held in the `webpage.event.key` object hash.

9. We call `getStageValue` again and print its value to `console` to provide evidence that our input has in fact been processed by the web page.

10. Lastly, we exit from PhantomJS.

There's more...

As discussed in the *Simulating mouse clicks in PhantomJS* recipe (earlier in this chapter), PhantomJS considers these to be *real* events and *not* synthetic DOM events. To reuse the analogy from that recipe: if PhantomJS is a headless browser, then we can think of `webpage.sendEvent` as coming from an invisible or infinitely small keyboard.

The signature for the `sendEvent` method is as follows:

```
sendEvent(keyboardEventType, input, null, null, modifier)
```

Here, `keyboardEventType` and `input` are required, the third and fourth arguments are ignored, and the `modifier` argument takes a hexadecimal integer that specifies a modifier key.

> Note that `sendEvent` is used for sending both keyboard and mouse events, but there is not complete parity between the function signatures required for both usages. As such, the third and fourth parameters, which *are* useful for sending mouse events, serve no purpose here. When sending keyboard events, the third and fourth arguments are ignored, but should be sent as `null`.

The three keyboard event types include:

- `keydown`
- `keyup`
- `keypress`

All of these events have a one-to-one correspondence with the keyboard events we are accustomed to dealing with in our normal web programming.

The `input` argument can take several forms. The most convenient form is the first one illustrated in our preceding example—pass a string as the argument, and PhantomJS will automatically convert that singular call to `sendEvent` into *N* keyboard events (where *N* is the length of the string). Alternatively, we can pass an integer, one that corresponds with the `charCode` of the key press we are simulating; this is precisely what we did in our example's second call to `sendEvent`, albeit behind the veneer of the `webpage.event.key` object.

Individual webpage instances will have an event object which has a key object that holds key/value pairs for the keys we expect to use. The keys have human-readable names for their characters (for example, Ampersand, Colon, Escape, and more); the values are the integers corresponding with the charCode for those characters. An example of their use appears in the preceding sample code as:

```
webpage.sendEvent('keypress',
    webpage.event.key.Enter);
```

The event.key object can be viewed as part of the webpage.js module in the PhantomJS source code.

As previously noted, the third and fourth arguments are ignored.

The final argument is for any modifier key we may want to include as part of our keyboard event. Similar to webpage.event.key, a shorthand object is provided for the modifier keys in the form of webpage.event.modifier. These modifier keys include:

Modifier	Value
shift	0x02000000
ctrl	0x04000000
alt	0x08000000
meta	0x10000000
keypad	0x20000000

Modifier keys can be combined using a bitwise OR operator. For example, to send *Alt + Shift + s*, use the following command:

```
webpage.sendEvent('keypress', 's', null, null,
    webpage.event.modifier.alt | webpage.event.modifier.shift);
```

See also

- The *Simulating mouse clicks in PhantomJS* recipe
- The *Simulating scrolling in PhantomJS* recipe
- The *Simulating mouse hovers in PhantomJS* recipe

Simulating scrolling in PhantomJS

This recipe introduces the scrollPosition property and how we can use it to simulate scrolling in PhantomJS.

Getting ready

To run this recipe, we will need a script that loads a web page tall enough (or wide enough) to scroll, and our script needs to expect to scroll the page.

The script in this recipe is available in the downloadable code repository as `recipe09.js` under `chapter03`. If we run the provided example script, we must change to the root directory for the book's sample code. Lastly, for this example to work, we will need an Internet connection.

How to do it...

Consider the following script:

```
var webpage = require('webpage').create();

webpage.viewportSize = { width: 1280, height: 800 };
webpage.scrollPosition = { top: 0, left: 0 };

webpage.open('https://twitter.com/founddrama', function(status) {
  if (status === 'fail') {
    console.error('webpage did not open successfully');
    phantom.exit(1);
  }

  var i = 0,
      top,
      queryFn = function() {
        return document.body.scrollHeight;
      };

  setInterval(function() {
    var filename = 'twitter-' + (++i) + '.png';
    console.log('Writing ' + filename + '...');
    webpage.render(filename);

    top = webpage.evaluate(queryFn);

    console.log('[' + i + '] top = ' + top);
    webpage.scrollPosition = { top: top + 1, left: 0 };

    if (i >= 5) {
      phantom.exit();
    }
  }, 3000);
});
```

Given the preceding script, enter the following at the command line:

```
phantomjs chapter03/recipe09.js
```

The script's console output will enumerate the names of the files it generates, and also the height (in pixels) of the web page during each iteration. It will print out something like the following:

```
Writing twitter-1.png...
[1] top = 2728
Writing twitter-2.png...
[2] top = 5071
Writing twitter-3.png...
[3] top = 6860
Writing twitter-4.png...
[4] top = 8911
Writing twitter-5.png...
[5] top = 11602
```

How it works...

As we can see in our rendered screenshots, we pitted our script against Twitter's infinite scroll in order to prove our scroll simulation implementation. Our preceding example script performs the following actions:

1. It creates a `webpage` instance and assigns it to a variable with the same name.

2. It sets `webpage.viewportSize` as a way of controlling the size of the viewport on our virtual screen.

3. It sets our initial `webpage.scrollPosition` to the extreme top/left (where we expect it to be).

4. It calls `webpage.open` with our target URL (`https://twitter.com/founddrama`) and callback function.

5. In our callback function, it checks the `status` argument first; if it equals `fail`, then it prints a message and exits from PhantomJS.

6. It sets up the variables that we will use during our scroll iterations:

   ❑ `i` is our counter (initialized to `0`)

   ❑ `top` holds the current `scrollHeight` of the page

   ❑ `queryFn` holds the function we will use to query the web page for its `scrollHeight`

7. We call `setInterval` with our scrolling function and a 3000 millisecond interval.

> Note that we are using `setInterval` here in order to give the web page enough time to load the next batch of tweets after we "reach the bottom".

In our scrolling function, we write the name of the rendered file to the console, and then we render the current view. Then, we call `webpage.evaluate` with `queryFn`, assigning the result to `top`. Next, we write the current value of `top` to the console and update `webpage.scrollPosition`. Lastly, we check `i` to see whether we have reached our limit, exiting PhantomJS after five iterations.

There's more...

The key to simulating scrolling in PhantomJS is to update the `webpage.scrollPosition` object, which contains the `top` and `left` properties that correspond roughly to the `scrollTop` and `scrollLeft` properties on the `body` element. Updating this object tells PhantomJS that it has a new scroll position and to reinterpret the web page appropriately.

With respect to scrolling, use of the word *simulation* is more appropriate than it was with mouse or keyboard events. If we refer back to the previous two recipes, we will remember that `webpage.sendEvent` sends "real" and not "synthetic" DOM events to the web page. However, things are trickier with the PhantomJS viewport and the way it handles scrolling.

Remember that PhantomJS is a headless web browser. As such, the DOM tree that it parses and renders is not constrained by any physical device's viewport; even setting `webpage.viewportSize` is more of a hint than a mandate. This explains why our rendered screenshots are "super tall" and exceed our specified viewport size by thousands of pixels.

> PhantomJS *does* provide a way for taking a snapshot of just the portion of the page that we want (with `webpage.clipRect`), but this is extra ceremony and is only meaningful for calls to `webpage.render`, and it has nothing to do with scrolling.

So what does that mean? In a nutshell, it means that for most pages, `webpage.scrollPosition` has very little utility. If we consider that traditional web pages load all of their content as a single DOM tree, and we get it all on the first load, then PhantomJS is happy to render the whole page as one continuous image. Where `webpage.scrollPosition` becomes more interesting is in places where the scroll position is used as a trigger for other events, such as infinite scroll.

See also

- ▶ The *Inspecting page content from a PhantomJS script* recipe
- ▶ The *Simulating mouse clicks in PhantomJS* recipe

- ▶ The *Simulating keyboard input in PhantomJS* recipe
- ▶ The *Simulating mouse hovers in PhantomJS* recipe
- ▶ The *Rendering images from PhantomJS* recipe in *Chapter 7, Generating Images and Documents with PhantomJS*
- ▶ The *Generating clipped screenshots from PhantomJS* recipe in *Chapter 7, Generating Images and Documents with PhantomJS*

Simulating mouse hovers in PhantomJS

This recipe demonstrates how to simulate hovers and similar mouse events using `webpage.sendEvent`.

Getting ready

To run this recipe, we will need a script that loads a web page with *hover effects* or similar features that are sensitive to the `mousemove` event; our script needs to expect to interact with these `mousemove` events.

The script in this recipe is available in the downloadable code repository as `recipe10.js` under `chapter03`. If we run the provided example script, we must change to the root directory for the book's sample code.

Lastly, the script in this recipe runs against the demo site that is included with the cookbook's sample code repository. To run that demo site, we must have Node.js installed. In a separate terminal, change to the `phantomjs-sandbox` directory (in the sample code's directory), and start the app with the following command:

```
node app.js
```

How to do it...

Consider the following script:

```
var webpage = require('webpage').create();

webpage.viewportSize = { width: 1280, height: 800 };

webpage.onConsoleMessage = function(m) {
  console.log(m);
  phantom.exit();
};

webpage.open('http://localhost:3000/hover-demo', function(status) {
```

```
  if (status === 'fail') {
    console.error('webpage did not open successfully');
    phantom.exit(1);
  }

  var coords = webpage.evaluate(function() {
    var box = document.querySelector('.hover-demo');

    return { x: box.offsetLeft, y: box.offsetTop };
  });

  webpage.sendEvent('mousemove', coords.x + 10, coords.y + 10);
});
```

Given the preceding script, enter the following at the command line:

phantomjs chapter03/recipe10.js

The script should print out the following:

[hover-demo] pointer has entered .hover-demo... [80 × 79]

How it works...

Note the page in the following screenshot:

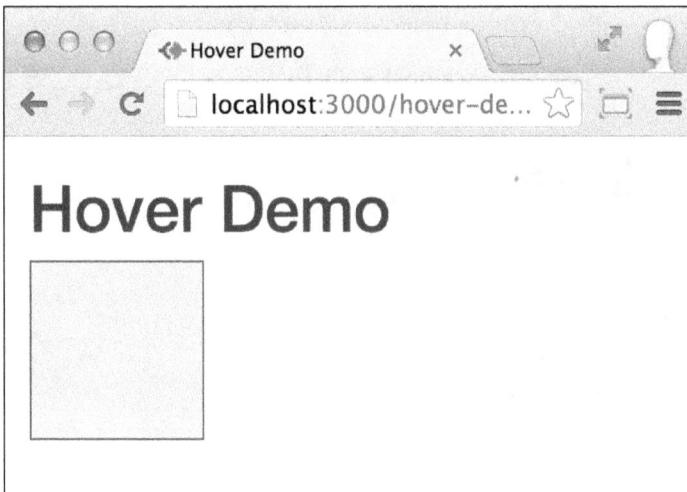

Our preceding example script performs the following actions:

1. It creates a `webpage` instance and assigns it to a variable with the same name.

2. It sets `webpage.viewportSize` as a way of controlling the size of the viewport on our virtual screen.

3. The target web page will write a message to the console when it processes the `mousemove` events. It attaches a callback function to `webpage.onConsoleMessage` in order to intercept and forward those messages to the PhantomJS context. After recording that console message, it exits from PhantomJS.

4. It calls `webpage.open` with our target URL (`http://localhost:3000/hover-demo`) and callback function.

5. In our callback function, it checks the `status` argument first; if it equals `fail`, then it prints a message and exits from PhantomJS.

6. It gets the coordinates of our target element from the web page context by calling `webpage.evaluate` and assigning the return value to the `coords` variable. In that callback function, it queries the DOM for our element of interest (`.hover-demo`) and returns an object with its `offsetLeft` and `offsetTop` values.

7. It calls `webpage.sendEvent` for our `mousemove` event; this triggers the event handler on the page to write to the web page's `console` that will be caught and forwarded by the `webpage.onConsoleMessage` callback.

This causes the hover effect to trigger as seen in the following screenshot:

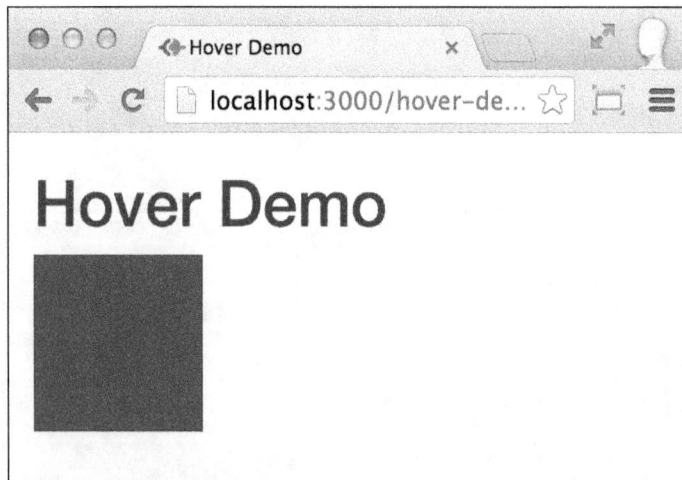

There's more...

As mentioned in the previous recipes regarding `webpage.sendEvent`, these are considered *real* events and *not* synthetic DOM events. As such, this helps to avoid some of the problems seen with synthetic DOM events not properly triggering their handlers.

The method signature for `sendEvent` was discussed in the *Simulating mouse clicks in PhantomJS* recipe (earlier in this chapter), but it bears repeating that when we pass the event type argument as `mousemove`, that the `button` argument is ignored.

An interesting side effect of calling `sendEvent` with `mousemove` is that it will also trigger `mouseover` events on that element, though not `mouseenter` events; similarly, calling `sendEvent` with coordinates that take us *out* of an element, will trigger `mouseout` events, but not `mouseleave` events.

> We can trigger these additional pointer events by calling `sendEvent` with the proper string passed as the `eventType` argument; for example:
>
> ```
> webpage.sendEvent('mouseenter', coords.x, coords.y);
> ```
>
> However, given the nature of PhantomJS as a headless browser, and given that there is no actual mouse cursor, these events are not necessarily semantically meaningful and may yield unexpected results.
>
> For more information on `mouseenter` and `mouseleave`, and the difference between them and `mouseover` and `mouseout`, see the `QuirksMode.org` article on the subject at `http://www.quirksmode.org/js/events_mouse.html#mouseenter`.

See also

- ▸ The *Simulating mouse clicks in PhantomJS* recipe
- ▸ The *Simulating keyboard input in PhantomJS* recipe
- ▸ The *Simulating scrolling in PhantomJS* recipe

Blocking CSS from downloading

In this recipe, we will demonstrate how to use the `onResourceRequested` callback to block files from downloading. Although we can use this technique to block any resource type, we will specifically be blocking CSS here; this can be useful to generate snapshots of how our sites look when the CSS fails.

Getting ready

To run this recipe, we will need a script that loads a web page; that web page must use CSS so that we can block the style sheet resources.

The script in this recipe is available in the downloadable code repository as `recipe11.js` under `chapter03`. If we run the provided example script, we must change into the root directory for the book's sample code.

Lastly, the script in this recipe runs against the demo site that is included with the cookbook's sample code repository. To run that demo site, we must have Node.js installed. In a separate terminal, change to the `phantomjs-sandbox` directory (in the sample code's directory), and start the app with the following command:

```
node app.js
```

How to do it...

Consider the following script:

```
var webpage = require('webpage').create(),
    url     = 'http://localhost:3000/css-demo',
    cssRx   = /\.css\??.*$/i,
    count   = 0;

webpage.viewportSize = { width: 1280, height: 800 };

webpage.clipRect = {
  top:    0,
  left:   0,
  width:  1280,
  height: 800
};

webpage.onLoadStarted = function() {
  count += 1;
};

webpage.onResourceRequested = function(requestData, networkRequest) {
  if (count > 1 && cssRx.test(requestData.url)) {
    console.log('Dropping CSS for ' + url);
    networkRequest.abort();
  }
};

webpage.onLoadFinished = function(status) {
  if (status === 'fail') {
```

```
      console.error(url + ' did not open successfully');
      phantom.exit(1);
   }

   if (count <= 1) {
      console.log('Rendering ' + url + ' with CSS...');
      webpage.render('demo-with-css.png');
      webpage.reload();
   } else {
      console.log('Rendering ' + url + ' without CSS...');
      webpage.render('demo-without-css.png');
      phantom.exit();
   }
};

webpage.open(url);
```

Enter the following at the command line:

```
phantomjs chapter03/recipe11.js
```

The script will print out messages about its progress, and when it completes, it will also have rendered and saved two files (`demo-with-css.png` and `demo-without-css.png`) so that we can observe the consequences.

Consider the demo with CSS as shown in the following image:

Now, consider the following demo without the CSS:

CSS Demo

Laboris enim tempor velit cillum. Tempor nulla consequat nostrud consequat qui eiusmod nulla excepteur dolore laborum culpa. Sint dolore fugiat aute culpa veniam qui magna ea pariatur quis nulla officia duis nisi. Incididunt consectetur cillum qui dolore laborum duis id officia anim sit et. Dolor velit proident deserunt nulla ut ex.

Quis ex nostrud veniam esse ex in. Sit fugiat excepteur proident aute proident do est occaecat. Deserunt fugiat exercitation enim deserunt voluptate cupidatat cupidatat aliquip qui consectetur elit. Laborum laborum in laborum excepteur veniam. Sint ea exercitation id veniam ad anim ea aliqua. Nostrud tempor cupidatat ea in aliqua veniam ad ullamco laborum id. Enim fugiat deserunt veniam adipisicing do Lorem laboris ea sunt aliquip esse. Reprehenderit nulla ea laboris adipisicing consequat dolore. Sint cillum fugiat voluptate non amet eiusmod magna est consequat qui laborum. Irure exercitation consequat proident ipsum do sint duis incididunt. Non deserunt pariatur in mollit tempor aliqua consectetur irure. Cupidatat magna reprehenderit id qui labore eu in Lorem sunt nostrud amet anim aliqua excepteur. Id occaecat eiusmod adipisicing enim nulla ullamco aute esse nisi cillum consectetur do duis sit. Lorem exercitation eu ad fugiat laborum id voluptate eu proident. Exercitation ex ullamco et in occaecat id enim mollit sit excepteur duis Lorem. Sunt amet do ullamco laborum sunt mollit dolor ipsum voluptate aliquip ipsum velit nisi. Occaecat ex labore nulla et aliqua ipsum culpa anim. Amet incididunt amet dolor officia nostrud Lorem non proident. Nostrud occaecat ullamco laborum labore qui. Ut minim elit labore cillum in pariatur cillum sunt ex. In sit amet dolor laboris id nostrud excepteur ad consequat aute nulla veniam anim cupidatat. Magna anim nostrud qui reprehenderit Lorem ad dolor incididunt minim. Ut nostrud nisi commodo quis. Tempor et qui sunt consectetur ipsum. Proident aute ex pariatur labore dolor et amet non laborum velit. Pariatur occaecat cupidatat aute ullamco qui. Laboris velit dolor voluptate officia fugiat ipsum exercitation. Dolor aliqua magna sunt ex officia incididunt adipisicing cupidatat. Aliquip qui culpa occaecat exercitation do minim proident occaecat dolore qui reprehenderit. Tempor aute nisi Lorem duis pariatur enim ut. Aliquip non duis labore commodo duis dolore tempor eiusmod nisi qui sunt. Est ex ipsum nulla fugiat pariatur veniam. Do et officia non amet nulla ullamco dolor eiusmod aliqua laboris commodo labore qui elit. Aliquip elit Lorem Lorem veniam dolor dolor consectetur sint sunt ut non non culpa exercitation. Nulla veniam culpa ullamco officia. Duis id tempor pariatur nulla sunt eu velit non voluptate qui velit labore enim ullamco. Voluptate esse incididunt incididunt commodo elit officia in labore. Consectetur labore minim pariatur et non.

How it works...

Our preceding example script performs the following actions:

1. It sets up the variables we want to use over the life of our script. These variables include:

    ❑   `webpage`: This holds a `webpage` instance
    ❑   `url`: This holds our target URL
    ❑   `cssRx`: This holds a naïve regular expression for matching style sheets based on file extension
    ❑   `count`: This holds a count of the number of times we have requested our target URL

2. We set `webpage.viewportSize` as a way of controlling the size of the viewport on our virtual screen.

3. We set `webpage.clipRect` so that our screenshots are of a more manageable size.

4. We set an `onLoadStarted` callback function, whose only action is to increment `count`.

5. We set our `onResourceRequested` callback function to look for style sheets. It checks that `count` is greater than 1 (we want to get a snapshot of the page *with* the styles first, after all!), and then checks whether `requestData.url` matches `cssRx`. If both conditions are met, we call `networkRequest.abort` to block the CSS.

6. We set up an onLoadFinished callback function instead of passing it to our later call to webpage.open. We do this as follows:

    1. We check the status argument; if it equals fail, then we print a message and exit from PhantomJS.

    2. If count is less than or equal to 1, we print a message and render the web page *with* the CSS; we then reload the page.

    3. If count is greater than 1, we print a message and render the web page *without* the CSS; we then exit from PhantomJS.

    4. Lastly, we make our call to webpage.open with our target URL.

There's more...

As alluded to in the recipe's introduction, blocking the CSS has several practical applications. Taking a snapshot of the site without CSS can help to see whether it is still usable even when the CSS fails to download. In turn, this knowledge can help guide us toward better design decisions (for example, through progressive enhancement). What makes this possible is the onResourceRequested callback.

onResourceRequested

We use the onResourceRequested callback to monitor—and potentially modify—network requests in PhantomJS. Every time PhantomJS makes a network request, this callback is fired; it provides a hook into each network request made by that webpage instance.

The onResourceRequested callback function takes two arguments:

▸ The requestData object describes the resource requested; it contains the following properties:

    ❑ id: This is an integer identifying the request (effectively a counter)

    ❑ method: This is a string indicating the HTTP method used to make the request (usually GET)

    ❑ url: This is the URL of the request

    ❑ time: This is the date/time stamp of the request

    ❑ headers: These are any HTTP headers on the request

▸ The networkRequest object represents the network request; it exposes two methods:

    ❑ abort(): This aborts the request, which results in the onResourceError callback being invoked

    ❑ changeUrl(url): This allows us to change the URL on the request (for example, to proxy certain scripts with local equivalents)

onResourceReceived

Although not used in the example, it is also worth discussing onResourceReceived, the callback for successfully completed HTTP requests in PhantomJS. Just as we used onResourceRequested to spy on requests, we can use onResourceReceived to inspect responses. The onResourceReceived callback is fired at least twice for each response, once at the beginning (identified as start) and once at the end (identified as end); the callback may also fire for intermediate chunks.

The onResourceReceived callback function takes a single argument, response; it is an object with the following properties:

- id: This is an integer identifying the resource; this should correspond to the id property in onResourceRequested
- url: This is the URL of the completed request
- time: This is the date/time stamp of the response
- headers: These are the HTTP headers on the response
- bodySize: This is the size of the response (in bytes)
- contentType: This is the content type string sent by the server for this resource (if any)
- redirectURL: This is the redirect URL (if any)
- stage: This is a string identifier for which stage of the response we are in (start or end)
- status: This is the HTTP status code of the response
- statusText: This is the HTTP status text associated with the status code

See also

- The *Causing images to fail randomly* recipe

Causing images to fail randomly

In this recipe, we will continue with onResourceRequested, introduce the onResourceError callback, and use them to illustrate a strategy for randomly causing images to fail to download.

Getting ready

To run this recipe, we will need a script that loads a web page; that web page must contain images so that we can block them.

The script in this recipe is available in the downloadable code repository as `recipe12.js` under `chapter03`. If we run the provided example script, we must change to the root directory for the book's sample code.

Lastly, the script in this recipe runs against the demo site that is included with the cookbook's sample code repository. To run that demo site, we must have Node.js installed. In a separate terminal, change to the `phantomjs-sandbox` directory (in the sample code's directory), and start the app with the following command:

```
node app.js
```

How to do it...

Consider the following script:

```
var webpage          = require('webpage').create(),
    url              = 'http://localhost:3000/cache-demo',
    imgRx            = /\.(?:gif|png|jpe?g)$/i,
    requestsMade     = 0,
    requestsCanceled = 0;

webpage.viewportSize = { width: 1280, height: 800 };

webpage.onResourceRequested = function(requestData, networkRequest) {
  if (imgRx.test(requestData.url)) {
    requestsMade += 1;
    if (Math.floor(Math.random() * 10) % 3 === 0) {
      requestsCanceled += 1;
      networkRequest.abort();
    }
  }
};

webpage.onResourceError = function(resourceError) {
  console.error('Error with requested resource:\n' + JSON.
stringify(resourceError, undefined, 2));
};

console.log('Simulating poor network weather for ' + url);
webpage.open(url, function(status) {
```

```
    if (status === 'fail') {
      console.error(url + ' did not open successfully.');
      phantom.exit(1);
    }

    console.log('Canceled ' + requestsCanceled + ' of ' + requestsMade +
' image requests.');
    webpage.render('lost-images.png');
    phantom.exit();
});
```

Given the preceding script, enter the following at the command line:

phantomjs chapter03/recipe12.js

The script will print out a series of messages, including JSON representations of the network request errors.

How it works...

Our preceding example script performs the following actions:

1. It sets up the variables we want to use over the life of our script. These variables include:

   - webpage: It holds a webpage instance
   - url: It holds our target URL
   - imgRx: It holds a naïve regular expression for matching images based on file extension
   - requestsMade and requestsCanceled: Both are counters to track our requests

2. We set webpage.viewportSize as a way to control the size of the viewport on our virtual screen.

3. We set our onResourceRequested callback function. This function takes two arguments, requestData and networkRequest. In the body of the callback function, we check the URL of requestData, and if it is determined to be an image, we increment our requestsMade counter and randomly decide whether or not to abort the networkRequest (incrementing the requestsCanceled counter if we do).

4. We set our onResourceError callback function. This function takes one argument (resourceError), and with it we simply print it to the console.

5. We call webpage.open with our target URL (http://localhost:3000/cache-demo) and callback function.

6. In our callback function, we check the `status` argument first; if it equals `fail`, we print a message and exit from PhantomJS. Otherwise, we print a message to the console about the number of requests made versus canceled; we then exit from PhantomJS.

To summarize, our script makes a simple request to our target URL and then cancels a subset of the subsequent image requests. We tap into the `onResourceRequested` callback to examine (and cancel) requests, and we use `onResourceError` to confirm the cancellations.

There's more...

A script like this one can be useful for simulating poor network weather (for example, dropped or otherwise unreliable connections). However, more importantly, this script illustrates the basics of PhantomJS' resource failure callback.

onResourceError

We use the `onResourceError` callback to monitor and respond to errors with specific resources requested in PhantomJS. When a resource fails for any reason in PhantomJS, this callback is fired.

The `onResourceError` callback function takes a single argument, `resourceError`; it is an object with the following properties:

▸ `id`: This is an integer identifying the resource; this should correspond to the `id` property in `onResourceRequested`

▸ `url`: This is the URL of the failed request

▸ `errorCode`: This is the error code associated with the error type in PhantomJS (that is, an HTTP status code)

▸ `errorString`: This is a brief explanatory message about the error

See also

▸ The *Blocking CSS from downloading* recipe

Submitting Ajax requests from PhantomJS

This recipe introduces methods for submitting XHR (XMLHttpRequest) or Ajax requests from PhantomJS and describes how to deal with the responses.

Getting ready

To run this recipe, we will need a script that makes a direct request to a URL that expects XHR.

The script in this recipe is available in the downloadable code repository as recipe13.js under chapter03. If we run the provided example script, we must change to the root directory for the book's sample code.

Lastly, the script in this recipe runs against the demo site that is included with the cookbook's sample code repository. To run that demo site, we must have Node.js installed. In a separate terminal, change to the phantomjs-sandbox directory (in the sample code's directory), and start the app with the following command:

```
node app.js
```

How to do it...

Consider the following script:

```
var webpage = require('webpage').create();

webpage.onResourceReceived = function(response) {
  if (response.stage === 'end') {
    console.log('Content-Type: ' + response.contentType);
  }
};

webpage.open('http://localhost:3000/ajax-demo', function(status) {
  if (status === 'fail') {
    console.error('webpage did not open successfully');
    phantom.exit(1);
  }

  console.log(webpage.plainText);
  phantom.exit();
});
```

Enter the following at the command line:

```
phantomjs chapter03/recipe13.js
```

The script will print out the `Content-Type` header and the response body:

```
Content-Type: application/json; charset=utf-8
{
  "time": 1390098844062,
  "randomNumber": 22,
  "initials": "REF"
}
```

How it works...

Our preceding example script performs the following actions:

1. It creates a `webpage` instance and assigns it to a variable with the same name.
2. It sets up our `onResourceReceived` callback function. In that callback function, we check the `stage` property on the response object to see whether it equals `end`; if so, we output the `contentType`.
3. We call `webpage.open` with our target URL (`http://localhost:3000/ajax-demo`) and callback function.
4. In our callback function, we check the `status` argument first; if it equals `fail`, we print a message and exit from PhantomJS.
5. We write `webpage.plainText` to the console.
6. Lastly, we exit from PhantomJS.

There's more...

The first thing to note about our example is that it was a normal request—there was no "magic", and we did not even need to specify any special `X-Requested-With` header. However, it is also worth noting that because we received a `Content-Type` of `application/json`, there was no HTML delivered over the wire, and thus, no web page to evaluate.

> How we make requests from PhantomJS ultimately depends on what the server expects. Although this example did not include an `X-Requested-With` header, that could be a critical part of a request made against a different server. As always, it is important to know what the server on the other end expects, and write scripts with that in mind.

PhantomJS exposes two properties on the `webpage` instance to directly inspect the contents of the web page: `content` and `plainText`. All content (HTML tags, text, and so on) is returned by `webpage.content`, while `webpage.plainText` (which we used in our script) returns *only* the text content and none of the HTML tags.

Common sense will tell us that we will be fine if we use `webpage.content` here because the response body did not contain any HTML, but this would be a mistake. As PhantomJS is a web browser and expects HTML in the response, it will wrap the JSON response in some simple HTML before returning it. For example, in this case, `webpage.content` would give us:

```
<html><head></head><body><pre style="word-wrap: break-word;
  white-space: pre-wrap;">{
  "time": 1397442861438,
  "randomNumber": 20,
  "initials": "REF"
}</pre></body></html>
```

This is an important consideration when writing PhantomJS scripts that target URLs returning JSON or other non-HTML payloads.

Working with WebSockets in PhantomJS

This recipe discusses how to open and work with a WebSocket connection in PhantomJS.

Getting ready

To run this recipe, we will need a script that requests a host that also exposes WebSocket connections.

> Although PhantomJS version 1.9 *does* have WebSocket support, that support is limited to the hixie-76 draft of the protocol. PhantomJS 2.0 is scheduled to include the more modern RFC 6455 version of WebSockets. When writing scripts for PhantomJS that intend to use WebSocket connections, we must ensure that the server supports the hixie-76 version of the protocol.

> A good introduction to the WebSocket protocol and the HTML5 API can be found at `http://www.websocket.org/aboutwebsocket.html`.

The script in this recipe is available in the downloadable code repository as `recipe14.js` under `chapter03`. If we run the provided example script, we must change to the root directory for the book's sample code.

Lastly, the script in this recipe runs against the demo site that is included with the cookbook's sample code repository. To run that demo site, we must have Node.js installed. In a separate terminal, change to the `phantomjs-sandbox` directory (in the sample code's directory), and start the app with the following command:

```
node app.js
```

How to do it...

Consider the following script:

```
var webpage = require('webpage').create();

webpage.onConsoleMessage = function(m) {
  console.log(m);

  if (/^Closing WebSocket/.test(m)) {
    phantom.exit();
  }
};

webpage.open('http://localhost:3000/', function(status) {
  if (status === 'fail') {
    console.error('webpage did not open successfully');
    phantom.exit(1);
  }

  webpage.evaluateAsync(function() {
    var ws = new WebSocket('ws://localhost:3000/');

    function stringify(o) {
      return JSON.stringify(o, undefined, 2);
    }

    ws.onopen = function(event) {
      console.log('WebSocket opened...\n' + stringify(event));

      ws.send('ping');
    };
    ws.onmessage = function(event) {
      console.log('WebSocket message:\n' + stringify(event));
    };
    ws.onerror = function(event) {
      console.error('WebSocket error!\n' + stringify(event));
    };
    ws.onclose = function(event) {
      console.error('Closing WebSocket...\n' + stringify(event));
    };

    console.log('WebSocket created...\n' + stringify(ws));

    setTimeout(function() {
      ws.close();
```

```
    }, 1000);
  });
});
```

Enter the following at the command line:

phantomjs chapter03/recipe14.js

The script will print out the JSON representations of the WebSocket activity.

How it works...

Our preceding example script performs the following actions:

1. It creates a `webpage` instance and assigns it to a variable with the same name.

2. It sets up our `onConsoleMessage` callback function. This function forwards `console` messages from the web page context to the PhantomJS context. It also watches for messages starting with *Closing WebSocket*, and it exits PhantomJS when it encounters such a message.

3. It calls `webpage.open` with our target URL (`http://localhost:3000/`) and callback function.

4. In our callback function, it checks the `status` argument first; if it equals `fail`, then it prints a message and exits from PhantomJS.

5. Using `webpage.evaluateAsync`, it enters the web page context and creates a `WebSocket` object. After setting up our `stringify` shorthand function, it attaches listeners to the WebSocket's callbacks. Then, it prints a message indicating that it has created our WebSocket, and it instructs the web page context to terminate that WebSocket connection after one second.

Of particular interest to us are the `onopen`, `onmessage`, and `onclose` callbacks. Each of these callbacks writes a JSON version of the `event` object to `console` so that we can inspect them. In the case of `onmessage`, we can see the `data` property on the `event` object, which contains the payload data as sent from the server.

There's more...

Although PhantomJS technically has WebSocket support, WebSocket connections are not *directly* observable. We cannot successfully call `webpage.open` with a `ws://` prefixed URL. WebSocket communication does not show up in `onResourceRequested` or `onResourceReceived` callbacks, and there are no other methods that allow us to make scripted WebSocket connections from PhantomJS without entering the web page context.

However, because the internal `webpage` context supports WebSockets, so (by extension) does PhantomJS. It takes some scripting acrobatics—creating the connections in a web page context, forwarding the payload data to the console, spying on the console messages with `onConsoleMessage`, and so forth—but we *can* use PhantomJS to communicate with WebSockets.

As previously mentioned, the WebSocket connections are only indirectly observable. In this recipe's example script, we need to use `webpage.evaluateAsync` to access the WebSocket object and its messages from the web page context, and even then, we manually create the connection, and then manually assign the appropriate callback functions that we spied on, through an `onConsoleMessage` handler. If we try to inspect more sophisticated code in this way, we may find that we need to resort to even more elaborate techniques to observe it, such as metaprogramming or side-effect detection. Again, while not ideal, we *can* concoct ways to interact with WebSockets if we feel the need—though getting there is not for the faint of heart!

4
Unit Testing with PhantomJS

In this chapter, we will cover:

- ▶ Running Jasmine unit tests with PhantomJS
- ▶ Using TerminalReporter for unit testing in PhantomJS
- ▶ Creating a Jasmine test runner for PhantomJS and every other browser
- ▶ Running Jasmine unit tests with Grunt
- ▶ Watching your tests during development with Grunt
- ▶ Running Jasmine unit tests with the Karma test runner
- ▶ Generating code coverage reports with Istanbul and the Karma test runner
- ▶ Running Jasmine unit tests with Karma and PhantomJS from WebStorm
- ▶ Running QUnit tests with PhantomJS
- ▶ Running Mocha unit tests with PhantomJS

Introduction

One of the most popular uses of PhantomJS among front-end developers is as the primary testing environment for fast unit tests during development. Since PhantomJS is a headless web browser, it can sit invisibly on the command line waiting for tests to be triggered—totally unobtrusive until tests fail and it's time to raise the alarm.

In this chapter, we will learn about using PhantomJS as just such an environment for JavaScript unit tests. The chapter will focus on the Jasmine test framework, but will also introduce two other popular frameworks, QUnit and Mocha. The recipes in this chapter will look at a trivial string utilities library (`string-utils.js` under `lib` in the sample repository), and tests for that library will provide the subject matter that underlies each of the testing strategies discussed.

Running Jasmine unit tests with PhantomJS

This recipe will illustrate a basic Jasmine-based test suite and how to execute its test runner under PhantomJS while extracting useful test feedback.

Getting ready

To run this recipe, we will need JavaScript code to test, and the tests for that code. To test our code, we will use the Jasmine test framework.

> Jasmine is a JavaScript framework used for writing tests in a **behavior-driven development** (**BDD**) style. We will use it here because it is widely used, and the tests are generally easy to read. Jasmine is open source (MIT licensed) and we can find its documentation at `http://jasmine.github.io/`.
>
> We will be using Jasmine version 1.3.1; we can download this version at `https://github.com/pivotal/jasmine/tree/v1.3.1`.

The library code that we will test is available in the downloadable code repository as `string-utils.js` under `lib`; the accompanying tests are available as `string-utils-spec.js` under `lib`. The test runner is also available in the repository as `recipe01-runner.html` under `chapter04`. If we run the provided example, we must change to the root directory for the book's sample code.

Lastly, we will use the `run-jasmine.js` script that ships as part of the `examples` directory with the PhantomJS source code. The example uses the `$PHANTOMJS_SOURCE` environment variable, which refers to our clone of the PhantomJS source code.

> We will want to set `PHANTOMJS_SOURCE` as an environment variable in our shell. For example, if we cloned the PhantomJS source code to `/dev/phantomjs`, then we want `PHANTOMJS_SOURCE` to refer to that path. Many recipes in this cookbook will refer to the examples in the PhantomJS source code, and it will be useful to have this environment variable at our disposal.

How to do it...

Given our example library and its tests, let us call out the executor (the inline script) on the test runner that kicks off the Jasmine tests:

```
(function(jasmine) {
  var env = jasmine.getEnv();

  env.addReporter(new jasmine.HtmlReporter());
  env.execute();
}(jasmine));
```

Then, we enter the following at the command line:

```
phantomjs $PHANTOMJS_SOURCE/examples/run-jasmine.js
  chapter04/recipe01-runner.html
```

The script will output the test results to the console. They should look like the following:

```
'waitFor()' finished in 200ms.


string-utils.js
Passing 10 specs
```

How it works...

There are three main components at work in our example:

- Our tests, wrapped up inside the test runner
- The run-jasmine.js script that loads and bootstraps the test runner
- PhantomJS, which serves as the test environment

If we look at our tests (string-utils-spec.js), they are straightforward and use only the basic testing functions that Jasmine provides. We have a few nested describe blocks (one for each function on the txtr object), and a couple of it functions containing expect blocks to document our specifications.

For those unfamiliar with Jasmine, there are three fundamental building-block functions that make up the test:

- `describe`: These functions are **suites** and take a string (to describe what is in the suite) and a function; the function may contain more suites and/or specifications

- `it`: These functions are **specifications** and take a string (to describe what is in the specification) and a function; the function contains one or more expectations

- `expect`: These functions are **expectations** (also called *assertions*) that take a value (the **actual**); the expectation is then chained with a **matcher** function that takes the expected value

See the Jasmine documentation for more information at `http://jasmine.github.io/1.3/introduction.html`.

We can open our test runner (`recipe01-runner.html`) in a normal browser and see the results of the tests, as shown in the following screenshot:

Looking at the test runner, we can see that it performs the following actions:

1. It loads the CSS for the Jasmine test framework.

2. It loads the core Jasmine test framework and `HtmlReporter`.

> **Reporters** are functions in Jasmine that take care of presenting the test results to the user. One of Jasmine's built-in reporters, `HtmlReporter`, converts the results into an HTML document to be rendered in a web browser.

3. It loads the JavaScript code under test (`string-utils.js`).
4. It loads the tests (`string-utils-spec.js`).
5. It kicks off the Jasmine tests with the executor, which performs the following actions:
    1. Gets a reference to the Jasmine environment and assigns it to the variable `env`.
    2. Creates and registers an `HtmlReporter` with the Jasmine environment.
    3. Calls `execute` on the Jasmine environment to start the tests.

While these are arguably sufficient tests on their own, it seems excessive to open an extra browser window just to run and check the tests each time.

The test runner, however, is just an HTML document like any other. This makes it a prime candidate for being loaded and evaluated by PhantomJS.

Rather than writing our own PhantomJS script to load the page, we can tap into the `run-jasmine.js` script that ships in the `examples` directory of the PhantomJS source code. In a nutshell, the script works as follows:

1. It loads the `system` module so that we can inspect the script's arguments.
2. It sets up a `waitFor` function, which helps to monitor the page for the correct conditions to indicate that the tests are complete.
3. It checks the number of arguments, exiting if the correct number (2) is not supplied.
4. It creates a `webpage` instance and attaches a simple `onConsoleMessage` callback to forward console messages from the web page to the PhantomJS context.
5. The `webpage` instance opens the URL (supplied as the script's argument).
6. In the callback to `webpage.open`, it calls `waitFor`, first scanning the page for pending tests. After the last pending test has cleared, it uses `page.evaluate` to inspect the page for CSS classes that indicate failed tests.
7. If the script finds failed tests, it outputs the number of failed tests and messages about each one, exiting PhantomJS with a status of 1. Otherwise, it prints the total number of successful tests and exits with a status of 0.

PhantomJS provides the test environment itself. We invoke it on the command line, providing our script (`run-jasmine.js`) and our target URL. All the work takes place within the PhantomJS process, which will exit cleanly, not depending upon the outcome of the tests on the page.

There's more...

The example in this recipe is convenient because it allows us to start using PhantomJS to drive our existing browser-based Jasmine test suites without any conversion. This illustrates some of the power that is inherent when using PhantomJS as a testing platform—we can use the `webpage` API to inspect HTML documents and provide meaningful reports to the command line about the success or failure of the tests within. It is interesting to note here that the test runner even assumes that it will only ever be run as an HTML document—it uses Jasmine's `HtmlReporter` only, which constructs the markup, but otherwise has no expectation of providing command-line friendly output.

In many ways, this is great news. If we have existing Jasmine test suites written using only the basic, core reporters, then we can dive right into using PhantomJS for tests during development or as part of continuous integration. Additionally, PhantomJS is agnostic about how we load our test runners, and it accepts files (as in our previous example) just as easily as it accepts URLs over HTTP or HTTPS.

However, the `run-jasmine.js` script provides us with only the basic integration between Jasmine tests and PhantomJS as the test environment. The script takes only one URL at a time. As such, we must either pack every test into one test runner or wrap the script with another, which *can* accept multiple URLs. If our needs exceed that which `run-jasmine.js` can provide for us, there are more advanced options.

See also

▶ The *Using TerminalReporter for unit testing in PhantomJS* recipe
▶ The *Creating a Jasmine test runner for PhantomJS and every other browser* recipe

Using TerminalReporter for unit testing in PhantomJS

This recipe introduces the `jasmine-reporters` library, and it explains how to use `TerminalReporter` for clear and concise output on the command line when using PhantomJS.

Getting ready

To run this recipe, we will need the following items:

▸ JavaScript code to test, and the tests for that code

▸ The Jasmine testing framework

▸ The `jasmine-reporters` library

> The `jasmine-reporters` library is a collection of advanced reporters for the Jasmine test framework. It is an open source (MIT licensed) project and is available at `https://github.com/larrymyers/jasmine-reporters`.

The library code that we will use for our tests is available in the downloadable code repository as `string-utils.js` under `lib`; the accompanying tests are available as `string-utils-spec.js` under `lib`. The test runner is also available in the repository as `recipe02-runner.html` under `chapter04`. If we run the provided example, we must change to the root directory for the book's sample code.

Lastly, we will use a variation on the `phantomjs.runner.sh` launcher script, which is included with our example repository and is derived from the version that ships with the `jasmine-reporters` library.

How to do it...

Given our example library and its tests, let us call out the executor in the test runner using the following code snippet:

```
(function(jasmine) {
  var env = jasmine.getEnv();

  env.addReporter(new jasmine.TerminalReporter({
    verbosity: 3,
    color: true
  }));
  env.addReporter(new jasmine.TrivialReporter());
  env.execute();
} (jasmine));
```

Two things to note about the preceding code:

First, the executor function is from our HTML test runner, it is intended to be run in the browser context, and it is *not* (by itself) targeting PhantomJS.

Second, like the previously described `HtmlReporter`, `TrivialReporter` is a built-in Jasmine reporter that converts the test results into an HTML document. The output from `TrivialReporter` is simpler (and less "pretty") than that produced by `HtmlReporter`.

Then, we can enter the following at the command line:

```
lib/jasmine-reporters/phantomjs.runner.sh
  chapter04/recipe02-runner.html
```

The script will output the test results to the console, including a line-by-line report of successes and failures.

How it works...

One of the first things that we are likely to notice here is that we are not explicitly calling PhantomJS on the command line; we are calling the `phantomjs.runner.sh` script, which in turn calls PhantomJS. This is provided as a convenience as it can help to ensure that some of the "plumbing" around the test apparatus is initialized or cleaned.

Windows users will find that `phantomjs.runner.sh` expects to be run in a bash shell, and as such it may not work for them. On Windows, we can run the script from Cygwin (available at `http://www.cygwin.com/`) or a similar POSIX-like shell; this is outside the scope of this book.

Alternatively, we can achieve the critical functionality of the `phantomjs.runner.sh` script by entering the following at the command line:

```
phantomjs lib/jasmine-reporters/phantomjs-testrunner.js
file:///C:/Users/me/phantomjs-cookbook/chapter04/
recipe02-runner.html
```

Note that this requires the absolute path to the test runner, and that we must use forward slashes (/) instead of backslashes (\).

The crux of `phantomjs.runner.sh` is how it calls PhantomJS with the `phantomjs-runner.js` script. This performs many functions similar to the `run-jasmine.js` script from the previous recipe; it inspects the script arguments, monitors the page for conditions indicating that tests are "done", and sets up an `onConsoleMessage` callback. Additionally, `phantomjs-runner.js` also collapses certain related console messages onto a single line, sets up a stubbed file writer function on the window object (for capturing and exporting data for persisted test reports), and manages the `webpage` instance for reliable reporting to the console.

More interesting than the `phantomjs-runner.js` script, however, is the inline executor script on our test runner page. Just like in the previous recipe, the first thing that we do here is access the Jasmine environment. However, instead of using `HtmlReporter`, this time we use a combination of `TerminalReporter` and `TrivialReporter`. The `TrivialReporter` is needed by `phantomjs-runner.js`; it uses the DOM elements created by the reporter to infer when the tests on the page have finished running.

> Although the comments in `phantomjs-runner.js` tell us that `TrivialReporter` is required, this is not strictly true. The `phantomjs-runner.js` script can also infer the test suite's completion when using `JUnitXmlReporter`; this reporter will be introduced in *Chapter 8, Continuous Integration with PhantomJS*.

The `TerminalReporter` is the critical component here—it gives us test output that is specially formatted for the console, including an adjustable verbosity level, indented formatting for nested `describe` blocks, and optionally colorized output.

There's more...

The `TerminalReporter` constructor takes a configuration object as its sole argument; the configuration object has two options that we can set:

- `verbosity`: This takes an integer between 0 and 3 (greater values are more verbose)
- `color`: This takes a Boolean that indicates whether to colorize the console output or not

In addition to the `TerminalReporter`, the `jasmine-reporters` library also provides the following reporters:

- `ConsoleReporter`: This is a simpler Jasmine reporter for the console (no colorized output, no other configurable parameters)
- `JUnitXmlReporter`: This is a reporter that persists an XML-based test report to the filesystem for use in continuous integration (CI) systems such as CruiseControl or Jenkins
- `TapReporter`: This is a reporter for the Test Anything Protocol, which also targets CI systems
- `TeamcityReporter`: This is a reporter for the TeamCity CI system by JetBrains

- ▶ The *Running Jasmine unit tests with PhantomJS* recipe
- ▶ The *Creating a Jasmine test runner for PhantomJS and every other browser* recipe
- ▶ The *Generating JUnit reports* recipe in *Chapter 8, Continuous Integration with PhantomJS*
- ▶ The *Generating TAP reports* recipe in *Chapter 8, Continuous Integration with PhantomJS*

Creating a Jasmine test runner for PhantomJS and every other browser

This recipe illustrates how user-agent sniffing can switch between different Jasmine reporters so that we use the appropriate reporters under the appropriate circumstances.

Getting ready

To run this recipe, we will need the following items:

- ▶ JavaScript code to test, and the tests for that code
- ▶ The Jasmine testing framework
- ▶ The `jasmine-reporters` library

The library code that we will use for our tests is available in the downloadable code repository as `string-utils.js` under `lib`; the accompanying tests are available as `string-utils-spec.js` under `lib`. The test runner is also available in the repository as `recipe03-runner.html` under `chapter04`. If we run the provided example, we must change to the root directory for the book's sample code.

Lastly, we will use the version of `phantomjs.runner.sh` that is included with our example repository and is derived from the version in the `jasmine-reporters` library.

How to do it...

Given our example library and its tests, let us call out the executor in the test runner using the following code snippet:

```
(function(jasmine) {
    var env = jasmine.getEnv();

    if (/PhantomJS/.test(navigator.userAgent)) {
      env.addReporter(new
        jasmine.JUnitXmlReporter('target/test-reports/', false));
      env.addReporter(new jasmine.TerminalReporter({
        verbosity: 3,
        color: true
      }));
    } else {
      env.addReporter(new jasmine.HtmlReporter());
    }

    env.execute();
}(jasmine));
```

> Note the highlighted portion of the executor code; this is where we will determine which reporters to use at runtime.

Then, we can enter the following at the command line:

```
lib/jasmine-reporters/phantomjs.runner.sh
  chapter04/recipe03-runner.html
```

The script will output the test results to the console using the `TerminalReporter`, including a line-by-line report of successes and failures.

Alternatively, we can open the test runner in a normal web browser and see a "pretty" formatted report like we saw in the screenshot from the *Running Jasmine unit tests with PhantomJS* recipe earlier in this chapter.

How it works...

The key to this recipe's solution is the user-agent sniffing that we performed in the executor. If left unmodified, PhantomJS will reliably include the string `PhantomJS` in its user-agent string when queried, for example:

```
Mozilla/5.0 (Macintosh; Intel Mac OS X) AppleWebKit/534.34 (KHTML,
  like Gecko) PhantomJS/1.9.2 Safari/534.34
```

This allows us to take our tests and scripts from the previous recipes and build upon them so that, with this small modification, we now have something that we can run in PhantomJS, with suitable command-line output. This also allows us to open something in a normal browser and receive attractive output there as well.

See also

- The *Using TerminalReporter for unit testing in PhantomJS* recipe
- The *Generating JUnit reports* recipe in *Chapter 8, Continuous Integration with PhantomJS*

Running Jasmine unit tests with Grunt

In this recipe, we will learn about using Grunt to execute our Jasmine unit tests from the command line. Grunt is a popular JavaScript task runner and is useful for automating repetitive operations, such as scaffolding, minification, linting, and testing, on the command line.

Getting ready

To run this recipe, we will need the following items:

- JavaScript code to test, and the tests for that code
- Node.js and npm installed and on our PATH

> The Node.js package manager is npm; it is used to download and install Node.js packages for use in our projects. It is included as part of the core Node.js platform. The typical pattern for using npm looks like this:
>
> ```
> npm <command> [<options>] [<package-name>]
> ```
>
> For more information, enter the following on the command line:
>
> ```
> npm help
> ```

- ▶ The Grunt task runner (`grunt-cli`)

> Grunt is a popular JavaScript task runner for the command line. We can find out more about it at `http://gruntjs.com/`; we can install the command-line interface using `npm`, as follows:
>
> **`npm install --global grunt-cli`**
>
> Note that our project will also need Grunt installed locally. We do this by adding Grunt to our `package.json` using `npm`, as follows:
>
> **`npm install grunt --save-dev`**

- ▶ The `grunt-contrib-jasmine` module

> The `grunt-contrib-jasmine` module is what allows us to run Jasmine tests from Grunt. We can find out more about it at `https://npmjs.org/package/grunt-contrib-jasmine`; we can install it on the command line using `npm`, as follows:
>
> **`npm install grunt-contrib-jasmine --save-dev`**

The library code that we will use for our tests is available in the downloadable code repository as `lib/string-utils.js`; the accompanying tests are `lib/string-utils-spec.js`.

Grunt will need a `package.json` file (for Node.js and `npm`) and a Gruntfile in order to run its tasks; one of each has been provided in the downloadable code repository in the `chapter04` directory as `package.json` and `Gruntfile.js`, respectively.

> To install the packages predefined in `package.json`, run the following from the command line in the same directory as that file:
>
> **`npm install`**
>
> This will tell `npm` to retrieve the specified dependencies from over the Internet and install them in the `node_modules` directory within the current directory.

How to do it...

Given our example library and its tests, and given that we have installed Grunt and its Jasmine module, let us add the appropriate testing task to our Gruntfile:

```
module.exports = function(grunt) {
  grunt.initConfig({
    pkg: grunt.file.readJSON('package.json'),
    jasmine: {
```

```
      recipe04: {
        src: '../lib/string-utils.js',
        options: {
          specs: '../lib/string*-spec.js'
        }
      }
    }
  });

  grunt.loadNpmTasks('grunt-contrib-jasmine');
};
```

With our Jasmine task defined, we change to the `chapter04` directory and run the task from the command line, as follows:

grunt jasmine:recipe04

This should print the test results to the console; for example:

```
Running "jasmine:recipe04" (jasmine) task
Testing jasmine specs via phantom
..........
10 specs in 0.004s.
>> 0 failures


Done, without errors.
```

How it works...

As previously mentioned, Grunt is primarily a task runner and can assist with automating a wide array of development tasks—from setting up the directory structure for new projects and running JSHint to running tests (as we have done here) all the way through to packaging your assets for production. In the highlighted portion of our Gruntfile, we have defined the `jasmine` task with a sub-task called `recipe04`. In `recipe04`, we specify the location of our source files with the `src` property, and then we specify the location of the associated specifications/tests with the `specs` property (in the `options` object).

With our Jasmine task defined in our Gruntfile, it is a trivial matter to invoke it from the command line. We simply enter the name of the executable (`grunt`), followed by the name of the task (`jasmine:recipe04`); Grunt takes care of the rest.

One advantage that is quickly noticeable here is that we do not need to maintain any `.html` documents as test runners. We can specify our source files and their supporting tests (by using strings, lists, or matcher patterns), and the Jasmine module can construct the test runner dynamically. This eliminates a lot of the boilerplate that we otherwise need to create and maintain with respect to our test runner pages.

> As of version 0.6.0 of `grunt-contrib-jasmine`, the module only supports Jasmine version 2.0 and above.
>
> Although PhantomJS was not explicitly called out in this recipe, it is useful to know that it is used transparently by Grunt when running the Jasmine tasks. For example, when executing `npm install` in the `chapter04` directory, we may notice that `npm` automatically checks whether PhantomJS is installed. If it is, and the version is compatible, Grunt will delegate to the one on the `PATH`; otherwise, `npm` will download and install a compatible version into `node_modules` and configure Grunt to use it.

There's more...

The `grunt-contrib-jasmine` module provides a variety of configurable options, and this recipe has only scratched the surface. In addition to what has been previously illustrated, we can also instruct `grunt-contrib-jasmine` to perform the following actions:

▸ Load third-party libraries or helper utilities that support our code or tests

▸ Load CSS for the dynamically generated test runner page

▸ Specify the name of the dynamically generated test runner page (and then, specify whether to keep it after the test completes)

▸ Specify whether to write JUnit reports and whether or not to consolidate them

See also

▸ The *Watching your tests during development with Grunt* recipe

▸ The *Generating JUnit reports* recipe in *Chapter 8, Continuous Integration with PhantomJS*

Watching your tests during development with Grunt

This recipe expands upon our combined use of PhantomJS with Jasmine and Grunt by demonstrating how to automatically watch our files during development and re-execute those tests.

Getting ready

To run this recipe, we will need the following items:

- ▶ JavaScript code to test, and the tests for that code
- ▶ A text editor with which to edit our code
- ▶ Node.js and `npm` installed and on our `PATH`
- ▶ The Grunt task runner (`grunt-cli`)
- ▶ The `grunt-contrib-jasmine` module
- ▶ The `grunt-contrib-watch` module

> The `grunt-contrib-watch` module allows Grunt to watch our filesystem during development and rerun certain tasks when it detects changes. We can find out more about it at `https://npmjs.org/package/grunt-contrib-watch`; we can install it on the command line using `npm`, as follows:
>
> `npm install grunt-contrib-watch --save-dev`

The library code that we will use for our tests is available in the downloadable code repository as `string-utils.js` under `lib`; the accompanying tests are available as `string-utils-spec.js` under `lib`.

Grunt will need a `package.json` file (for Node.js and `npm`) and a Gruntfile in order to run its tasks; one of each has been provided in the downloadable code repository in the `chapter04` directory as `package.json` and `Gruntfile.js`, respectively.

How to do it...

Given our example library and its tests, and given the `jasmine` task that we set up in our Gruntfile in the previous recipe (*Running Jasmine unit tests with Grunt*), let us add a `watch` task to our Gruntfile:

```
module.exports = function(grunt) {
  grunt.initConfig({
    pkg: grunt.file.readJSON('package.json'),
    // jasmine task omitted from here
    watch: {
      scripts: {
        files: ['../lib/*.js'],
        tasks: ['jasmine']
      }
```

```
      }
    });

    grunt.loadNpmTasks('grunt-contrib-watch');
  };
```

With our `watch` task defined, we can run it from the command line, as follows:

grunt watch

This should print out a message indicating that it is in a ready state, as follows:

Running "watch" task

Waiting...

Since we already have tests for our library code, let's open up `string-utils.js` under `lib` in a text editor and break it, just to see what happens. Let's remove line 28 (`case 'number':`) and save the file.

Toggling back to our console window, we see that our `watch` task has triggered our Jasmine tests, as shown:

>> File "../lib/string-utils.js" changed.

Running "jasmine:recipe04" (jasmine) task

Testing jasmine specs via phantom

....X..X..

string-utils.js:: txtr.format(s, /*...*/):: formats a string with
  numbers: failed

  Expected 'Foo {0}' to be 'Foo 42'. (1)

string-utils.js:: txtr.format(s, /*...*/):: formats a string with
  multiple items: failed

  Expected 'Foo Bar {1} baz true' to be 'Foo Bar 42 baz true'. (1)

10 specs in 0.004s.

>> 2 failures

Warning: Task "jasmine:recipe04" failed. Use --force to continue.

Aborted due to warnings.

Completed in 1.951s at Thu Jan 30 2014 21:00:17 GMT-0500 (EST) -
  Waiting...

Back in our text editor, let's revert that breaking change. Toggling back to the console, we should see that our tests are passing once again.

When we are finished with the `watch` task, we can cancel it by pressing *CTRL + C*.

How it works...

The crux of this recipe is in adding the `watch` task to Grunt, which will automatically run our tests as files change. In our Gruntfile, we add the `watch` task and tell it which resources to monitor (the array of patterns assigned to the `files` property). Then, in the `tasks` property, we provide the list of tasks (in our case, `['jasmine']`) that we want Grunt to run when it detects changes.

By itself, `grunt-contrib-watch` does not provide very much; all it does is to watch the filesystem and then trigger *other* tasks defined by *other* Grunt modules. In that respect, it is still `grunt-contrib-jasmine` that does our unit testing, although we could just as easily use another testing framework. Again, the main advantage provided here by `grunt-contrib-watch` is the fact that we can start it, and it will provide continuous and nearly instantaneous feedback while we develop.

> As we noted in the *Running Jasmine unit tests with Grunt* recipe, PhantomJS is a critical but secondary component here. Although we are not invoking PhantomJS directly, using it helps to make watched tests less intrusive when they're passing. As we've stated before, as PhantomJS is a headless browser, it is the natural choice to use with command-line utilities such as Grunt.

There's more...

The Grunt task runner has an impressive ecosystem of modules, and many of these modules fit together easily, as we have already seen with `grunt-contrib-jasmine` and `grunt-contrib-watch`. An example of another Grunt module that would help to enhance a PhantomJS-based unit testing workflow is something such as `grunt-notify`.

The `grunt-notify` module is a module that can forward messages from Grunt into a variety of notification systems, including Growl, Snarl, the built-in OS X notifications, and Notify-Send. If the continuous test feedback in the console doesn't seem sufficiently obvious, try something such as `grunt-notify`.

Running Jasmine unit tests with the Karma test runner

This recipe introduces the Karma test runner and describes how to configure it to execute Jasmine tests in PhantomJS. Karma is a test runner that helps make test automation easier by managing the test environments and target browsers, and test reporting for us through simple configuration files.

Getting ready

To run this recipe, we will need the following items:

- JavaScript code to test, and the tests for that code
- Node.js and `npm` installed and on our `PATH`
- The Karma test runner installed

> Karma is a test runner that is agnostic to any underlying test framework or target browser. We can find out more about it at `http://karma-runner.github.io/`; we can install it on the command line using `npm`, as shown:
> ```
> npm install karma-cli --global
> npm install karma --save-dev
> ```

- And the following plugins (`npm` modules) for Karma:
  - ❑ `karma-jasmine`
  - ❑ `karma-phantomjs-launcher`

> Both of these Karma plugins can be installed as regular `npm` modules on the command line, as shown:
> ```
> npm install karma-jasmine --save-dev
> npm install karma-phantomjs-launcher --save-dev
> ```

The library code that we will use for our tests is available in the downloadable code repository as `string-utils.js` under `lib`; the accompanying tests are available as `string-utils-spec.js` under `lib`.

Karma will need a configuration file in order to run tests; a sample configuration file has been provided in the downloadable code repository in the `chapter04` directory as `recipe06.conf.js`. If we run the provided configuration file, we must change to the `chapter04` directory of the book's sample code.

How to do it...

Given our example library and its tests, and given that we have Karma installed, we can configure Karma with our configuration file, `recipe06.conf.js`:

```
module.exports = function(config) {
  config.set({
    frameworks: ['jasmine'],
    files: [
      '../lib/string-utils.js',
      '../lib/string-utils-spec.js'
    ],
    browsers: ['PhantomJS'],
    singleRun: true
  });
};
```

With our configuration file defined, we can run Karma from the command line, as follows:

```
karma start recipe06.conf.js
```

This will print the results of the Karma test runner's execution, showing something like the following:

```
INFO [karma]: Karma v0.10.9 server started at http://localhost:9876/

INFO [launcher]: Starting browser PhantomJS

INFO [PhantomJS 1.9.7 (Mac OS X)]: Connected on socket
  9oGHV5BryrH4seBDRZR2

PhantomJS 1.9.7 (Mac OS X): Executed 10 of 10 SUCCESS (0.02 secs /
  0.003 secs)
```

How it works...

Karma is one of the best testing tools available to front-end developers today, and it makes a fantastic companion to PhantomJS for streamlining day-to-day development workflows. Karma is a command-line test harness that consumes configuration files (which are themselves nothing more than JavaScript) and then uses that configuration to automate almost all of the boilerplate that goes into setting up and executing in the test environment. Similar to what we saw in the *Running Jasmine unit tests with Grunt* recipe in this chapter, Karma frees us from having to maintain the `.html` documents for our test runners; it constructs all of that dynamically based on parameters that we specify in the configuration file.

For our introduction to Karma, we have used a very simple configuration file. Walking through that configuration file, we perform the following actions:

1. We assign a function to `module.exports`, and that function takes a single argument (`config`). This is the function that Karma calls internally to configure itself at the beginning of the test run.

2. The main body of the function calls `config.set` with the *actual* configuration object, applying defaults wherever we do not otherwise specify certain critical values.

3. We set the `frameworks` property to use `jasmine`.

4. We indicate the set of `files` to inject into the dynamic test runner (note that this could be a glob pattern).

5. We specify what `browsers` we want to use; in our case, we want to start with just PhantomJS.

6. We specify `singleRun` here so that we don't end up in watch mode.

Confident about our configuration file, we can pass it on the command line to Karma when we otherwise trigger a test run via the `start` command. Once started, Karma consumes the configuration file, constructs the appropriate test environment (loads plugins, builds test runners, launches and slaves browsers), executes the tests, and returns the report.

There's more...

Like Grunt, Karma has a rich ecosystem of plugins and modules. A search at `https://npmjs.org` will reveal dozens of modules/plugins, including support for different test frameworks, reporters, preprocessors, browser launchers, and more. Similarly, there is also a `grunt-karma` module so that you can drive Karma from Grunt. There is too much to make a comprehensive survey of the Karma ecosystem here, but it's good to know that many of the tools we may want for Karma already exist.

Generating code coverage reports with Istanbul and the Karma test runner

This recipe expands on our use of the Karma test runner and introduces the Istanbul library for static analysis of test coverage. **Istanbul** is a code coverage tool for JavaScript that instruments the code under test and provides reports about statement, branch, function, and line test coverage.

Getting ready

To run this recipe, we will need the following items:

- ▸ JavaScript code to test, and the tests for that code
- ▸ Node.js and npm installed and on our PATH
- ▸ The Karma test runner installed
- ▸ The following plugins (npm modules) for Karma:
  - ❏ karma-jasmine
  - ❏ karma-phantomjs-launcher
  - ❏ karma-coverage

> The karma-coverage plugin uses Istanbul to provide reports on code coverage. We can learn more about Istanbul at http://gotwarlost.github.io/istanbul/; we can install it on the command line as:
>
> **npm install karma-coverage --save-dev**

The library code that we will use for our tests is available in the downloadable code repository as string-utils.js under lib; the accompanying tests are available as string-utils-spec.js under lib.

Karma will need a configuration file in order to run tests; a sample configuration file has been provided in the downloadable code repository in the chapter04 directory as recipe07.conf.js. If we run the provided configuration file, we must change to the root directory of the book's sample code.

How to do it...

Given our example library and its tests, and given that we have Karma and its coverage plugin installed, we can add code coverage to Karma by updating our configuration file. Let's examine the changes in recipe07.conf.js:

```
module.exports = function(config) {
  config.set({
    frameworks: ['jasmine'],
    files: ['../lib/string-utils*.js'],
    preprocessors: {
      '../lib/string-utils.js': 'coverage'
    },
    reporters: ['progress', 'coverage'],
```

```
        browsers: ['PhantomJS'],
        singleRun: true
    });
};
```

In particular, we have added two things to our configuration:

- ► We have specified use of the `coverage` preprocessor on a specific file (`string-utils.js`; though that could just as easily have been a matcher pattern)
- ► We have added the `coverage` reporter to the `reporters` list

With the configuration file updated, we can run Karma from the command line, as follows:

karma start chapter04/recipe07.conf.js

This will print the results of the Karma test runner's execution, but it will also generate a code coverage report in the `coverage` directory. If we open the report formatted as `.html`, we will see something as seen in the following screenshot:

We can then drill into directories and files to see the actual line and branch coverage as seen in the following screenshot:

How it works...

Adding Istanbul's code coverage to Karma involves installing the plugin and adding the preprocessor and reporter to the configuration file. Once these have been added, generating the code coverage reports is as simple as executing our tests as we normally would have, and then examining the code coverage reports.

There's more...

Code coverage reports, such as the ones generated by Istanbul, are powerful tools to have in our development toolkit. A solid testing strategy can help us to be more thoughtful in our code design and more confident while we refactor; but there's nothing quite like a code coverage report to reveal the dusty corners we may have overlooked.

One caution about using the `karma-coverage` plugin—if our Karma configuration file is set to run tests against multiple browsers (for example, PhantomJS *and* Chrome *and* Firefox), then a code coverage report is only produced for one of them—and it's unpredictable which one will get the report. Generally speaking, if we critically need the code coverage report, we should set up a specific Karma configuration file for generating it, preferring PhantomJS as the browser in which to do so.

Running Jasmine unit tests with Karma and PhantomJS from WebStorm

This recipe illustrates how to set up the Karma test runner to run within WebStorm so that we can receive feedback during development without leaving our IDE. WebStorm is an IDE by JetBrains that is focused on JavaScript development and other front-end technologies and tools.

Getting ready

To run this recipe, we will need the following items:

▸ JavaScript code to test, and the tests for that code

▸ Node.js and `npm` installed and on our `PATH`

▸ The Karma test runner (and its supporting plugins/modules) installed

▸ The WebStorm IDE

> WebStorm is an IDE by JetBrains that is oriented toward front-end developers and focused on JavaScript, CSS, and HTML. Support for the Karma test runner was added in version 7; we can find out more about WebStorm at `http://www.jetbrains.com/webstorm/`.

The library code that we will use for our tests is available in the downloadable code repository as `string-utils.js` under `lib`; the accompanying tests are available as `string-utils-spec.js` under `lib`.

Karma will need a configuration file in order to run tests. For this recipe, we will reuse `recipe07.conf.js`, which is provided in the `chapter04` directory of the downloadable code repository.

How to do it...

Given our example library and its tests, we can add our project to WebStorm.

> The JetBrains WebStorm help site has detailed instructions for how to import the existing code as a project at `http://www.jetbrains.com/webstorm/webhelp/importing-project-from-existing-source-code.html`.

The first time we want to run the Karma test runner from WebStorm, we will need to add a Run Configuration for it, as follows:

1. In the **Run** menu, click on **Edit Configurations...**; alternatively, you can click on **Edit Configurations...** under the Run item in the navigation bar.

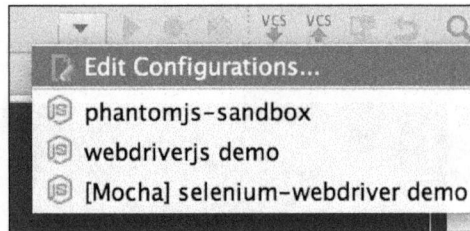

2. In the **Run/Debug Configurations** dialog, click on the **+** button, and then select the **Karma** option.

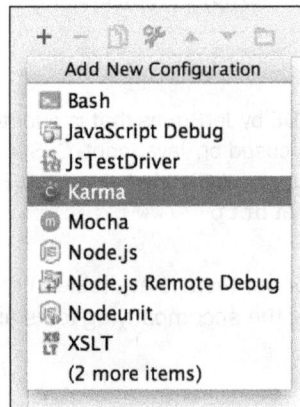

3. In the **Run/Debug Configurations** dialog, configure the **Karma** run configuration:

    1. Give the Run Configuration a name (for example, `Chapter 4 : Recipe 8`).

    2. Set the path to the Node.js interpreter (although this should be set automatically).

    3. Set the path to the Karma `npm` module (preferring the one local to the project, if possible).

    4. Set the path to the Karma configuration file (for example, `recipe07.conf.js`).

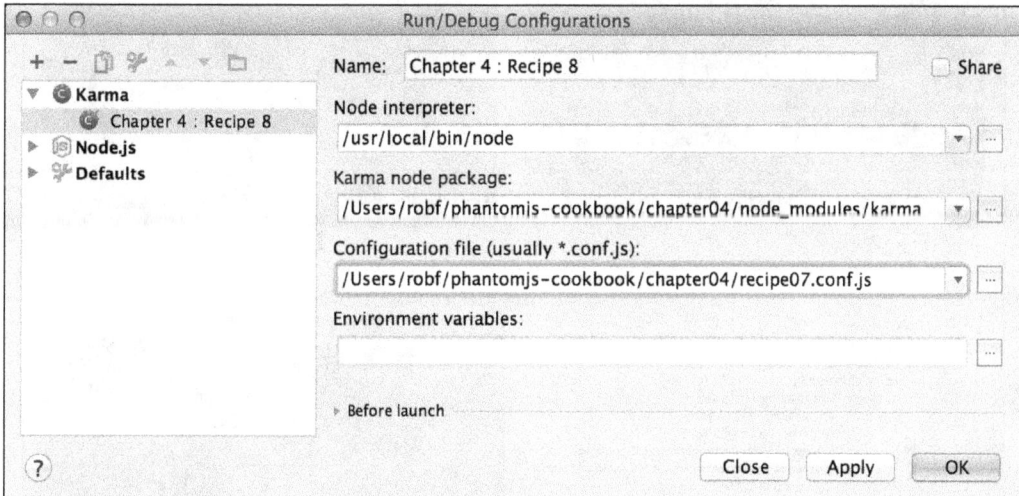

4. Click on **OK** and return to WebStorm's editor context.

Now (and every time after this initial set up) we can run our tests using Karma, right from within our IDE. We can select our **Chapter 4 : Recipe 8** configuration from the Run Configuration menu, and then click on the Run button.

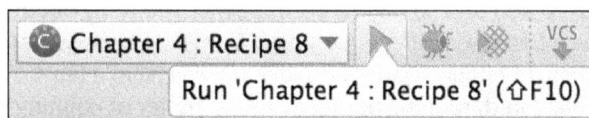

Clicking on the Run button will start Karma, which loads the specified configuration file, launches PhantomJS (and/or other browsers), and then executes the tests, displaying the results right in the IDE.

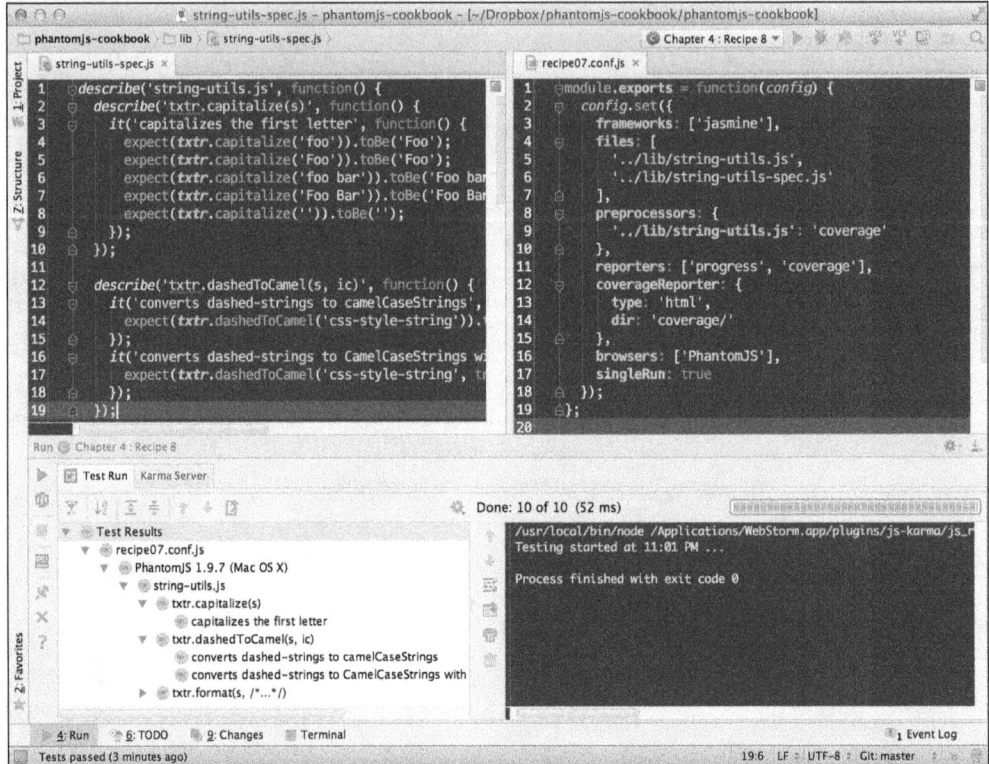

How it works...

As an IDE that is oriented towards the front-end development workflow, WebStorm has made it an almost trivial task to add and configure Karma tests. The **Run/Debug Configuration** menu treats Karma as a first-class citizen, putting it alongside Node.js, JsTestDriver, and other well-known utilities. In effect, all we needed to do was fill in a few boxes and save our configuration. Once configured, running our tests was a matter of pointing and clicking. Although WebStorm does not honor the `autoWatch` configuration property (to keep the tests running in the background), it is quite convenient to be able to click through the report in the IDE and have it navigate directly to the test in question.

Running QUnit tests with PhantomJS

In this recipe, we will illustrate how to run QUnit-based unit tests through PhantomJS as an alternative to Jasmine.

Getting ready

To run this recipe, we will need JavaScript code to test, and the tests for that code. To test our code, we will use the QUnit test framework.

> QUnit (maintained by the jQuery Foundation) is a JavaScript framework for writing unit tests; its assertion methods conform to the CommonJS unit testing specification (see `http://wiki.commonjs.org/wiki/Unit_Testing/1.0`). QUnit is open source (MIT licensed) and is available at `http://qunitjs.com/`.
>
> We will be using QUnit version 1.14.0.

The library code that we will use for our tests is available in the downloadable code repository as `string-utils.js` under `lib`; the accompanying QUnit tests are available as `string-utils-tests.js` under `lib`. The test runner is also available in the repository as `recipe09-runner.html` under `chapter04`. If we run the provided example, we must change to the root directory for the book's sample code.

Lastly, we will use the `run-qunit.js` script that ships with the PhantomJS source code in the `examples` directory. The recipe uses the `$PHANTOMJS_SOURCE` environment variable, which refers to our clone of the PhantomJS source code.

How to do it...

Given our example library, we can execute its tests by launching the test runner in PhantomJS from the command line:

```
phantomjs $PHANTOMJS_SOURCE/examples/run-qunit.js
  chapter04/recipe09-runner.html
```

The script will output the test results to the console. They should look something like the following:

```
'waitFor()' finished in 202ms.

Tests completed in 18 milliseconds.

16 assertions of 16 passed, 0 failed.
```

How it works...

There are three main components at work in our example:

- Our tests, wrapped inside of the test runner
- The `run-qunit.js` script that loads and bootstraps the test runner
- PhantomJS that serves as the test environment

If we look at our tests (`string-utils-tests.js`), they are straightforward, they use only the basic testing functions that QUnit provides, and they are assertion-for-assertion equivalents to the Jasmine specifications we have used throughout the rest of this chapter. We have partitioned the suite based on which method is being tested by using the `module` function; then, we set up several tests using the `test` function, with one or more `equal` assertions inside.

We can open our test runner (`recipe09-runner.html`) in a normal browser and see the results of the tests:

Looking at the test runner, we can see that it:

1. Loads the CSS for the QUnit test framework.
2. Contains two div nodes (qunit and `qunit-fixture`) as required by QUnit.
3. Loads the QUnit test framework.
4. Loads the JavaScript code under test (`string-utils.js`).
5. Loads the tests (`string-utils-tests.js`).

As we noted with our Jasmine examples, opening the test runner in a normal browser could be sufficient. However, given that our aim is to streamline our development workflow on the command line, we need a script that can load our test runner into PhantomJS, run the tests, and interpret the results. Once again, the PhantomJS source code ships with a script to manage `run-qunit.js`. The `run-qunit.js` script functions almost identically as the `run-jasmine.js` script that we analyzed in the *Running Jasmine unit tests with PhantomJS* recipe; the only notable differences are in the CSS selectors that it uses to inspect the page for failures.

PhantomJS provides the test environment itself. We invoke it on the command line, providing our script (`run-qunit.js`) and our target URL. All the work takes place within the PhantomJS process, which will exit cleanly, or not, depending upon the outcome of the tests on the page.

There's more...

As we saw in the *Running Jasmine unit tests with PhantomJS* recipe in this chapter, one of the advantages of using the `run-qunit.js` script is that we can start using our existing QUnit tests immediately. We do not need to perform any conversion or migration, and there is no additional adapter to install onto the test runner; `run-qunit.js` is already equipped to scrape the results from the page and output them to the console.

Additionally, if we've adopted Grunt as part of our development workflow, we can add the `grunt-contrib-qunit` module to our project, and with a couple of lines added to our Gruntfile, we can drive our QUnit tests in PhantomJS with Grunt.

> We can find out more about `grunt-contrib-qunit` at `https://npmjs.org/package/grunt-contrib-qunit`; we can install it on the command line using npm, as follows:
>
> ```
> npm install grunt-contrib-qunit --save-dev
> ```

See also

▸ The *Running Jasmine unit tests with PhantomJS* recipe
▸ The *Running Jasmine unit tests with Grunt* recipe

Running Mocha unit tests with PhantomJS

This recipe demonstrates how to run Mocha-based unit tests through PhantomJS as an alternative to Jasmine and QUnit.

Getting ready

To run this recipe, we will need the following items:

- JavaScript code to test, and the tests for that code
- Node.js and npm installed and on our PATH
- The Mocha test framework (included in `lib/mocha`)

> Mocha is the "simple, flexible, and fun" JavaScript unit-testing framework that runs in Node.js or in the browser. It is open source (MIT licensed), and we can learn more about it at `http://visionmedia.github.io/mocha/`; we can install Mocha on the command line using npm, as follows:
>
> ```
> npm install --global mocha
> ```

- The Chai assertion library (included in `lib/chai`)

> Chai is a platform-agnostic BDD/TDD assertion library featuring several interfaces (for example, `should`, `expect`, and `assert`). It is open source (MIT licensed), and we can learn more about it at `http://chaijs.com/`; we can install Chai on the command line using npm, as follows:
>
> ```
> npm install chai --save-dev
> ```

- The `mocha-phantomjs` module

> The `mocha-phantomjs` module provides PhantomJS test runners with Mocha. We can learn more about it at `https://github.com/metaskills/mocha-phantomjs`; we can install it on the command line using npm, as follows:
>
> ```
> npm install --global mocha-phantomjs --save-dev
> ```

The library code that we will use for our tests is available in the downloadable code repository as `string-utils.js` under `lib`; the accompanying `Mocha/Chai` tests are available as `string-utils-expectations.js` under `lib`. The test runner is also available in the repository as `recipe10-runner.html` under `chapter04`. If we run the provided example, we must change to the root directory for the book's sample code.

How to do it...

Given our example library and its tests, let us call out the two inline JavaScript blocks in our test runner. The first such block configures Mocha and exposes Chai to the tests as a global variable, as shown in the following code snippet:

```
mocha.ui('bdd');
mocha.reporter('html');
expect = chai.expect;
```

The second such block is our executor, as shown:

```
if ('mochaPhantomJS' in window) {
  mochaPhantomJS.run();
} else {
  mocha.run();
}
```

With Mocha configured and our executor in place, we can launch the test runner from the command line, as shown:

mocha-phantomjs chapter04/recipe10-runner.html

The script will output the test results to the console. They should look something like the following:

```
string-utils.js
  txtr.capitalize(s)
    √ capitalizes the first letter
  txtr.dashedToCamel(s, ic)
    √ converts dashed-strings to camelCaseStrings
    √ converts dashed-strings to CamelCaseStrings with an initial capital
when specified
  txtr.format(s, /*...*/)
    √ formats a string with strings
    √ formats a string with numbers
    √ formats a string with a function
    √ formats a string with a boolean
    √ formats a string with multiple items
    √ returns the token itself when there are not enough arguments to
substitute for them all
```

√ returns the token itself when it cannot otherwise recognize or
handle the substitution

10 passing

How it works...

The `mocha-phantomjs` module provides the bridge between our test runner and the PhantomJS test runtime. After setting up our tests using Mocha's BDD style and the Chai assertions, we can open our test runner (`recipe10-runner.html`) in a normal browser and see the results of the tests:

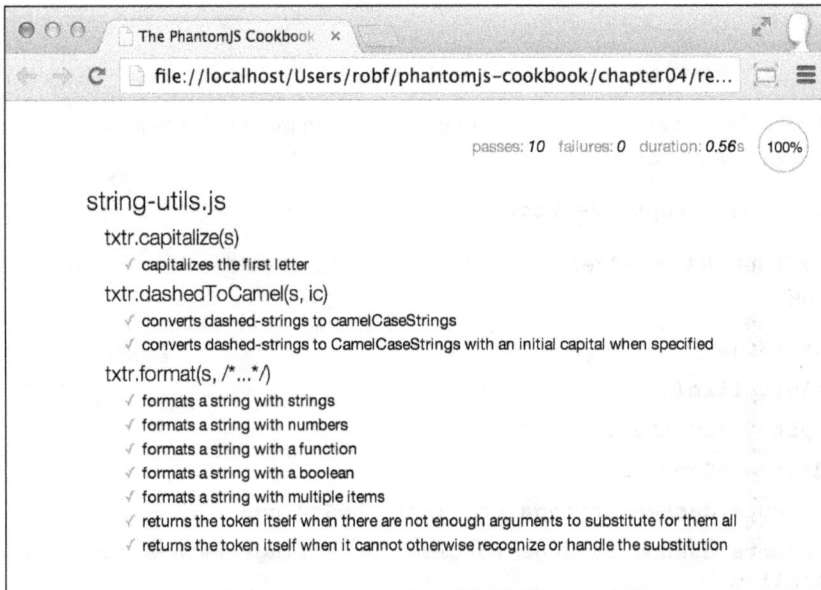

Looking at the test runner, we can see that it performs the following actions:

1. Sets the page's charset as UTF-8 with a meta tag (important for proper encoding of certain characters used in the test framework).

2. Loads the CSS for the Mocha test framework.

3. Contains a div (`mocha`) as required by Mocha.

4. Loads the Chai assertion library and the Mocha test framework.

5. Configures Mocha (setting it to use the BDD style and an `html` reporter) and exposes the `chai.expect` object as the global `expect` with an inline script.

6. Loads the JavaScript code under test (`string-utils.js`).

7. Loads the tests (`string-utils-expectations.js`).

8. Runs the Mocha executor that kicks off `mochaPhantomJS.run` (if we are running the `mocha-phantomjs` module); it kicks off `mocha.run` otherwise.

With the test runner properly set up, it can now execute tests in a normal browser (as before) or in PhantomJS through the `mocha-phantomjs` module. Launching the tests in `mocha-phantomjs` is as simple as entering the module's exported binary's name on the command line followed by the path to the test runner.

There's more...

In addition to providing its core test runner for PhantomJS, `mocha-phantomjs` provides hooks into the underlying Mocha framework. From the command line, we can specify that `mocha-phantomjs` uses alternative reporters. For example, instead of the default `spec` reporter, we can specify the `-R` flag on the command line followed by the name of our preferred reporter (for example, `dot`, `tap`, `xunit`, or others), and `mocha-phantomjs` will forward that along to Mocha when executing the tests. The `mocha-phantomjs` module can also accept command-line arguments that are forwarded along to the underlying PhantomJS instance, configuring aspects of the browser as well (for example, a cookie object, a viewport size, and other settings).

Additionally, if we've adopted Grunt as part of our development workflow, then we can add the `grunt-mocha-phantomjs` module to our project, and with a couple of lines added to our Gruntfile, we can drive our Mocha tests in PhantomJS with Grunt.

> Find out more about grunt-mocha-phantomjs at `https://npmjs.org/package/grunt-mocha-phantomjs`; we can install it on the command line using npm, as follows:
>
> **npm install grunt-mocha-phantomjs --save-dev**

See also

- The *Running Jasmine unit tests with PhantomJS* recipe
- The *Running Jasmine unit tests with Grunt* recipe

5
Functional and End-to-end Testing with PhantomJS

In this chapter, we will cover:

- ▶ Running Selenium tests with PhantomJS and GhostDriver
- ▶ Using WebdriverJS as a Selenium client for PhantomJS
- ▶ Adding Poltergeist to a Capybara suite
- ▶ Taking screenshots during tests with Poltergeist
- ▶ Simulating precise mouse clicks with Poltergeist
- ▶ Installing CasperJS
- ▶ Interacting with web pages using CasperJS
- ▶ End-to-end testing with CasperJS
- ▶ Exporting test results from CasperJS in the XUnit format
- ▶ Detecting visual regressions using PhantomCSS

Introduction

In addition to being a popular solution for fast front-end unit tests, PhantomJS has emerged as a compelling component of functional or end-to-end test solutions. As we have noted several times already, the headless nature of PhantomJS gives it some unique characteristics that can help streamline the testing process, especially on certain systems where setting up test automation with traditional browsers may be more cumbersome.

In this chapter, we will learn about functional testing strategies with PhantomJS. We will survey several different functional testing tools, including Selenium, Poltergeist (a driver for Capybara), and CasperJS. We will also learn how to apply PhantomJS as part of the overall testing stack.

Running Selenium tests with PhantomJS and GhostDriver

This recipe introduces GhostDriver, an implementation of the WebDriver wire protocol, and explains how to use it to run Selenium tests with PhantomJS as the target browser.

Getting ready

To run this recipe, we will need Selenium available on our system; our recipe will use version 2.39.0 of the Selenium Java server, but we must use version 2.33.0 or later to be able to use GhostDriver. Our examples in this recipe will use the Java bindings for Selenium.

> Selenium is a big enough topic on its own to be an entire book, so we will not dive in deep here. As such, this recipe assumes that we already have some knowledge of Selenium as a testing utility.
>
> Also, as we use the Selenium Java bindings, we assume at least some basic knowledge of Java.

To simplify working with Java, we will need Maven installed and on our `PATH`.

> Maven is a software project management and comprehension tool that can be used to simplify working with and building Java-based projects. We can learn more about Maven at `http://maven.apache.org/`.

We will need a test suite (a set of Java test classes) that makes use of the `RemoteWebDriver` class to connect with the remote PhantomJS instance for running our functional tests. Our example will use the `phantomjs.cookbook.RemoteWebDriverTest` class in the `recipe01` folder under `chapter05` in the downloadable code repository. If we run the provided example tests, we must change to the `chapter05/recipe01` directory for the book's sample code.

GhostDriver must be available on our system. If we have PhantomJS 1.8 or greater installed, then GhostDriver is already built-in.

> GhostDriver is an implementation of the remote WebDriver wire protocol that uses PhantomJS as the target browser. If we need to deal with GhostDriver independently from PhantomJS, or otherwise wish to learn more about it, the project home page can be found at `https://github.com/detro/ghostdriver`.

Lastly, the functional test in this recipe runs against the demo site that is included with the cookbook's sample code repository. To run that demo site, we must have Node.js installed. In a separate terminal, change to the `phantomjs-sandbox` directory (in the sample code's directory), and start the app with the following command:

`node app.js`

How to do it...

First, we must spawn a PhantomJS instance and put it into a state where it is receptive to remote WebDriver requests. We can initialize PhantomJS on the command line, as follows:

`phantomjs --webdriver=4444`

Second, consider the following test class:

```
package phantomjs.cookbook;

import org.junit.Test;
import org.openqa.selenium.By;
import org.openqa.selenium.Keys;
import org.openqa.selenium.WebDriver;
import org.openqa.selenium.WebElement;
import org.openqa.selenium.remote.DesiredCapabilities;
import org.openqa.selenium.remote.RemoteWebDriver;
import java.net.URL;
import static org.junit.Assert.assertEquals;

public class RemoteWebDriverTest {
    private static final String THE_TEXT = "PhantomJS + GhostDriver";

    @Test
    public void testGhostDriver() throws Exception {
        WebDriver driver = new RemoteWebDriver(
                new URL("http://localhost:4444/"),
                DesiredCapabilities.phantomjs());

        driver.get("http://localhost:3000/input-demo");

        WebElement demo = driver.findElement(By.id("demo"));
```

```
        demo.sendKeys(THE_TEXT);
        demo.sendKeys(Keys.ENTER);

        WebElement stage = driver.findElement(By.id("stage"));

        final String stageText = stage.getText();

        assertEquals(THE_TEXT, stageText);
    }
}
```

In a new terminal window, we can execute our test on the command line using Maven, as follows:

```
mvn clean test -Dtest=RemoteWebDriverTest
```

> Maven may need to download some dependencies before it can execute the tasks. This could take a little while depending on our Internet connection speed, the state of the remote Maven server, and other factors; so, let's be patient. When we run the preceding command, Maven will first check whether it has dependencies to resolve, it will then resolve those dependencies, build the project, and run the Selenium tests.

The testing task's output will appear in the console and should look something like the following screenshot:

```
●○○                      recipe01 (bash)

 T E S T S

Running phantomjs.cookbook.RemoteWebDriverTest
Tests run: 1; Failures: 0, Errors: 0, Skipped: 0, Time elapsed: 0.528 sec

Results :

Tests run: 1, Failures: 0, Errors: 0, Skipped: 0

[INFO] ------------------------------------------------------------------------
[INFO] BUILD SUCCESS
[INFO] ------------------------------------------------------------------------
[INFO] Total time: 2.317 s
[INFO] Finished at: 2014-04-22T21:46:41-05:00
[INFO] Final Memory: 21M/180M
[INFO] ------------------------------------------------------------------------
$
```

How it works...

The first thing that we do in our recipe is start a PhantomJS instance using the `webdriver` command-line argument, putting it into a state where it is receptive to remote WebDriver connections on the specified port. We specify the port as the value following the `webdriver` argument key. Specifying this argument tells PhantomJS to engage GhostDriver when it launches, and it allows the browser to be controlled by remote Selenium automation.

Secondly, we launch our functional test from Maven using the `test` goal, indicating the specific class (`RemoteWebDriverTest`) with the `test` argument.

> Note that we also specified the `clean` goal in our example. While not strictly necessary, it is a good idea to run `clean` first, in order to sanitize the testing environment and minimize the risk of complications.

Our test class, `phantomjs.cookbook.RemoteWebDriverTest`, contains a single method (`testGhostDriver`) that performs the following actions:

1. It creates a new `RemoteWebDriver` instance and assigns it to the `driver` variable. This instance is created with a URL of `http://localhost:4444/` (the port where our PhantomJS instance is listening for WebDriver connections) and a Selenium `Capabilities` object that requests a PhantomJS browser instance.

2. With the `driver` instance created, we have it request the URL `http://localhost:3000/input-demo`—part of our Node.js-based demo app.

3. Once loaded, we have our `driver` instance find the #demo element on the page and save it to a variable with the name `demo`.

4. The `RemoteWebDriver` instance (`driver`) sends keyboard input to the `demo` element; first, we send the string `PhantomJS + GhostDriver`, and the script sends an *Enter* keypress.

5. We have our `driver` instance find the `#stage` element and save it to a variable with the name `stage`. Then, we get the text from within `stage`, and save it to the variable `stageText`.

6. Lastly, we assert that `stageText` does in fact match the text we input in step 4.

Maven runs the test class and outputs the results, informing us whether it passed or failed.

There's more...

Although this recipe's example is as trivial as a functional test can be, it should convey the simplicity of incorporating PhantomJS into our overall Selenium testing strategies. Adding PhantomJS is just a matter of requesting a `RemoteWebDriver` instance with PhantomJS capabilities and having a PhantomJS instance listening on the appropriate port. In this way, we can take our existing Selenium functional tests and start running them in PhantomJS with very little effort.

There are more options available to us. For example, we do not necessarily need to have a PhantomJS instance running; instead of using the `RemoteWebDriver` class and requesting PhantomJS capabilities, we can use the `PhantomJSDriver` class that provisions and manages its own PhantomJS instance. Looking in the `chapter05/recipe01` directory again, we see an example of this with the `PhantomJSDriverTest` class. The only significant difference between `RemoteWebDriverTest` and `PhantomJSDriverTest` is the constructor used to create the `WebDriver` instance. To demonstrate how `PhantomJSDriver` manages its own PhantomJS instances, we can kill our PhantomJS process, and then launch the test class from the command line:

```
mvn clean test -Dtest=PhantomJSDriverTest
```

Watching the command-line output, we should see where the test class creates a PhantomJS instance, binds to it, and then successfully executes its assertions.

Lastly, it is worth noting that although our examples here use Selenium's Java bindings, the recipe should be equally applicable for any of the other language bindings, such as for C#, Python, Ruby, or JavaScript.

Using WebdriverJS as a Selenium client for PhantomJS

This recipe demonstrates how to use WebdriverJS as a JavaScript-based Selenium client. We will run tests and discuss how to use the combination of WebdriverJS and PhantomJS for ubiquitous JavaScript.

Getting ready

To run this recipe, we will need a Selenium server available and running on our system; our recipe will use version 2.41.0 of the Selenium Java server, but we must use version 2.33.0 or later to be able to use GhostDriver.

> The Selenium Standalone Server JAR can be downloaded from the Selenium project website at `http://docs.seleniumhq.org/download/`.
>
> Once downloaded, the server can be started (listening on port `4444` by default) with Java on the command line, as follows:
>
> ```
> java -jar selenium-server-standalone-2.41.0.jar
> ```
>
> Selenium is open source and distributed under the Apache License 2.0.

We will need WebdriverJS installed. WebdriverJS is a JavaScript-based Selenium client with a fluent API that implements the WebDriver wire protocol.

> WebdriverJS can be installed with the Node.js package manager, `npm`, as follows:
>
> ```
> npm install webdriverjs
> ```
>
> Our example project (located in the `chapter05/recipe02` directory) already lists WebdriverJS as a dependency in its `package.json` file. We can learn more about WebdriverJS at `http://webdriver.io/`.

The Mocha test framework must be installed; we will use the `mocha` binary to execute our tests. We demonstrated how to install Mocha globally with `npm` in the *Running Mocha unit tests with PhantomJS* recipe in *Chapter 4, Unit Testing with PhantomJS*.

We need GhostDriver available on our system. If we have PhantomJS 1.8 or greater installed, then GhostDriver is already built-in.

The script for the functional test in this recipe is available in the downloadable code repository as `webdriverjs-test.js` under `chapter05/recipe02/`. If we run the provided example script, we must change to the root directory for the book's sample code.

Lastly, the functional test in this recipe runs against the demo site that is included with the cookbook's sample code repository. To run that demo site, we must have Node.js installed. In a separate terminal, change to the `phantomjs-sandbox` directory (in the sample code's directory), and start the app with the following command:

```
node app.js
```

How to do it...

Consider our functional test script:

```
var assert   = require('assert'),
    driver   = require('webdriverjs'),
    client,
```

```
      THE_TEXT = 'PhantomJS + GhostDriver';

describe('input-demo', function() {
  beforeEach(function(done) {
    client = driver.remote({
      desiredCapabilities: {
        browserName: 'phantomjs'
      }
    }).init();
    client.url('http://localhost:3000/input-demo', done);
  });

  afterEach(function(done) {
    client.end(done);
  });

  it('gets input from #demo and puts it onto #stage', function(done) {
    client
      .setValue('#demo', THE_TEXT + '\uE007')
      .getText('#stage', function(err, text) {
        assert(text === THE_TEXT, '#stage innerText equals ' + THE_
TEXT);
      })
      .call(done);
  });
});
```

Assuming that we already have our Selenium server running, we can execute our functional test on the command line, as follows:

mocha chapter05/recipe02/webdriverjs-test.js

Mocha will execute the tests in the script and output the results to the console. Note that the test output is not verbose and will look something like the following:

1 passing (2s)

> We may get errors that read something like:
>
> ```
> /input-demo "after each" hook:
>     Uncaught TypeError: Cannot read property
>       'sessionId' of undefined
> ```
>
> In this case, we may need to reinstall the Node.js modules. In these instances, try deleting the node_modules directory (in chapter05/recipe02) and reinstalling the modules from the command line, as follows:
>
> **npm install**

How it works...

At a high level, Mocha serves as the test runner for our functional test script, automatically provisioning the PhantomJS instance and connecting it to the Selenium server. More specifically, our script does the following:

1. It imports our required modules: `assert` (the built-in Node.js assertion library) and `webdriverjs` (our Selenium client).

2. It declares the `client` variable that will hold our WebdriverJS instance, and it also assigns our specimen text to `THE_TEXT`.

3. It creates a BDD-style `describe` block to hold our test expectations.

4. It sets up a `beforeEach` function to initialize a WebdriverJS instance with PhantomJS capabilities, and it directs it to our target URL (`http://localhost:3000/input-demo`).

5. It sets up an `afterEach` function to signal to the client that we have finished.

6. It creates a test expectation that:

   1. Sets the value of the `#demo` element to `THE_TEXT`.
   2. Gets the value of the `#stage` element.
   3. Asserts that the `#demo` input is the same as the `#stage` content.
   4. Calls `done` to complete the test.

On the command line, we execute the functional test script using the `mocha` binary that provides the test framework to the script. From within the script, WebdriverJS then provisions the PhantomJS instance and connects to Selenium.

There's more...

One of the advantages of using a Selenium client such as WebdriverJS is that we can have ubiquitous JavaScript in our project if we desire. For example, we may be more comfortable, and thus, more productive writing JavaScript; or perhaps, we have our own internal JavaScript libraries that we need to share between different environments. Whatever the reason, it is useful to know that this option exists.

In addition to WebdriverJS, which we have discussed in this recipe, there is also `selenium-webdriver`, the Selenium project's official JavaScript bindings for the WebDriver wire protocol. We can find out more about `selenium-webdriver` at `https://www.npmjs.org/package/selenium-webdriver`; an example of it appears in the downloadable code repository as `selenium-webdriver-test.js` under `chapter05/recipe02`. We can run that example from the command line as:

```
mocha chapter05/recipe02/selenium-webdriver-test.js
```

Adding Poltergeist to a Capybara suite

In this recipe we introduce Poltergeist, the PhantomJS driver for Capybara tests. We will illustrate a simple end-to-end test using Capybara and explain how to run such tests in PhantomJS using Poltergeist.

Getting ready

To run this recipe, we will need a recent version of Ruby installed and on our PATH.

> Ruby is a dynamic programming language that is both popular and expressive. We use it here for these reasons. Capybara requires version 1.9.3 or greater, but version 2.1.0 or greater is advised. See the Ruby website for information about how to obtain and install the runtime at https://www.ruby-lang.org/.

We will need the RubyGems package management framework for Ruby installed and on our PATH.

> We can find information about downloading and installing RubyGems at http://rubygems.org/pages/download.

We will need Capybara installed.

> Capybara is a Ruby library for simulating user interactions and automating browsers. It is too large a topic to go into depth here. As such, this recipe assumes that we already have some knowledge of Capybara as a testing utility. We can find out more about Capybara at http://jnicklas.github.io/capybara/.
>
> We can install Capybara on the command line:
>
> `gem install capybara`
>
> Some Mac users may find that they need to install gems with administrator privileges. In these cases, simply add sudo in front of the installation command and enter our password when prompted. For example, to install Capybara:
>
> `sudo gem install capybara`

We will need Poltergeist installed.

> Poltergeist is a driver for Capybara that allows it to control the
> PhantomJS browser. We can find out more about Poltergeist at
> `https://github.com/jonleighton/poltergeist`.
>
> We can install Poltergeist on the command line:
>
> **`gem install poltergeist`**

We will need our suite of Capybara functional tests. The example tests are available in the
downloadable code repository as `recipe03.rb` under `chapter05`. If we run the provided
example, we must change to the root directory for the book's sample code.

Lastly, the functional test in this recipe runs against the demo site that is included with the
cookbook's sample code repository. To run that demo site, we must have Node.js installed.
In a separate terminal, change to the `phantomjs-sandbox` directory (in the sample code's
directory), and start the app with the following command:

`node app.js`

How to do it...

Consider the following Ruby script:

```ruby
require 'rubygems'
require 'capybara'
require 'capybara/dsl'
require 'capybara/poltergeist'

Capybara.run_server = false
Capybara.default_driver = :poltergeist
Capybara.app_host = 'http://localhost:3000'

THE_TEXT = 'PhantomJS + Capybara + Poltergeist'

module CookbookCapybaraDemo
  class Demo
    include Capybara::DSL
    def test_input_demo
      visit '/input-demo'
      fill_in 'demo', :with => THE_TEXT
      find('#demo').native.send_key(:Enter)
      find('#stage').text
    end
  end
```

```
end

demo = CookbookCapybaraDemo::Demo.new
text = demo.test_input_demo

puts "=> input '#{THE_TEXT}' and #stage received '#{text}' (same =
    #{text == THE_TEXT})"
```

Given the preceding script, enter the following at the command line:

ruby chapter05/recipe03.rb

This script should print out the following:

```
=> input 'PhantomJS + Capybara + Poltergeist' and #stage received
    'PhantomJS + Capybara + Poltergeist' (same = true)
```

How it works...

Much like Selenium, Capybara does not provide us with a test framework; instead, it provides a **domain-specific language** (**DSL**) that allows us to specify user interactions that it automates in the browser. Put more simply, Capybara is *not* a test framework, but it *is* a mechanism for controlling the browser.

Our preceding example script performs the following actions:

1. It imports the Ruby gems (libraries) that we need, using a series of `require` statements.

2. It configures Capybara, as follows:

    1. It turns off `run_server` because we are using a remote host.

    2. It sets Poltergeist to be our `default_driver`.

    3. It specifies our application's host.

> If we already have an existing functional test suite in place that is configured to use Capybara, then 2.2 is the key step. If we require `capybara/poltergeist`, then setting `:poltergeist` as Capybara's driver should be sufficient for most scripts.

3. As `THE_TEXT`, it specifies a text fixture to use throughout our test.

4. It creates our module (`CookbookCapybaraDemo`) and the `Demo` class inside of that. Our `Demo` class includes the Capybara DSL, and we define a single method (`test_input_demo`).

5. Our `test_input_demo` method performs the following:

    1. It visits the `/input-demo` URL.

    2. It fills in the `#demo` input with `THE_TEXT`.

    3. It sends an *Enter* keypress to `#demo`.

    4. It gets the text from the `#stage` element and returns it.

6. It creates a new instance of our `Demo` class and assigns it to `demo`; then, it executes its `test_input_demo` method and assigns the results to text.

7. Lastly, it writes our message to the console.

Taking screenshots during tests with Poltergeist

This recipe illustrates how to take screenshots from Capybara using Poltergeist, and it points out a couple of things that differ from taking screenshots under PhantomJS.

Getting ready

To run this recipe, we will need the following items installed and available on the system:

▸ Ruby 1.9.3 or greater, and the RubyGems package management framework

▸ Capybara

▸ Poltergeist

▸ A suite of functional tests or browser automation scripts set to run in Capybara

> Details on how to locate and install the preceding software are discussed in the *Adding Poltergeist to a Capybara suite* recipe earlier in this chapter.

The script we will use in this chapter is available in the downloadable code repository as `recipe04.rb` under `chapter05`. If we run the provided example, we must change to the root directory for the book's sample code.

Lastly, the functional test in this recipe runs against the demo site that is included with the cookbook's sample code repository. To run that demo site, we must have Node.js installed. In a separate terminal, change to the `phantomjs-sandbox` directory (in the sample code's directory), and start the app with the following command:

```
node app.js
```

How to do it...

Consider the following Ruby script:

```ruby
require 'rubygems'
require 'capybara'
require 'capybara/dsl'
require 'capybara/poltergeist'

Capybara.run_server = false
Capybara.default_driver = :poltergeist
Capybara.app_host = 'http://localhost:3000'

module CookbookCapybaraDemo
  class Demo
    include Capybara::DSL
    def capture_viewport
      page.driver.resize 1280, 1024
      visit '/css-demo'demo'
      screenshot_name = 'chapter05-recipe04-viewport.png'
      save_screenshot(screenshot_name)
      puts "=> Captured as '#{screenshot_name}'"
    end
  end
end

demo = CookbookCapybaraDemo::Demo.new
demo.capture_viewport
```

Enter the following at the command line:

ruby chapter05/recipe04.rb

The script will render the viewport to disk as `chapter05-recipe04-viewport.png`, and it will print a message to the console.

How it works...

Much of this script follows the pattern described in the previous recipe (*Adding Poltergeist to a Capybara suite*), which we can summarize as follows: the script imports the necessary gems, configures Capybara, creates an instance of our `Demo` class, and executes the method. To get more specific about our `capture_viewport` method, it performs the following actions:

1. It sets the viewport size to 1280 × 1024 pixels (the default is 1024 × 768).
2. It visits the `/css-demo` resource.

3. It instructs Poltergeist to take a screenshot.

4. It prints a message about the screenshot we just took.

There's more...

The first observation that we make is that Poltergeist's screenshots are (by default) bound by the viewport, whereas PhantomJS' are not. (We were first introduced to PhantomJS' `webpage.render` method in the *Simulating scrolling in PhantomJS recipe in Chapter 3, Working with webpage Objects*.) That being said, it is a good idea for us to set the viewport size appropriately before proceeding with the screenshot.

Poltergeist also provides two other (mutually exclusive) options for the call to `save_screenshot`: `:full` and `:selector`.

The `:full` option tells Poltergeist to take a "full content" screenshot, much like PhantomJS' default `webpage.render` behavior. We can use it as follows:

```
save_screenshot(screenshot_name, :full => true)
```

The `:selector` option allows us to pass a CSS selector to the method, which will scope the screenshot to the specified element. This can be useful if we are only interested in grabbing a screenshot of a specific part of the page. We can use it as follows:

```
save_screenshot(screenshot_name, :selector => '#id .class')
```

> Calling `save_screenshot` with `:selector` is the equivalent of using something like the DOM's `querySelector` method; we will get back only the first element that matches the selector.

> Examples of using both `:full` and `:selector` appear in the downloadable code repository in `recipe04.rb` under `chapter05` as `capture_full_page` and `capture_element`, respectively.

See also

▶ The *Simulating scrolling in PhantomJS* recipe in *Chapter 3, Working with webpage Objects*

▶ The *Adding Poltergeist to a Capybara suite* recipe

▶ *Chapter 7, Generating Images and Documents with PhantomJS*

Simulating precise mouse clicks with Poltergeist

This recipe shows how to simulate precise mouse clicks from within a Capybara-backed test using Poltergeist.

Getting ready

To run this recipe, we will need the following items installed and available on the system:

- Ruby 1.9.3 or greater, and the RubyGems package management framework
- Capybara
- Poltergeist
- A suite of functional tests or browser automation scripts set to run in Capybara

> Details on how to locate and install the above software are discussed in the *Adding Poltergeist to a Capybara suite* recipe earlier in this chapter.

The script we will use in this chapter is available in the downloadable code repository as `recipe05.rb` under `chapter05`. If we run the provided example, we must change to the root directory for the book's sample code.

Lastly, the functional test in this recipe runs against the demo site that is included with the cookbook's sample code repository. To run that demo site, we must have Node.js installed. In a separate terminal, change to the `phantomjs-sandbox` directory (in the sample code's directory), and start the app with the following command:

```
node app.js
```

How to do it...

Consider the following Ruby script:

```ruby
require 'rubygems'
require 'capybara'
require 'capybara/dsl'
require 'capybara/poltergeist'

Capybara.run_server = false
Capybara.default_driver = :poltergeist
Capybara.app_host = 'http://localhost:3000'
```

```
module CookbookCapybaraDemo
  class Demo
    include Capybara::DSL
    def precise_click
      page.driver.resize 1280, 1024
      visit '/precision-click'
      page.driver.click 1280 - 21, 1024 - 21
    end
  end
end

demo = CookbookCapybaraDemo::Demo.new
demo.precise_click
```

Given the preceding script, enter the following at the command line:

ruby chapter05/recipe05.rb

The script will print a message to the console that looks something like this:

[precision-click] pointer has click #precision-click... [1259 × 1003]

How it works...

Much of this script follows the same pattern described in an earlier recipe (*Adding Poltergeist to a Capybara suite*), which we can summarize as follows: the script imports the necessary gems, configures Capybara, creates an instance of our Demo class, and executes the method. To get more specific about our `precise_click` method, it performs the following actions:

1. It sets the viewport size to 1280 × 1024 pixels (the default is 1024 × 768).

2. It visits the `/precision-click` resource.

3. It instructs Poltergeist to click on specific coordinates.

> In our example, we calculate the coordinates to click based on the viewport size (see step 1) and the known absolute position of our target element (see `precision-click.ejs` under `phantomjs-sandbox/views` for the CSS defining the element's position).

4. Poltergeist automatically forwards the resulting JavaScript `console.log` statement to STDOUT as a console message.

There's more...

More often than not, we will not need to click on "precise coordinates" as we have done in our example here. In fact, we could have accomplished the same thing with the following:

```
find('#precision-click-demo').click
```

However, for the instances when we do need this ability, it is good to know that it is there.

See also

▶ The *Adding Poltergeist to a Capybara suite* recipe

Installing CasperJS

In this recipe, we introduce CasperJS—a scripting and testing utility that targets PhantomJS—and demonstrate how to install it. We can think of CasperJS as a **domain-specific language** (**DSL**) that simplifies the code that we write to target PhantomJS; in particular, it makes it easier to reason about the asynchronous nature of PhantomJS.

Getting ready

Before we can install CasperJS, we need Python 2.6 or greater installed and on our PATH. Windows users will need the .NET Framework 3.5 or greater (or Mono 2.10.8 or greater) installed.

We will need Node.js and npm installed and on our PATH; we will also need an Internet connection.

> CasperJS requires PhantomJS version 1.8.2 or greater; however, as this book assumes that we are running version 1.9 or greater of PhantomJS, this should be fine.

How to do it...

The easiest way to install CasperJS is to use the Node.js package manager, npm. Enter the following at the command line:

```
npm install -g casperjs
```

We should see the console output from npm as it resolves CasperJS and its dependencies. After the installation is complete, we can type the following at the command line to verify CasperJS' successful installation:

```
casperjs
```

If the installation was successful, CasperJS will print its help message to the console.

> If the console output from npm does not indicate that there were any problems during installation, but typing casperjs does not produce the help message, then it is possible that the CasperJS binary did not get added to the PATH. Double-check where npm installed CasperJS and ensure that its path is added to our system's PATH.

How it works...

Even though CasperJS is not a Node.js package in itself, the binary is distributed through npm as a convenience. Since we already have npm installed and configured, and because npm is used (in part) to install packages, it is well suited to helping us get CasperJS onto our machines. By installing CasperJS with npm, we can allow that utility to manage the download, and to manage situating it on the filesystem. Afterward, the casperjs binary should automatically be on our PATH because we allowed npm to put it there; installing it with the -g (or --global) command-line argument also means that it is now available system-wide.

There's more...

Although our best bet when installing CasperJS is to do so with npm, we also have other options. OS X users can install it using Homebrew; users on all platforms can clone the Git repository and reference the binary included there. More detailed instructions are available in the CasperJS documentation at http://docs.casperjs.org/en/latest/installation.html.

Interacting with web pages using CasperJS

This recipe demonstrates how to open and interact with web pages using CasperJS. It introduces the CasperJS API and discusses where to go for more information.

Getting ready

To run this recipe, the CasperJS binary must be installed and on our PATH; we will also need a script that expects to use the CasperJS API for accessing, inspecting, or manipulating web pages.

The script in this recipe is available in the downloadable code repository as `recipe07.js` under `chapter05`. If we run the provided example script, we must change to the root directory for the book's sample code.

Lastly, the script in this recipe runs against the demo site that is included with the cookbook's sample code repository. To run that demo site, we must have Node.js installed. In a separate terminal, change to the `phantomjs-sandbox` directory (in the sample code's directory), and start the app with the following command:

node app.js

How to do it...

Consider the following script:

```
var casper = require('casper').create();

casper.start('http://localhost:3000/', function() {
  this.clickLabel('/input-demo', 'a');
});

casper.then(function() {
  this.sendKeys('#demo', 'PhantomJS + CasperJS',
      {keepFocus: true});
  this.sendKeys('#demo', casper.page.event.key.Enter,
      {keepFocus: true});

  this.echo('#stage text is:');
  this.echo(this.getHTML('#stage'));
});

casper.run();
```

Given the preceding script, enter the following at the command line:

casperjs chapter05/recipe07.js

The script will print out something like the following:

#stage text is:

PhantomJS + CasperJS

How it works...

Our script performs the following actions:

1. It instantiates an instance of a `Casper` object.

2. It starts our `Casper` instance, providing `http://localhost:3000/` as our destination. It also provides a callback function specifying that CasperJS should click the link with the text `/input-demo`.

[🔍 Note that the `this` object inside of a `Casper` object's callback is bound to that `Casper` object instance.]

3. It specifies a `then` function that indicates to CasperJS that the step should be run *after* the previous one is complete. In that `then` function, the script performs the following steps:

   1. It sends the keyboard input `PhantomJS + CasperJS` to the `#demo` input element using `sendKeys` on the `Casper` instance.

   2. It uses `sendKeys` again, this time to send an *Enter* keystroke to `#demo`.

   3. It gets the inner HTML of the `#stage` element (using `getHTML` on the `Casper` instance) and prints it to the console using `echo`.

4. Lastly, it triggers the specified steps with a call to `casper.run`.

There's more...

In many ways, CasperJS itself is syntactic sugar around the PhantomJS API. Although a trivial example, this recipe's demonstration illustrates the basics of CasperJS, including the following:

- Navigating to web pages
- Selecting and clicking on links
- Sending keyboard input
- Inspecting elements

All of these actions could be performed in a "raw" PhantomJS script, but they are arguably easier with CasperJS. For most tasks we may want to perform in a PhantomJS script, the CasperJS API includes an equivalent convenience function or a proxy method that delegates to the underlying `webpage` object. Furthermore, the CasperJS API abstracts away some of the asynchronous programming necessary in PhantomJS, making the scripts easier to comprehend.

In addition to APIs for working with web pages, CasperJS also provides modules for working with content client-side (`clientutils`), utilities for colorizing console output (`colorizer`), a module to streamline mouse operations (`mouse`), a module for assertions and testing functions (`tester`), and a module for general-purpose helpers and utilities (`utils`).

> For more information about the CasperJS API, refer to the project's robust online documentation at `http://docs.casperjs.org/en/latest/modules/index.html`.

See also

▸ The *Installing CasperJS* recipe

End-to-end testing with CasperJS

This recipe expands on CasperJS by introducing how to work with its testing API. We will demonstrate how to create and run a simple end-to-end test.

Getting ready

To run this recipe, the CasperJS binary must be installed and on our PATH; we will also need a script that expects to use the CasperJS API, particularly the tester module for executing assertions and tests.

The script in this recipe is available in the downloadable code repository as `recipe08.js` under `chapter05`. If we run the provided example script, we must change to the root directory for the book's sample code.

Lastly, the script in this recipe runs against the demo site that is included with the cookbook's sample code repository. To run that demo site, we must have Node.js installed. In a separate terminal, change to the `phantomjs-sandbox` directory (in the sample code's directory), and start the app with the following command:

```
node app.js
```

How to do it...

Consider the following script:

```
casper.test.begin('Chapter 5 : Recipe #8', function(test) {
  var THE_TEXT = 'PhantomJS + CasperJS Testing';

  casper
    .start('http://localhost:3000/', function() {
```

```
        test.assertExists('[href="/input-demo"]');

        this.clickLabel('/input-demo', 'a');
    })
    .then(function() {
      var getDemoValue = (function() {
        return this.evaluate(function() {
          return __utils__.getFieldValue('demo');
        });
      }).bind(this);

      test.assertEquals(getDemoValue(), '',
          '#demo begins with no value set');
      test.assertSelectorHasText('#stage', '',
          '#stage begins with no text');

      this.sendKeys('#demo', THE_TEXT, {keepFocus: true});
      test.assertEquals(getDemoValue(), THE_TEXT,
          'value of #demo equals "' + THE_TEXT + '"');

      this.sendKeys('#demo', casper.page.event.key.Enter,
          {keepFocus: true});
      test.assertSelectorHasText('#stage', THE_TEXT,
          'innerHTML of #stage equals "' + THE_TEXT + '"');
    })
    .run(function() {
      test.done();
    });
});
```

Given the preceding script, enter the following at the command line:

casperjs test chapter05/recipe08.js

The script will print the test results to the console. With colorized output, our console should look something like the following screenshot:

How it works...

Our example test recipe builds on the one from *Interacting with web pages using CasperJS*; it adds only the assertions, and is otherwise different in a couple of small but significant ways. Walking through the script:

1. We tell the CasperJS environment that we are running a test scenario, initializing the test with a call to `casper.test.begin`. Our arguments to `casper.test.begin` include a string describing the scenario and the callback function that encapsulates that scenario (the scenario's callback function has the `test` object passed in as its argument).

    > Note that we do *not* make any calls to `require` in this test script. This is an important difference from our previous recipe. When called with the `test` argument on the command line, CasperJS will manage the `casper` module on its own and assign it to a variable with that name; any attempt on our part to initialize the module will result in this error being printed to the console:
    >
    > **Fatal: you can't override the preconfigured casper instance in a test environment.**

2. We assign our test text to the variable `THE_TEXT`.

3. We set up the first part of our CasperJS test with a call to `casper.start`. As we did in the previous recipe, we start off by pointing CasperJS at `http://localhost:3000/`.

4. In the callback to `casper.start`, we make our first assertion using `test.assertExists` and look for an element that matches the selector `[href="/input-demo"]`. Assuming this assertion passes, we click on our link (with a call to `this.clickLink`) to proceed to the next step in the end-to-end test.

5. Chaining the steps in the test together, we see that our next step is enclosed in a call to `casper.then`.

6. In the callback to `casper.then`, the first thing that we do is create a function (`getDemoValue`) that uses the `casper` instance's `evaluate` function (and the `__utils__` suite injected into the web page context) to extract the value of the `#demo` field.

    > Note that we use a call to `bind` here, passing the `this` object of the `then` callback, so that our call to `evaluate` is called from the proper context.

7. Next, we make two preliminary assertions, one using `test.assertEquals` (to verify that #demo starts with no preset value) and another using `test.assertSelectorHasText` (to verify that #stage contains no text).

8. We input text to #demo using `this.sendKeys` (like we did in our previous recipe); immediately afterward, we assert that #demo contains `THE_TEXT` using `test.assertEquals`.

9. We send an *Enter* keypress to #demo using `this.sendKeys` (again, like we did in our previous recipe); immediately afterward, we assert that #stage contains `THE_TEXT` using `test.assertSelectorHasText`.

10. With the `then` block ended, the next call in the chain is to `casper.run`, which sets the script in motion. Lastly, the callback to `casper.run` makes a call to `test.done` to signal that the test is complete.

Outside of the script itself, there is one other small but significant difference between this recipe and the previous one. Whereas in the *Interacting with web pages using CasperJS* recipe, we called the `casperjs` binary with the script as its only argument, here we call `casperjs` followed by `test` and the path to the script. Adding the `test` argument on the command line is necessary to put CasperJS into test mode. Again, putting all this together, it looks like the following:

```
casperjs test chapter05/recipe08.js
```

There's more...

Although CasperJS is an excellent tool for writing web automation scripts, it really shines as an end-to-end test utility. The fluent API and built-in assertion library are powerful tools that allow us to quickly write comprehensive tests for our web applications.

CasperJS' `tester` module (the `test` instance in our recipe's example script) is both a robust assertion library oriented towards the DOM and end-to-end testing and a framework for managing those end-to-end tests. The module is well documented on the CasperJS website at `http://docs.casperjs.org/en/latest/modules/tester.html`.

See also

▶ The *Installing CasperJS* recipe
▶ The *Interacting with web pages using CasperJS* recipe

Exporting test results from CasperJS in the XUnit format

In this recipe, we demonstrate how to capture the CasperJS test output and persist it to disk in the XUnit format. This is important for tracking test performance over time and integrating CasperJS with continuous integration servers.

Getting ready

To run this recipe, the CasperJS binary must be installed and on our PATH; we will also need a script that expects to use the CasperJS API, particularly the `tester` module for executing assertions and tests. Lastly, we need to make sure that we have write permissions on the directory where CasperJS will write the XUnit report.

We will reuse the script from the previous recipe here. That script is available in the downloadable code repository as `recipe08.js` under `chapter05`. If we run the provided example script, we must change to the root directory for the book's sample code.

Lastly, the script in this recipe runs against the demo site that is included with the cookbook's sample code repository. To run that demo site, we must have Node.js installed. In a separate terminal, change to the `phantomjs-sandbox` directory (in the sample code's directory), and start the app with the following command:

```
node app.js
```

How to do it...

Given our end-to-end test script (`chapter05/recipe08.js`), we can enter the following at the command line:

```
casperjs test chapter05/recipe08.js --xunit=recipe09.xml
```

This will print the test results to the console the same way that it did in our previous recipe. However, it will also write the test results to disk as an XML file in the XUnit format.

How it works...

Our previous recipe (*End-to-end testing with CasperJS*) includes the description of the testing script; we can refer to that description if we need a discussion of its mechanics.

The key difference here is in how the test is invoked on the command line. Once again, we execute the `casperjs` binary with the `test` argument and the path to the script; however, this time we also use the `--xunit` argument and give it the report's desired filename as its value.

Behind the scenes, the `--xunit` argument tells the CasperJS test to call `casper.test.renderResults` after all tests have been completed, converting the suite results into XML and persisting that XML to disk as the test report. These XML reports are important to get CasperJS properly integrated into many continuous integration environments.

> We can learn more about the CasperJS command-line arguments (and how it honors the PhantomJS command-line arguments) on the documentation site at `http://casperjs.readthedocs.org/en/latest/cli.html#casperjs-native-options`.

See also

▸ The *Installing CasperJS* recipe
▸ The *End-to-end testing with CasperJS* recipe

Detecting visual regressions using PhantomCSS

This recipe introduces the PhantomCSS library for CasperJS and illustrates how to test for visual regressions in web pages.

Getting ready

To run this recipe, the CasperJS binary must be installed and on our `PATH`; we will also need a script that expects to use the CasperJS API to navigate to and inspect a web page.

We will need the PhantomCSS library, and we will need to make it available to our CasperJS script.

> PhantomCSS is a module for CasperJS that can automate visual regression testing. It is an open source (MIT licensed) project and is available at the following GitHub repository at `https://github.com/Huddle/PhantomCSS`.

> The PhantomCSS script is available in the downloadable code repository as `lib/phantomcss/phantomcss.js`.

The script in this recipe is available in the downloadable code repository as `recipe10.js` under `chapter05`. If we run the provided example script, we must change to the root directory for the book's sample code.

Lastly, the script in this recipe runs against the demo site that is included with the cookbook's sample code repository. To run that demo site, we must have Node.js installed. In a separate terminal, change to the `phantomjs-sandbox` directory (in the sample code's directory), and start the app with the following command:

```
node app.js
```

How to do it...

Consider the following script:

```
var phantomcss = require('./../lib/phantomcss/phantomcss.js');

phantomcss.init({
  libraryRoot: './lib/phantomcss'
});

casper
  .start('http://localhost:3000/css-demo')
  .viewport(1280, 1024)
  .then(function() {
    phantomcss.screenshot('.jumbotron', 'jumbotron');
    phantomcss.compareAll();
  })
  .run(function(){
    casper.test.done();
    phantom.exit(phantomcss.getExitStatus());
  });
```

Given the preceding script, enter the following at the command line:

```
casperjs test chapter05/recipe10.js
```

CasperJS will print results to the console. The initial message (which appears in the following screenshot) indicates that we have performed our first run and created the baseline images for later comparisons.

To demonstrate the power of PhantomCSS' visual comparisons, we will need to change the appearance of the targeted selector. In `phantom-sandbox/views/css-demo.ejs`, change the h1 tag by deleting the `<%= title %>` directive and adding the text `PhantomCSS FTW`.

> Note that we do not need to restart the Node.js server; the
> markup/text change will be picked up automatically. We may
> also wish to open `http://localhost:3000/css-demo` in
> a browser so that we can see the change for ourselves first.

Rerun PhantomCSS by entering the same command-line input as before. CasperJS should
print a message to the console; this time, the message should indicate that it failed the test
suite because it detected a change in the appearance of the targeted selector. With colorized
output, our console should look something like the following screenshot:

```
○ ○ ○                    phantomjs-cookbook (bash)
$ casperjs test chapter05/recipe10.js
Test file: chapter05/recipe10.js

Must be your first time?
Some screenshots have been generated in the directory ./screenshots
This is your 'baseline', check the images manually. If they're wrong, delete the
  images.
The next time you run these tests, new screenshots will be taken.  These screens
hots will be compared to the original.
If they are different, PhantomCSS will report a failure.
$ casperjs test chapter05/recipe10.js
Test file: chapter05/recipe10.js


FAIL Visual change found for screenshot ./screenshots/jumbotron_0.png (6.97% mis
match)
#     type: fail
#     file: chapter05/recipe10.js
#     subject: false

PhantomCSS found 1 tests, 1 of them failed.

PhantomCSS has created some images that try to show the difference (in the direc
tory ./failures). Fuchsia colored pixels indicate a difference betwen the new an
d old screenshots.
$
```

In addition to this console output, PhantomCSS persists the images to disk so that we can review them and see the visual regressions for ourselves. Most importantly, PhantomCSS generates an "image diff" that highlights the differences between the two test runs, producing something that looks like the following:

The image shows our failure diff and writes the image to disk as jumbotron_0.fail.png

How it works...

In a nutshell, PhantomCSS uses CasperJS (as backed by PhantomJS) to navigate through the designated web pages, rendering the specified selectors, and then comparing the current rendered image against the previous one to look for visual regressions; the tests pass or fail based on whether we have introduced any visual regressions with our changes.

Walking through our script:

1. We import the PhantomCSS library, using `require` to read the module from the filesystem and putting it into context as `phantomcss`.

2. Once imported, we initialize `phantomcss` by calling its `init` function. Here, we also pass a configuration object to `init`, specifying the `libraryRoot` that we need to use.

> Note that the `libraryRoot` path is relative to the directory from which the script is run, and it is not relative to the script's path on the filesystem.
>
> Additionally, there are a total of 11 configurable options that can be passed to PhantomCSS. Although these are not explicitly documented, the `testsuite.js` file under `demo` in the PhantomCSS repository lists them all.

3. We point our CasperJS instance (`casper`) at our target URL (`http://localhost:3000/css-demo`) in our call to `start`; we then set the viewport to 1280 × 1024.

4. In our `then` callback, we call `phantomcss.screenshot`, instructing PhantomCSS to render the specified selector (`.jumbotron`) to the specified filename (`jumbotron`).

5. We call `phantomcss.compareAll` to take all of the images we have generated (only one in our case) and compare them against the previous renderings.

6. Lastly, we kick off the script with our call to `casper.run`. In the callback function, we make sure to call `casper.test.done` (to signal that the tests have completed) and then forward the pass/fail status to PhantomJS with a call to `phantom.exit` (getting the appropriate exit status with a call to `phantomcss.getExitStatus`).

There's more...

PhantomCSS is an excellent tool for creating test automation around our web applications' CSS and overall visual appearance. Although the library itself does not have extensive documentation, the main module (`phantomcss.js`) is relatively small (about 440 lines), and the exported API methods are all conveniently listed at the top of the file. Our preceding example highlights the critical methods.

> For more information about use cases and the motivations behind PhantomCSS, check out the introductory blog post by the library's author, James Cryer, at `http://tldr.huddle.com/blog/css-testing/`.

See also

▸ The *Loading custom modules in PhantomJS* recipe in *Chapter 2, PhantomJS Core Modules*

▸ The *Installing CasperJS* recipe

▸ The *End-to-end testing with CasperJS* recipe

▸ *Chapter 7, Generating Images and Documents with PhantomJS*

6
Network Monitoring and Performance Analysis

In this chapter, we will cover:

- ▶ Generating HAR files from PhantomJS
- ▶ Listing CSS properties
- ▶ Generating an appcache manifest
- ▶ Executing a simple performance analysis
- ▶ Executing a detailed performance analysis
- ▶ Executing a YSlow performance analysis with a custom ruleset
- ▶ Automating performance analysis with YSlow and PhantomJS

Introduction

As a command-line utility, PhantomJS is ideally situated to handle a variety of test automation tasks; as a web browser, PhantomJS' chief performance bottleneck is the same as every other web browser's: network latency. Taken together, and in light of the mechanisms that it exposes for monitoring network activity, this puts PhantomJS in an excellent position to carry out performance analysis tasks.

We were introduced to these mechanisms earlier in this book. In *Chapter 3, Working with webpage Objects*, we worked through two recipes: *Blocking CSS from downloading* and *Causing images to fail randomly*. These recipes introduced the `onResourceRequested`, `onResourceReceived`, and `onResourceError` callbacks, and they provide the foundation for network monitoring and performance analysis in PhantomJS.

In this chapter, we will learn how to use PhantomJS for just such performance analysis tasks. We will explore topics such as how to generate a HAR file for waterfall analysis, and how to use libraries such as `confess.js` and YSlow to get feedback about our page performance.

Generating HAR files from PhantomJS

This recipe illustrates how to generate an **HTTP Archive** (**HAR**) file from the requests made within PhantomJS. We will also introduce tools to visualize and analyze these HAR files.

Getting ready

To run this recipe, we will use the `netsniff.js` script that ships as part of the `examples` directory with the PhantomJS source code. Our example here assumes that `$PHANTOMJS_SOURCE` refers to our clone of the PhantomJS source code. We will also need the URL of a web page to provide to the `netsniff.js` script.

To visualize the resource waterfall, we will need to have a HAR Viewer; this recipe uses the Ruby HAR Library.

> With Ruby and RubyGems installed on our system, we can easily install the Ruby HAR Library as follows:
>
> **gem install har**
>
> Visit the project home page for more information about the HAR Viewer at `http://www.softwareishard.com/blog/har-viewer/`.

> Alternatively, if we don't mind sending our HAR data over the Internet in clear text, we can simply copy and paste our results into the online HAR Viewer at `http://www.softwareishard.com/har/viewer/`.

Lastly, the script in this recipe runs against the demo site that is included with the book's sample code repository. To run that demo site, we must have Node.js installed. In a separate terminal, change to the `phantomjs-sandbox` directory (in the sample code's directory), and start the app with the following command:

```
node app.js
```

How to do it...

With the Node.js demo app running, enter the following on the command line:

```
phantomjs $PHANTOMJS_SOURCE/examples/netsniff.js
  http://localhost:3000/css-demo > css-demo.har
```

This will generate the JSON for the HAR and persist it to disk as `css-demo.har`.

Now, we can open the HAR file by entering the following on the command line:

```
har css-demo.har
```

This will open the HAR Viewer in a new browser window as shown in the following screenshot:

Each item in the **Preview** tab of the HAR Viewer can be expanded to view details about each request and response. We can also toggle to the **HAR** tab to navigate a tree view of the HAR data itself.

How it works...

The preceding example makes use of the `netsniff.js` script that ships with the PhantomJS examples. In a nutshell, the `netsniff.js` script performs the following actions:

1. It takes in a URL as an argument from the command line.

2. It loads that URL as the target of the script's `webpage` object.

3. Using the `onResourceRequested` and `onResourceReceived` callbacks, PhantomJS records information about every request and its associated response. These data are collected in a JavaScript object that adheres to the HAR specification.

   ❑ In the `onResourceRequested` callback, the script sets a key on the `page.resources` object using the `id` of the current request; the object's entry includes the request itself and two properties: `startReply` and `endReply` (initially `null`).

   ❑ In the `onResourceReceived` callback, the script examines the response's `stage` property, assigning the response object to the `startReply` property when `res.stage` equals `start`, and assigning the response object to the `endReply` property when `res.stage` equals `end`.

> PhantomJS assigns numeric IDs to requests and responses, and the related requests and responses will share that ID. As such, we can safely use that `id` property to match them in this fashion.

4. Once the target page has finished loading, PhantomJS logs the HAR object to the console.

When PhantomJS logs the HAR data to the console, it channels the data to `stdout`. As we want to capture the data, our command-line invocation includes redirecting the output to the specified file (`css-demo.har`).

With our data written to disk, we can pass it to the Ruby HAR Library, which loads it into an instance of the HAR Viewer and constructs a waterfall graph, as well as visualizations for several other useful statistics about this page load event.

There's more...

The goal of the **HTTP Archive** (**HAR**) specification is to define a format that HTTP monitoring tools can use to collect, export, and visualize HTTP request/response data. These HAR files can be used to capture specific request instances and play them back later using tools such as the HAR Viewer to construct waterfall graphs, or to perform other analyses on them. For more information about the HAR 1.2 specification, see `http://www.softwareishard.com/blog/har-12-spec/`.

Listing CSS properties

This recipe introduces the confess.js library and demonstrates how to use it to identify which CSS properties are being used on a page.

Getting ready

To run this recipe, we will need a target URL for a website that uses CSS.

We will use the `confess.js` script to analyze the site and produce a report of the CSS properties used on the page.

> The confess.js library is an open source project by James Pearce that provides several performance-related tasks to run under PhantomJS. At this time, confess.js does not currently have a copyright license listed in the repository; however, it can be obtained on GitHub at `https://github.com/jamesgpearce/confess`.
>
> After downloading the `confess` repository, we want to place it in the `lib` directory of our downloadable sample code repository. Note that if we download the `.zip` archive of the repository, we may need to rename the folder from `confess-master` to `confess`.

Lastly, the script in this recipe runs against the demo site that is included with the book's sample code repository. To run that demo site, we must have Node.js installed. In a separate terminal, change to the `phantomjs-sandbox` directory (in the sample code's directory), and start the app with the following command:

```
node app.js
```

How to do it...

With the Node.js demo app running, make sure we are in the root directory for the book's sample code, and enter the following on the command line:

```
phantomjs lib/confess/confess.js http://localhost:3000/css-demo
    cssproperties lib/confess/config.json
```

Output similar to the following will be printed by confess.js:

```
Config:
  task: cssproperties
  userAgent: Mozilla/5.0 (X11; Linux x86_64) AppleWebKit/535.11
     (KHTML, like Gecko) Chrome/17.0.963.12 Safari/535.11
```

```
wait: 0
consolePrefix: #
verbose: true
url: http://localhost:3000/css-demo
configFile: lib/confess/config.json

CSS properties used:
-webkit-animation-delay
-webkit-animation-direction
-webkit-animation-duration
-webkit-animation-fill-mode
-webkit-animation-iteration-count
# and 102 more...
```

How it works...

The `cssproperties` task in confess.js tallies all of the CSS properties that are used in the document and writes that list to the console. Internally, the `cssproperties` task makes a call to the `getCssProperties` method (on the `confess` object) in the `onLoadFinished` callback for the `webpage` instance. The `getCssProperties` method takes a single argument, the `webpage` instance, and performs an `evaluate` on it, first accumulating the properties cited in `document.styleSheets`; then it iterates over every element in the document and determines what styles are applied in the DOM. The method returns an object with the CSS properties as the keys and their tallies as the values; the `onLoadFinished` callback, however, flattens this list and simply prints each one to the console.

On the command line, we invoke confess.js as we would any other PhantomJS script—with the script name as the first argument after the `phantomjs` binary, and its arguments following that. The following arguments are expected by confess.js:

- The target URL
- The task name
- (Optionally) the path to the configuration file

> If we leave off the configuration file, then it will look for a `config.json` file in the working directory.

There's more...

On the surface, the `cssproperties` task may seem more of a curiosity than anything else, but the inventory of CSS properties can be revealing, especially on large projects. With respect to performance concerns, this inventory can provide a place to start when trying to profile web applications with sluggish or unresponsive user interfaces. Some CSS properties (or combinations of properties) are widely believed to cause front-end performance issues, such as declining frame rates. The inventory of CSS properties can reveal whether these properties are present, and as such, they can give us a place to start our profiling.

See also

- ▸ The *Recording debugger messages* recipe in *Chapter 3, Working with webpage Objects*
- ▸ The *Generating an appcache manifest* recipe
- ▸ The *Executing a simple performance analysis* recipe

Generating an appcache manifest

This recipe expands on our usage of confess.js and shows how to use it to generate an **application cache** (**appcache**) manifest for our web applications.

Getting ready

To run this recipe, we will need a target URL. We will use confess.js to analyze the site and produce an appcache manifest.

> Details about how to obtain confess.js are included in the *Listing CSS properties* recipe earlier in this chapter.

Lastly, the script in this recipe runs against the demo site that is included with the book's sample code repository. To run that demo site, we must have Node.js installed. In a separate terminal, change to the `phantomjs-sandbox` directory (in the sample code's directory), and start the app with the following command:

```
node app.js
```

How to do it...

With the Node.js demo app running, make sure we are in the root directory for the book's sample code, and enter the following on the command line:

```
phantomjs lib/confess/confess.js http://localhost:3000/appcache-demo
  appcache lib/confess/config.json >
  phantomjs-sandbox/static/demo.appcache
```

> Note that we are using redirection here to write the script's output to the disk.

If we open the target URL (for example, in a regular browser), we will notice in the Node.js console that the GET request to demo.appcache results in a 200 success and a delivered file with that name. We will also notice that subsequent refreshes in the browser only request demo.appcache (which results in a 304 redirect) and that we can even kill the Node.js process entirely and the web page will continue to function.

How it works...

The appcache task in confess.js inspects the target web page and generates the manifest based on the resources that it detects; then it writes that manifest to the console. Internally, the appcache task hooks into the onResourceRequested and onLoadFinished callbacks to generate the list of external resources to cache. If the confess.js configuration has urlsFromRequests set to true, then it gathers the URLs of every requested resource based on those requests. If the confess.js configuration has urlsFromDocument set to true, then it gathers the URLs of each resource that it identifies in its call to getResourceUrls, which inspects the web page itself. In both cases, the resource URLs are accumulated as keys on an object (confess.appcache.resourceUrls), so we can be confident that we are only getting one reference to each. Once the set of resource URLs has been generated, confess.js prints the URLs to the console.

On the command line, we invoke confess.js as we would any other PhantomJS script—with the script name as the first argument after the phantomjs binary, and its arguments following that. The following arguments are expected by confess.js:

▶ The target URL

▶ The task name

▶ (Optionally) the path to the configuration file

> If we leave off the configuration file, then it will look for a config.json in the working directory.

As we have noted previously, since confess.js is printing the output to the console, and is thus printing it to `stdout`, we need to capture it. Although it may be fine to copy and paste from the terminal, a better option (and the one illustrated in our example) is to use text redirection and forward the output to an appropriate file. In our example, we redirect the text to the `demo.appcache` file in our `phantomjs-sandbox` application's static assets directory.

There's more...

The application cache (appcache) manifest is an HTML5 specification that allows developers to enumerate resources (as a list of URLs) that compatible browsers will download and cache to enable offline access to the master or parent resource (the web page). An appcache manifest is simply a text file (served with a `Content-Type` of `text/cache-manifest`) that contains that list of URLs.

> Even though the application cache specification is relatively small, it is too large a subject to discuss in detail here, and we are simplifying some things for the sake of brevity. The Web has many excellent in-depth discussions of the appcache; a good place to start is *A Beginner's Guide to Using the Application Cache* by Eric Bidelman at `http://www.html5rocks.com/en/tutorials/appcache/beginner/`.

If we decide that our application needs offline support, and that an appcache is the right solution, then the confess.js `appcache` task is something that we should consider working into our build process. The script takes the tedium out of what is otherwise a laborious and manual task.

> It is worth noting that application cache manifests have some specific rules about how they can be formatted. Although confess.js is less likely to foul up the formatting than if we were to do it by hand, it is still worth running the output through a validator; try this one from `http://manifest-validator.com/`.
>
> As the saying goes: Trust, but verify.

Configuration options

Although we have alluded to the confess.js configuration file several times before now, it is worth describing it in a bit more detail here. The confess.js configuration file is a JSON document that PhantomJS reads at runtime when executing a given confess.js task. We can supply the path to the configuration file on the command line as the last argument to the script; by default, confess.js will look for a `config.json` file in the working directory.

Although the configurable options are well defined in the `README.md` for the confess.js repo, we should pay special attention to the following options:

- `appcache.urlsFromDocument`: This is a Boolean (defaults to `true`) that indicates whether confess.js should inspect the DOM and CSSOM for resources to add to the appcache

- `appcache.urlsFromRequests`: This is a Boolean (defaults to `false`) that indicates whether confess.js should monitor requests for resources to add to the appcache

- `appcache.cacheFilter`: This is a regular expression that tells confess.js which resources to *include* in the appcache

- `appcache.networkFilter`: This is a regular expression that tells confess.js which resource to *exclude* from the appcache

See also

- The *Recording debugger messages* recipe in *Chapter 3, Working with webpage Objects*

- The *Listing CSS properties* recipe

- The *Executing a simple performance analysis* recipe

Executing a simple performance analysis

In this recipe, we will demonstrate how to execute a simple performance analysis using confess.js.

Getting ready

To run this recipe, we will need a target URL.

We will use confess.js to analyze that target URL and produce a lightweight performance report.

> Details about how to obtain confess.js are included in the *Listing CSS properties* recipe, earlier in this chapter.

Lastly, the script in this recipe runs against the demo site that is included with the book's sample code repository. To run that demo site, we must have Node.js installed. In a separate terminal, change to the `phantomjs-sandbox` directory (in the sample code's directory), and start the app with the following command:

```
node app.js
```

How to do it...

With the Node.js demo app running, make sure we are in the root directory for the book's sample code, and enter the following on the command line:

```
phantomjs lib/confess/confess.js http://localhost:3000/css-demo
  performance lib/confess/config.json
```

Something similar to the following screenshot will be printed by confess.js to the console:

```
○ ○ ○                                    robf (bash)
Config:
 task: performance
 userAgent: Mozilla/5.0 (X11; Linux x86_64) AppleWebKit/535.11 (KHTML, like Gecko) Chrome/17.0.963.12 Safari/5
 35.11
 wait: 0
 consolePrefix: #
 verbose: true
 url: http://localhost:3000/css-demo
 configFile: lib/confess/config.json

Elapsed load time:     39ms
   # of resources:      7

 Fastest resource:     2ms; http://localhost:3000/components/bootstrap/dist/css/bootstrap.min.css
 Slowest resource:    12ms; http://localhost:3000/css-demo
  Total resources:    57ms

Smallest resource:    4051b; http://localhost:3000/css-demo
 Largest resource:   99548b; http://localhost:3000/components/bootstrap/dist/css/bootstrap.min.css
  Total resources:  431279b

 1|--------------------------======
 2|                            ------
 3|                                      ------=================
 4|                                      ----------------============
 5|                                      --------------------========
 6|                                      ---------------------======
 7|                                      --------------------========

 1:    12ms;    4051b; http://localhost:3000/css-demo
 2:     2ms;   99548b; http://localhost:3000/components/bootstrap/dist/css/bootstrap.min.css
 3:     9ms;   65536b; http://localhost:3000/images/152824439_ffcc1b2aa4_b.jpg
 4:     9ms;   65536b; http://localhost:3000/images/357292530_f225d7e306_b.jpg
 5:     9ms;   65536b; http://localhost:3000/images/391560246_f2ac936f6d_b.jpg
 6:     7ms;   65536b; http://localhost:3000/images/583519989_1116956980_b.jpg
 7:     9ms;   65536b; http://localhost:3000/images/872027465_2519a358b9_b.jpg
$
```

An example of the confess.js performance task output, including the ASCII waterfall chart

How it works...

The `performance` task in confess.js monitors the resources requested and received by the target web page, captures timing and size information about each one, and writes that information to the console. Internally, the `performance` task hooks into the `onLoadStarted`, `onResourceRequested`, `onResourceReceived`, and `onLoadFinished` callbacks to capture the complete request/response lifecycle. In `onLoadStarted`, it initiates the overall timings, recording the start time of the leading web page request. In `onResourceRequested`, it captures the starting information about each requested resource. In `onResourceReceived`, it matches a given response to the initiating request and records the ending time and size of that resource. In `onLoadFinished`, the script loops through the collected resources and prints the timing and size information for each one; optionally (if `verbose` is `true` in the configuration file) confess.js will also print an ASCII version of the waterfall graph.

On the command line, we invoke confess.js as we would any other PhantomJS script—with the script name as the first argument after the `phantomjs` binary, and its arguments following that. The following arguments are expected by confess.js:

- The target URL
- The task name
- (Optionally) the path to the configuration file

> If we leave off the configuration file, then it will look for a `config.json` file in the working directory.

There's more...

The confess.js `performance` task provides us with a lightweight, command-line equivalent to the Network panel that we find in the Chrome DevTools or the Net panel in Firebug. As in those tools, the ASCII waterfall chart can give us an at-a-glance view of what our page's load time looks like and where our bottlenecks might be. It gives us a leading summary about the overall start-to-finish load time, how many resources we loaded, which resources were fastest and slowest, and which resources were the smallest and largest. It also produces an inventory of all the requested resources that we can trivially parse with a script. (Assuming, of course, that we did not desire the level of detail that we would get from the HAR produced by `netsniff.js`.) Despite the fact that it provides only a high level of detail, the confess.js `performance` task can serve as an early warning sign that we have performance concerns which we need to investigate.

Configuration options

Although the ASCII waterfall is one of the most interesting bits of output from the confess.js `performance` task, it is also optional. If we set `verbose` to `false` in our configuration file, it will be omitted from the console output.

See also

- ▸ The *Recording debugger messages* recipe in *Chapter 3, Working with webpage Objects*
- ▸ The *Generating HAR files from PhantomJS* recipe
- ▸ The *Listing CSS properties* recipe
- ▸ The *Generating an appcache manifest* recipe
- ▸ The *Executing a detailed performance analysis* recipe

Executing a detailed performance analysis

This recipe introduces the YSlow library for PhantomJS and illustrates how to perform a detailed performance analysis of a web page.

Getting ready

To run this recipe, we will need a target URL.

We will use the PhantomJS port of the YSlow library to execute the performance analysis on our target web page.

> YSlow is a library that analyzes web pages and produces a report on that page's performance, grading it against benchmarks and rules established by Yahoo! web performance experts. We can find out more about YSlow for PhantomJS on the project site at `http://yslow.org/phantomjs/`.
>
> The examples that follow assume version 3.1.8 of the YSlow library, which is included with the sample code repository.
>
> YSlow is open source and distributed under the New BSD License.

Lastly, the script in this recipe runs against the demo site that is included with the book's sample code repository. To run that demo site, we must have Node.js installed. In a separate terminal, change to the `phantomjs-sandbox` directory (in the sample code's directory), and start the app with the following command:

```
node app.js
```

How to do it...

With the Node.js demo app running, make sure we are in the root directory for the book's sample code, and enter the following on the command line:

```
phantomjs lib/yslow.js -i grade -f tap http://localhost:3000/css-demo
```

YSlow will then print something like the following commands to the console:

```
TAP version 13
1..24
ok 1 B (89) overall score
ok 2 A (100) ynumreq: Make fewer HTTP requests
not ok 3 F (40) ycdn: Use a Content Delivery Network (CDN)
  ---
  message: There are 6 static components that are not on CDN. <p>You
  can specify CDN hostnames in your preferences. See
  <a href="https://github.com/marcelduran/yslow/wiki/FAQ#wiki-faq_
cdn">YSlow FAQ</a> for details.</p>
  offenders:
    - "localhost: 6 components, 2753.1K"
  ...
ok 4 A (100) yemptysrc: Avoid empty src or href
not ok 5 F (23) yexpires: Add Expires headers
  ---
  message: There are 7 static components without a far-future
    expiration date.
  offenders:
    - "http://localhost:3000/components/bootstrap/dist/css/bootstrap.min.
css"
    - "http://localhost:3000/images/152824439_ffcc1b2aa4_b.jpg"
    - "http://localhost:3000/images/357292530_f225d7e306_b.jpg"
    - "http://localhost:3000/images/391560246_f2ac936f6d_b.jpg"
    - "http://localhost:3000/images/583519989_1116956980_b.jpg"
    - "http://localhost:3000/images/872027465_2519a358b9_b.jpg"
    - "http://localhost:3000/favicon.ico"
  ...
not ok 6 C (78) ycompress: Compress components with gzip
  ---
  message: There are 2 plain text components that should be sent
    compressed
  offenders:
```

```
    - "http://localhost:3000/css-demo"
    - "http://localhost:3000/components/bootstrap/dist/css/bootstrap.min.
css"
    ...
ok 7 A (100) ycssstop: Put CSS at top
ok 8 A (100) yjsbottom: Put JavaScript at bottom
ok 9 A (100) yexpressions: Avoid CSS expressions
ok 10 N/A (-1) yexternal: Make JavaScript and CSS external # SKIP
    score N/A
    ---
    message: Only consider this if your property is a common user home
       page.
    ...
ok 11 A (100) ydns: Reduce DNS lookups
    ---
    offenders:
       - "localhost: 8 components, 2759.5K"
    ...
ok 12 A (100) yminify: Minify JavaScript and CSS
ok 13 A (100) yredirects: Avoid URL redirects
ok 14 A (100) ydupes: Remove duplicate JavaScript and CSS
ok 15 A (100) yetags: Configure entity tags (ETags)
ok 16 A (100) yxhr: Make AJAX cacheable
ok 17 A (100) yxhrmethod: Use GET for AJAX requests
ok 18 A (100) ymindom: Reduce the number of DOM elements
ok 19 A (100) yno404: Avoid HTTP 404 (Not Found) error
ok 20 A (100) ymincookie: Reduce cookie size
ok 21 A (100) ycookiefree: Use cookie-free domains
ok 22 A (100) ynofilter: Avoid AlphaImageLoader filter
ok 23 A (100) yimgnoscale: Do not scale images in HTML
ok 24 A (100) yfavicon: Make favicon small and cacheable
```

How it works...

As mentioned before, performance-focused engineers at Yahoo! created YSlow as a tool to assess web page performance using a set of established best practices. Since its inception, YSlow has been ported to many different flavors; today it exists as an extension for Chrome, Firefox, Opera, and Safari, as a bookmarklet, as a Node.js application, as a command-line tool, and as a PhantomJS script. The YSlow script works by loading the target URL and analyzing it (including all its resources) and assessing each one against a specified ruleset that defines what is acceptable, and what is not.

In the simplest case, we can invoke YSlow on the command line without any additional arguments—just the `phantomjs` binary, the path to the YSlow script itself, and the target URL. However, in this form, YSlow produces JSON, which is not terribly easy to read on the console. In our example, we executed YSlow using the `-i` (information) and `-f` (format) arguments. We asked for the `grade` information and `tap` formats respectively; these options make the output significantly easier to read while still being something a machine can manageably parse.

Regardless of the output format selected, YSlow will give us a detailed evaluation of the target URL compared to the ruleset provided. YSlow will summarize its findings with an overall score (for example, `B (89)`), but also lists grades and scores for each of the rules in the ruleset. This detailed analysis allows us to home in on our web application's problem areas. Given our preceding example, we can see that we perform well across several dimensions (for example, our content has no empty `src` or `href` attributes, none of our resources are giving a 404 error, and that we have minified our JavaScript and CSS assets), but that there are others where we have not done well (for example, we are not using any CDNs, we have not added `Expires` headers, and we are not using gzip compression on our plain text assets). Armed with this report, we can formulate an informed plan for improving our web application's performance.

More importantly, now we have baseline metrics with which to do before-and-after tests!

There's more...

YSlow gives us many more options than just the ones we have explored in the preceding example. Let's explore some of YSlow's command-line options:

Information

Specified with the `-i` or `--info` flag, followed by the level value, the information argument controls YSlow's verbosity. The output levels include the following:

- `basic`: This is the simplest level, `basic` displays only the summary information (overall score)
- `stats`: This displays the summary information, as well as high-level statistics broken down by resource type
- `grade`: This displays the grade and score for each rule in the ruleset, along with any messages or offending resources
- `comps`: This displays a report about the page's components or resources, similar to what we would find in a HAR; however, it does not provide any summary statistics
- `all`: (The default level) this displays a report that combines the `grade`, `stats`, and `comps` reports into one

Format

Specified with the -f or --format flag, followed by the format value, the format argument instructs YSlow how to format the script's output. The supported formats include the following:

- json: (The default format) this gets the output of the YSlow results in JSON
- xml: This gets the output in a simple XML format

> The element names in the YSlow xml format, and property names in the YSlow json format align with the parameter names of the YSlow beacon.

> For more definitions and more information, see http://yslow.org/user-guide/#yslow_beacon.

- plain: This gets the output in a simple, plain text format
- tap: This gets the output using **TAP (Test Anything Protocol)**
- junit: This gives us the results using the xUnit style of XML for continuous integration servers

Ruleset

Specified with the -r or --ruleset flag, followed by the ruleset value, this argument configures YSlow to use a particular ruleset for its performance analysis. A ruleset is a collection of performance rules that YSlow uses to grade a given website. The available rulesets include the following:

- ydefault: (This is the default ruleset) it includes the 23 rules that Yahoo!'s Exceptional Performance team has identified as making 25-50 percent web page response-time improvements
- yslow1: This is also known as *YSlow Classic*; this includes the original 13 of the now 23 "Exceptional Performance" rules
- yblog: This is a set of 14 performance rules that are targeted at small websites such as blogs

> For more information about the rulesets, see http://yslow.org/user-guide/.

> In the *Executing a YSlow performance analysis with a custom ruleset* recipe (later in this chapter), we will also discuss how to create our own custom rulesets.

User agent

Specified with the `-u` or `--ua` flag, followed by the quoted value, the user agent argument allows us to specify or override the user agent that PhantomJS uses when representing itself to the server. This is particularly useful when we know that the server is doing some user agent string checking and serving particular content as a result. For example, if we wanted PhantomJS to represent itself as an iPad, we might use the following command:

```
phantoms lib/yslow.js --ua "Mozilla/5.0 (iPad; CPU OS 6_0 like Mac OS
  X) AppleWebKit/536.26 (KHTML, like Gecko) Version/6.0 Mobile/10A5355d
  Safari/8536.25" http://localhost:3000/
```

Viewport

Specified with the `-vp` or `--viewport` flag, followed by `x` delimited dimensions, the viewport argument allows us to specify the viewport size that PhantomJS will use for rendering the web page. This can be useful when performance testing responsive designs that target multiple viewports through fluid grids or media queries. For example, if we wanted to run YSlow against a "mobile" viewport, we might use the following command:

```
phantomjs lib/yslow.js --viewport 320x356 http://localhost:3000/
```

Headers

Specified with the `-ch` or `--headers` flag, the headers argument allows us to specify a JSON string that contains the custom headers we want to apply to our requests. For example, if we wanted to pass along a cookie, we might use the following command:

```
phantomjs lib/yslow.js --headers '{"Cookie":"favorite=oatmeal-raisin"}'
  http://localhost:3000/
```

CDNs

Specified with the `--cdns` flag, the CDNs argument allows us to provide a list of domains, where we know those domains to be content delivery networks and edge caches. For example, if we have a site that uses photos from Flickr and JavaScript assets from CDNJS, then we might use the following command:

```
phantomjs lib/yslow.js --cdns "staticflickr.com,cdnjs.cloudflare.com"
  http://localhost:3000/cdn-demo
```

See also

- ▸ The *Generating HAR files from PhantomJS* recipe
- ▸ The *Executing a YSlow performance analysis with a custom ruleset* recipe
- ▸ The *Automating performance analysis with YSlow and PhantomJS* recipe

Executing a YSlow performance analysis with a custom ruleset

In this recipe, we will create a custom-defined ruleset for YSlow and execute a performance analysis with it.

Getting ready

To run this recipe, we will need a target URL.

We will use the PhantomJS port of the YSlow library to execute the performance analysis on our target web page. However, as we are creating a custom ruleset, we must build the library from source. To obtain the YSlow library source code, we change directories into the sample code repository and initialize the submodule as shown in the following command:

```
git submodule init && git submodule update
```

> Alternatively, we can click the download link on the project's GitHub page `https://github.com/marcelduran/yslow`.
>
> If we download the `.zip` from the GitHub project page, we may need to rename the folder from `yslow-master` to `yslow` before we move it into the `lib` directory.

We will need a custom ruleset for the YSlow library. An example of such a custom ruleset is included in the sample code repository as `recipe06.js` in the `chapter06` directory.

To compile the YSlow library into a single package that includes our custom ruleset, we will need the `make` binary.

> **Make** is a mature, general-purpose command-line build tool used to compile source files and perform other tasks. A project such as the YSlow library may contain a **Makefile** that defines the tasks that Make can execute for that project.
>
> Many systems include the `make` binary by default; however, if we need to install it or wish to find out more about it, we can do so at the project website `https://www.gnu.org/software/make/`.

Lastly, the script in this recipe runs against the demo site that is included with the book's sample code repository. To run that demo site, we must have Node.js installed. In a separate terminal, change to the `phantomjs-sandbox` directory (in the sample code's directory), and start the app with the following command:

```
node app.js
```

How to do it...

Consider the following custom ruleset:

```
YSLOW.registerRuleset({
  id: 'cookbook',
  name: 'PhantomJS Cookbook Example Ruleset',
  rules: {
    ynumreq: {},
    yexpires: {},
    ycompress: {},
    ycsstop: {},
    yjsbottom: {},
    ydupes: {},
    ymindom: {},
    yno404: {},
    yemptysrc: {}
  },
  weights: {
    ynumreq: 8,
    yexpires: 2,
    ycompress: 4,
    ycsstop: 2,
    yjsbottom: 2,
    ydupes: 4,
    ymindom: 2,
    yno404: 2,
    yemptysrc: 4
  }
});
```

From the root of the sample code repository, we should copy the custom ruleset into place:

```
cp chapter06/recipe06.js lib/yslow/src/common/rulesets/cookbook.js
```

With our ruleset copied to the proper place, we need to add it into a custom build of the YSlow library. From the root of the YSlow repository (`lib/yslow`), we enter the following on the command line:

```
make phantomjs
```

After the build has completed, we should change to the root directory of the book's sample code repository. From there, we can run our performance analysis with our custom ruleset from the command line as follows:

```
phantomjs lib/yslow/build/phantomjs/yslow.js -f plain -i basic
  -r cookbook http://localhost:3000/css-demo
```

YSlow will then print something like the following to the console:

```
version: 3.1.8
size: 2758.9K (2758978 bytes)
overall score: A (91)
url: http://localhost:3000/css-demo
# of requests: 8
ruleset: cookbook
page load time: 82
```

How it works...

Our example of a custom ruleset is admittedly a bit liberal, but it is sufficient for demonstrating how to create one and incorporate it into our build of YSlow.

The first thing that we need to do when creating our custom ruleset is to decide what rules to include. The rules themselves are defined in the YSlow source; we can find 23 standard rules defined in `src/common/rules.js`. Each rule is defined with a call to `YSLOW.registerRule` and includes the following:

- The `id` that we will use in our ruleset to specify that rule
- A `url` that provides background information on that rule
- A `category` array that contains the general category to which the rule belongs
- A `config` object to help define aspects of the rule and how we might evaluate scripts in light of that rule
- A `lint` function that consumes the `config` object and performs the actual evaluation of the script for that rule

> For a detailed discussion of each rule identified by Yahoo!'s Exceptional Performance team, see `http://developer.yahoo.com/performance/rules.html`.
>
> There are 35 rules discussed on that web page, including the 23 "testable" rules that comprise YSlow's default ruleset.

> The three default rulesets (`ydefault`, `yslow1`, and `yblog`) are also defined in `src/common/rules.js`.

Once we have decided which rules to include in our ruleset, we can add our definition to the file (for example, `cookbook.js` in our case). A ruleset is defined with a call to `YSLOW.registerRuleset`; the single argument expected by `registerRuleset` is a configuration object defining our ruleset. The properties of this configuration object include the following:

- `id`: This is the string we will use to specify our ruleset on the command line
- `name`: This is a short, descriptive name that we can use as documentation for the ruleset
- `rules`: This is an object that uses the individual rule IDs as its keys and overrides for that rule's configuration object as the value
- `weights`: This is an object that defines the weights to assign to each rule when determining the overall grade and score for performance analysis

Once we have defined our ruleset, we need to create a custom build of the YSlow library that incorporates that ruleset. Fortunately, the YSlow source code includes a `Makefile` that already contains the instructions necessary to compile the library from the `src` directory. We simply invoke `make` on the command line and specify the `phantomjs` target; Make will print out a notice when the build is complete. By default, Make will place the compiled library in `build/phantomjs`.

Once compiled, we can use our custom build of the library the same as we would the standard one. To use our custom ruleset, we simply specify it by name using the `-r` flag.

There's more...

For most cases, using one of the three standard rulesets will be sufficient. In particular, the `ydefault` ruleset is already a nearly comprehensive analysis and can give us an accurate picture of our front-end performance and where we can improve. However, what if there are aspects of `ydefault` that do not apply to our situation? What if using the `GET` method for our XHR is not feasible? What if we have made a deliberate choice to inline our JavaScript and CSS assets? What if we have written a new performance rule that we want to *add* to what would otherwise be `ydefault`? This is where custom rulesets become important—in helping us to execute the most appropriate analyses for our applications based on our knowledge of *our* needs and constraints.

See also

- The *Generating HAR files from PhantomJS* recipe
- The *Executing a detailed performance analysis* recipe
- The *Automating performance analysis with YSlow and PhantomJS* recipe

Automating performance analysis with YSlow and PhantomJS

This recipe demonstrates how to set up an automated performance analysis task on a continuous integration server (for example, Jenkins CI) using PhantomJS and the YSlow library.

Getting ready

To run this recipe, the `phantomjs` binary will need to be accessible to the continuous integration server, which may not necessarily share the same permissions or `PATH` as our user. We will also need a target URL.

We will use the PhantomJS port of the YSlow library to execute the performance analysis on our target web page. The YSlow library must be installed somewhere on the filesystem that is accessible to the continuous integration server. For our example, we have placed the `yslow.js` script in the `tmp` directory of the `jenkins` user's home directory.

> To find the `jenkins` user's home directory on a POSIX-compatible system, first switch to that user using the following command:
> ```
> sudo su - jenkins
> ```
> Then print the home directory to the console using the following command:
> ```
> echo $HOME
> ```

> See the *Executing a detailed performance analysis* recipe, earlier in this chapter, for how to obtain the YSlow library.

We will need to have a continuous integration server set up where we can configure the jobs that will execute our automated performance analyses. The example that follows will use the open source Jenkins CI server.

> Jenkins CI is too large a subject to introduce here, but this recipe does not assume any working knowledge of it. For information about Jenkins CI, including basic installation or usage instructions, or to obtain a copy for your platform, visit the project website at `http://jenkins-ci.org/`.
> Our recipe uses version 1.552.

> The combination of PhantomJS and YSlow is in no way unique to Jenkins CI. The example aims to provide a clear illustration of automated performance testing that can easily be adapted to any number of continuous integration server environments.

The recipe also uses several plugins on Jenkins CI to help facilitate our automated testing. These plugins include:

- Environment Injector Plugin
- JUnit Attachments Plugin
- TAP Plugin
- xUnit Plugin

Lastly, the script in this recipe runs against the demo site that is included with the book's sample code repository. To run that demo site, we must have Node.js installed. In a separate terminal, change to the `phantomjs-sandbox` directory (in the sample code's directory), and start the app with the following command:

```
node app.js
```

How to do it...

To execute our automated performance analyses in Jenkins CI, the first thing that we need to do is set up the job as follows:

1. Select the **New Item** link in Jenkins CI. Give the new job a name (for example, `YSlow Performance Analysis`), select **Build a free-style software project**, and then click on **OK**.

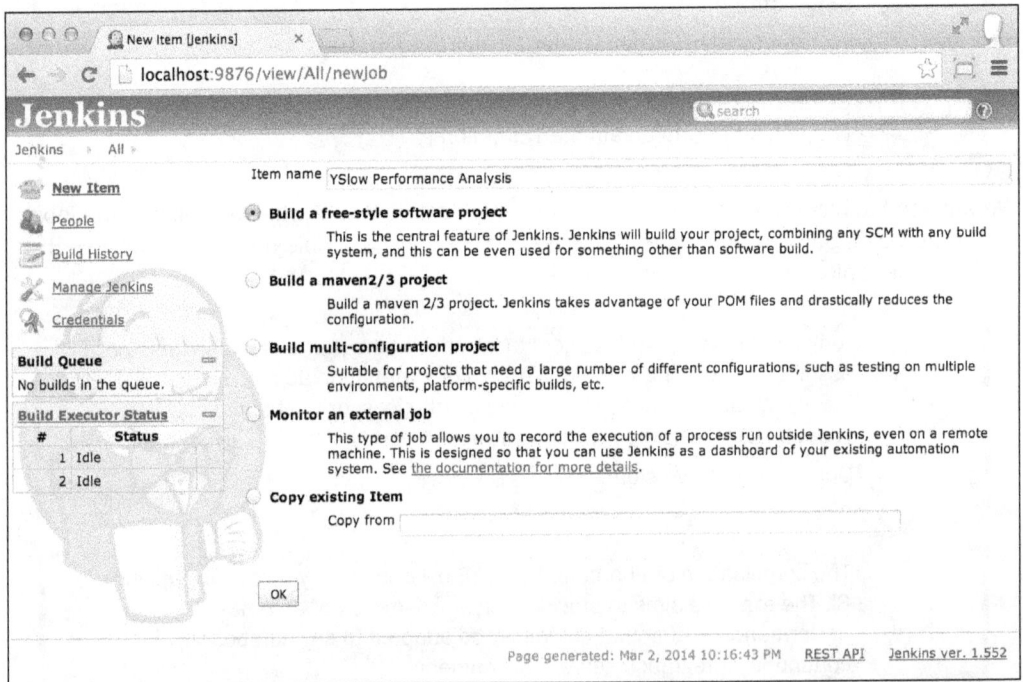

2. To ensure that the performance analyses are automated, we enter a **Build Trigger** for the job. Check off the appropriate **Build Trigger** and enter details about it. For example, to run the tests every two hours, during business hours, Monday through Friday, check **Build periodically** and enter the **Schedule** as H 9-16/2 * * 1-5.

3. In the **Build** block, click **on Add build step** and then click on **Execute shell**. In the **Command** text area of the Execute Shell block, enter the shell commands that we would normally type at the command line, for example:

```
phantomjs ${HOME}/tmp/yslow.js -i grade -threshold "B" -f
    junit http://localhost:3000/css-demo > yslow.xml
```

4. In the **Post-build Actions** block, click on **Add post-build action** and then click on **Publish JUnit test result report**. In the **Test report XMLs** field of the Publish JUnit Test Result Report block, enter `*.xml`.

5. Lastly, click on **Save** to persist the changes to this job.

Our performance analysis job should now run automatically according to the specified schedule; however, we can always trigger it manually by navigating to the job in Jenkins CI and clicking on **Build Now**. After a few of the performance analyses have completed, we can navigate to those jobs in Jenkins CI and see the results shown in the following screenshots:

The landing page for a performance analysis project in Jenkins CI

Note the Test Result Trend graph with the successes and failures.

The Test Result report page for a specific build

Note that the failed tests in the overall analysis are called out and that we can expand specific items to view their details.

The All Tests view of the Test Result report page for a specific build

Note that all tests in the performance analysis are listed here, regardless of whether they passed or failed, and that we can click into a specific test to view its details.

How it works...

The driving principle behind this recipe is that we want our continuous integration server to periodically and automatically execute the YSlow analyses for us so that we can monitor our website's performance over time. This way, we can see whether our changes are having an effect on overall site performance, receive alerts when performance declines, or even fail builds if we fall below our performance threshold.

The first thing that we do in this recipe is set up the build job. In our example, we set up a new job that was dedicated to the YSlow performance analysis task. However, these steps could be adapted such that the performance analysis task is added onto an existing multipurpose job.

Next, we configured when our job will run, adding **Build Trigger** to run the analyses according to a schedule. For our schedule, we selected H 9-16/2 * * 1-5, which runs the analyses every two hours, during business hours, on weekdays.

> While the schedule that we used is fine for demonstration purposes, we should carefully consider the needs of our project—chances are that a different **Build Trigger** will be more appropriate. For example, it may make more sense to select **Build after other projects are built**, and to have the performance analyses run only *after* the new code has been committed, built, and deployed to the appropriate QA or staging environment. Another alternative would be to select **Poll SCM** and to have the performance analyses run only after Jenkins CI detects new changes in source control.

With the schedule configured, we can apply the shell commands necessary for the performance analyses. As noted earlier, the **Command** text area accepts the text that we would normally type on the command line. Here we type the following:

- `phantomjs`: This is for the PhantomJS executable binary
- `${HOME}/tmp/yslow.js`: This is to refer to the copy of the YSlow library accessible to the Jenkins CI user
- `-i grade`: This is to indicate that we want the "Grade" level of report detail
- `-threshold "B"`: This is to indicate that we want to fail builds with an overall grade of "B" or below
- `-f junit`: This is to indicate that we want the results output in the JUnit format
- `http://localhost:3000/css-demo`: This is typed in as our target URL
- `> yslow.xml`: This is to redirect the JUnit-formatted output to that file on the disk

What if PhantomJS isn't on the `PATH` for the Jenkins CI user? A relatively common problem that we may experience is that, although we have permission on Jenkins CI to set up new build jobs, we are not the server administrator. It is likely that PhantomJS is available on the same machine where Jenkins CI is running, but the `jenkins` user simply does not have the `phantomjs` binary on its `PATH`. In these cases, we should work with the person administering the Jenkins CI server to learn its path. Once we have the PhantomJS path, we can do the following: click on **Add build step** and then on **Inject environment variables**; drag-and-drop the **Inject environment variables** block to ensure that it is *above* our **Execute shell** block; in the **Properties Content** text area, apply the PhantomJS binary's path to the `PATH` variable, as we would in any other script as follows:

```
PATH=/path/to/phantomjs/bin:${PATH}
```

After setting the shell commands to execute, we jump into the **Post-build Actions** block and instruct Jenkins CI where it can find the JUnit XML reports. As our shell command is redirecting the output into a file that is directly in the workspace, it is sufficient to enter an unqualified `*.xml` here.

Once we have saved our build job in Jenkins CI, the performance analyses can begin right away! If we are impatient for our first round of results, we can click on **Build Now** for our job and watch as it executes the initial performance analysis.

As the performance analyses are run, Jenkins CI will accumulate the results on the filesystem, keeping them until they are either manually removed or until a discard policy removes old build information. We can browse these accumulated jobs in the web UI for Jenkins CI, clicking on the **Test Result** link to drill into them.

There's more...

The first thing that bears expanding upon is that we should be thoughtful about what we use as the target URL for our performance analysis job. The YSlow library expects a single target URL, and as such, it is not prepared to handle a performance analysis job that is otherwise configured to target two or more URLs. As such, we must select a strategy to compensate for this, for example:

- **Pick a representative page**: We could manually go through our site and select the single page that we feel best represents the site as a whole. For example, we could pick the page that is "most average" compared to the other pages ("most will perform at about this level"), or the page that is most likely to be the "worst performing" page ("most pages will perform better than this"). With our representative page selected, we can then extrapolate performance for other pages from this specimen.

- **Pick a critical page**: We could manually select the single page that is most sensitive to performance. For example, we could pick our site's landing page (for example, "it is critical to optimize performance for first-time visitors"), or a product demo page (for example, "this is where conversions happen, so this is where performance needs to be best"). Again, with our performance-sensitive page selected, we can optimize the general cases around the specific one.

- **Set up multiple performance analysis jobs**: If we are not content to extrapolate site performance from a single specimen page, then we could set up multiple performance analysis jobs—one for each page on the site that we want to test. In this way, we could (conceivably) set up an exhaustive performance analysis suite. Unfortunately, the results will not roll up into one; however, once our site is properly tuned, we need to only look for the telltale red ball of a failed build in Jenkins CI.

The second point worth considering is—where do we point PhantomJS and YSlow for the performance analysis? And how does the target URL's environment affect our interpretation of the results? If we are comfortable running our performance analysis against our production deploys, then there is not much else to discuss—we are assessing exactly what needs to be assessed. But if we are analyzing performance in production, then it's already too late—the slow code has already been deployed! If we have a QA or staging environment available to us, then this is potentially better; we can deploy new code to one of these environments for integration and performance testing before putting it in front of the customers. However, these environments are likely to be different from production despite our best efforts. For example, though we may be "doing everything else right", perhaps our staging server causes all traffic to come back from a single hostname, and thus, we cannot properly mimic a CDN, nor can we use cookie-free domains. Do we lower our threshold grade? Do we deactivate or ignore these rules? How can we tell apart the false negatives from the real warnings? We should put some careful thought into this—but don't be disheartened—better to have results that are slightly off than to have no results at all!

Using TAP format

If JUnit formatted results turn out to be unacceptable, there is also a TAP plugin for Jenkins CI. **Test Anything Protocol** (**TAP**) is a plain text-based report format that is relatively easy for both humans and machines to read. (We saw an example of TAP output from YSlow in the *Executing a detailed performance analysis* recipe, earlier in this chapter.) With the TAP plugin installed in Jenkins CI, we can easily configure our performance analysis job to use it. We would just make the following changes to our build job:

1. In the **Command** text area of our **Execute shell** block, we would enter the following command:

```
phantomjs ${HOME}/tmp/yslow.js -i grade -threshold "B" -f tap
    http://localhost:3000/css-demo > yslow.tap
```

2. In the **Post-build Actions** block, we would select **Publish TAP Results** instead of **Publish JUnit test result report** and enter `yslow.tap` in the **Test results** text field.

Everything else about using TAP instead of JUnit-formatted results here is basically the same. The job will still run on the schedule we specify, Jenkins CI will still accumulate test results for comparison, and we can still explore the details of an individual test's outcomes. The TAP plugin adds an additional link in the job for us, **TAP Extended Test Results**, as shown in the following screenshot:

One thing worth pointing out about using TAP results is that it is much easier to set up a single job to test multiple target URLs within a single website. We can enter multiple tests in the Execute Shell block (separating them with the `&&` operator) and then set our Test Results target to be `*.tap`. This will conveniently combine the results of all our performance analyses into one.

See also

▸ The *Generating HAR files from PhantomJS* recipe
▸ The *Executing a detailed performance analysis* recipe
▸ The *Executing a YSlow performance analysis with a custom ruleset* recipe
▸ *Chapter 8, Continuous Integration with PhantomJS*

7
Generating Images and Documents with PhantomJS

In this chapter, we will cover:

- ▸ Rendering images from PhantomJS
- ▸ Saving images as Base64 from PhantomJS
- ▸ Rendering and rasterizing SVGs from PhantomJS
- ▸ Generating clipped screenshots from PhantomJS
- ▸ Saving a web page from PhantomJS as a PDF
- ▸ Applying custom headers and footers to PDFs generated from PhantomJS
- ▸ Testing responsive designs with PhantomJS

Introduction

Up to this point, our discussion on PhantomJS focused on its headless nature; while there are many advantages to it, there is also one obvious disadvantage—you can't see anything when you need to.

Fortunately, the PhantomJS `webpage` API exposes a couple of methods for rendering web page content as images and documents. We have seen a couple of these methods already; in this chapter, we will explore them in more detail, and discuss how to apply them. We will see strategies for exporting different types of images, PDFs, rasterizing SVGs, and everything else we need to know to get visual information back out of PhantomJS.

Rendering images from PhantomJS

This recipe introduces the `render` method from the `webpage` module in PhantomJS; we will use `render` to generate images of our web page content.

Getting ready

To run this recipe, we will need a script that intends to access a web page. We also need permissions to write to the filesystem in that script's working directory.

The script in this recipe is available in the downloadable code repository as `recipe01.js` under `chapter07`. If we run the provided example script, we must change to the root directory for the book's sample code.

Lastly, the script in this recipe runs against the demo site that is included with the cookbook's sample code repository. To run the demo site, we must have Node.js installed. In a separate terminal, change to the `phantomjs-sandbox` directory (in the sample code's directory), and start the app with the following command:

```
node app.js
```

How to do it...

Consider the following script:

```
var webpage  = require('webpage').create(),
    filename = 'index.png';

webpage.viewportSize = { width: 1024, height: 384 };

webpage.open('http://localhost:3000/', function(status) {
  if (status === 'fail') {
    console.error('webpage did not open successfully');
    phantom.exit(1);
  }

  webpage.render(filename);

  console.log('webpage rendered as ' + filename);

  phantom.exit();
});
```

Given the preceding script, enter the following at the command line:

```
phantomjs chapter07/recipe01.js
```

The script should print out the following:

```
webpage rendered as index.png
```

We can locate `index.png` in the root directory for the book's sample code; when we open the image, we should see something like the following screenshot:

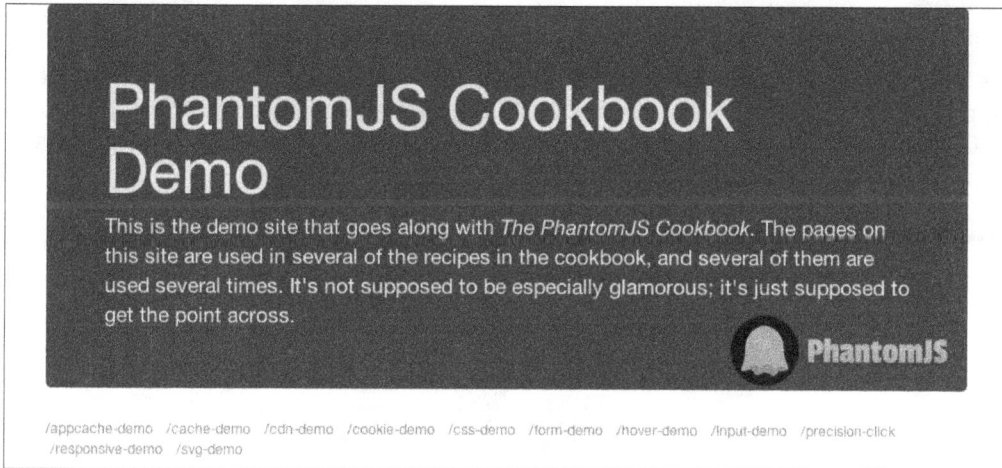

How it works...

Our preceding example script performs the following actions:

1. It creates a `webpage` instance and assigns it to a variable with the same name. It also assigns our target image filename to the `filename` variable.

2. It sets the size of the viewport on the `webpage` instance by setting its `viewportSize` property.

3. It calls `webpage.open` on our target URL (`http://localhost:3000/`) and passes it a callback function. In the callback function, it exits PhantomJS with an error status if the web page fails to load.

4. If the web page loads successfully, it makes a call to `webpage.render`, passing it the name of the file we want for the output (`filename`).

> PhantomJS infers the file format from the file extension passed to
> `webpage.render`. In this case, our target filename ends in `.png`,
> so PhantomJS will render the image in the **Portable Network Graphics
> (PNG)** format.

5. After the call to `webpage.render` is complete, we write a message to the console
    and exit from PhantomJS.

There's more...

The `render` method on `webpage` instances is about as simple and intuitive as can be. We
simply call it with a filename, and a rendering of the current web page content is written to
disk. There is a little bit more to the method, which we will discuss in the following sections
of the chapter.

First, `render` can output in the following formats:

- GIF
- JPEG
- PNG
- PDF

> We will discuss generating PDFs in more detail in the *Saving a web page
> from PhantomJS as a PDF* recipe later in this chapter.

> Behind the scenes, PhantomJS uses the QImage class (from the Qt
> project) to render web page content as an image. As such, `webpage.`
> `render` can technically output any format that QImage can; however, only
> the preceding four formats listed are documented as supported by the
> PhantomJS API. If our needs dictate another format (for example, TIFF),
> then we can experiment with it.

On the subject of formats, and as we noted before, PhantomJS infers the file format from
the extension on the filename that is passed as the first argument to `webpage.render`.
However, we can override the actual format that is rendered by applying a `format` property
in the second argument to `webpage.render`, for example:

```
webpage.render('index.png', { format: 'jpg' });
```

This will render a JPG image with a filename of `index.png`. In other words, the `format`
property (in the second argument) takes precedence over whatever is implied through
the filename.

> If we supply a filename that does not have a file extension, and we do not supply a format in the second argument, then the call to `webpage.render` will fail silently. However, if we supply a filename without an extension, but do supply a format in the second argument, then the file will be written to disk (though without the extension).

When exporting JPEG images, we can also supply a `quality` property in the second argument. The `quality` property takes an integer between 0 and 100, which will be used as the quality setting when compressing the JPEG image, for example:

```
webpage.render('something.jpg', { quality: 90 });
```

This will render the current web page content as `something.jpg` with a 90 percent quality rating.

Lastly, if we ever get something that we do not expect from our web page content rendering, we should troubleshoot using questions such as:

- **Are we trying to capture a web page with a plugin?** Remember that plugins such as Flash and Silverlight cannot run within PhantomJS. As such, if our target web page makes use of such a plugin, we will not be able to render it.

- **Are we capturing a single-page app?** Many web pages written in a single-page app style may have lazily-loaded content. As such, if our script is set up to make its call to `webpage.render` immediately after the page finishes loading, then it's possible that not all of its components have finished loading or painting. In a case such as this, we should consider what other events we may listen to before making our call to `webpage.render`. If all else fails, we can always try waiting a few hundred milliseconds.

- **Does our target page perform an immediate redirect?** Another possibility is that our target URL performs an immediate redirect (for example, it returns a 301). As the HTTP status code returned is less than 400, PhantomJS will interpret this as a success. In such cases, we may need to ascertain what URL we are redirected to, and then reconfigure our scripts so that we render the content for the downstream destination page and not the original target.

- **Are we trying to take screenshots of something animated?** Are we trying to capture the web page state before the animation has started? Are we capturing it during or after the process? This puts us in a position similar to the one when we were trying to render a single-page app. We may need to inspect the web page manually and come up with a strategy for timing the call to `webpage.render`. Is there an event we can listen for, or do we need to set a timeout and wait?

See also

▶ The *Saving images as Base64 from PhantomJS* recipe

▶ The *Generating clipped screenshots from PhantomJS* recipe

▶ The *Saving a web page from PhantomJS as a PDF* recipe

Saving images as Base64 from PhantomJS

This recipe continues our discussion of rendering web page content by introducing the `renderBase64` method from the `webpage` module in PhantomJS.

Getting ready

To run this recipe, we will need a script that intends to access a web page.

The script in this recipe is available in the downloadable code repository as `recipe02.js` under `chapter07`. If we run the provided example script, we must change to the root directory for the book's sample code.

Lastly, the script in this recipe runs against the demo site that is included with the cookbook's sample code repository. To run the demo site, we must have Node.js installed. In a separate terminal, change to the `phantomjs-sandbox` directory (in the sample code's directory), and start the app with the following command:

```
node app.js
```

How to do it...

Consider the following script:

```
var webpage = require('webpage').create(),
    args    = require('system').args,
    format  = args[1] || 'jpeg';

webpage.viewportSize = { width: 1024, height: 768 };

webpage.open('http://localhost:3000/', function(status) {
  if (status === 'fail') {
    console.error('webpage did not open successfully');
    phantom.exit(1);
  }

  console.log(webpage.renderBase64(format));
```

```
    phantom.exit();
});
```

Enter the following at the command line:

phantomjs chapter07/recipe02.js png

The script will print a Base64 encoded string of the web page's rendering (as a PNG) to standard out.

How it works...

Our preceding example script performs the following actions:

1. It creates a `webpage` instance and assigns it to a variable with the same name. Next, it grabs the command-line arguments from the `system` module and assigns them to the `args` variable; it also takes the first argument as the targeted rendering format or falls back to JPEG.

2. It sets the size of the viewport on the `webpage` instance by setting its `viewportSize` property.

3. It calls `webpage.open` on our target URL (`http://localhost:3000/`) and passes it a callback function. In our callback function, it exits PhantomJS with an error status if the web page fails to load.

4. If the web page loads successfully, it makes a call to `webpage.renderBase64`, passing it the format we want for the output and writing that output to the console.

5. After the call to `webpage.renderBase64` is complete, it exits from PhantomJS.

There's more...

The `renderBase64` method on `webpage` instances takes a single argument, and that argument is used to specify the image format used to render the web page content. The supported formats for this method include BMP, GIF, JPEG (JPG is also acceptable), PNG, PPM, TIFF, XBM, and XPM.

> At the time of writing this book, many PhantomJS users have been reporting problems using the GIF format. Given the low overall quality of GIF images, we should prefer PNG or JPEG images anyway. See the issue on GitHub for more information at `https://github.com/ariya/phantomjs/issues/10888`.

If no argument is supplied to `webpage.renderBase64`, it falls back to the default PNG format. If an unacceptable or unrecognized format is passed, the method will fail gracefully and return an empty string.

Unlike `webpage.render`, the `renderBase64` method does not interact with the filesystem and brokers strictly in strings. Note that our example script needed to take the returned string immediately and use it as the argument to `console.log` for us to see any evidence of its operation at all. This is important to keep in mind as we consider using `renderBase64` in our scripts.

See also

▸ The *Rendering images from PhantomJS* recipe

Rendering and rasterizing SVGs from PhantomJS

In this recipe, we introduce how to load **Scalable Vector Graphics** (**SVG**) content into PhantomJS and save rasterized versions of those images.

Getting ready

To run this recipe, we will need a script that accesses a web page and a target URL that either is or contains SVG content. We also need write permissions to the filesystem in that script's working directory.

The script in this recipe is available in the downloadable code repository as `recipe03.js` under `chapter07`. If we run the provided example script, we must change to the root directory for the book's sample code.

Lastly, the script in this recipe runs against the demo site that is included with the cookbook's sample code repository. To run the demo site, we must have Node.js installed. In a separate terminal, change to the `phantomjs-sandbox` directory (in the sample code's directory), and start the app with the following command:

```
node app.js
```

How to do it...

Consider the following script:

```
var webpage  = require('webpage').create(),
    filename = 'eyes.png';

webpage.open('http://localhost:3000/svg/eyes.svg',
  function(status) {
    if (status === 'fail') {
      console.error('webpage did not open successfully');
      phantom.exit(1);
    }

    webpage.render(filename);

    console.log('webpage rendered as ' + filename);

    phantom.exit();
});
```

Given the preceding script, enter the following at the command line:

phantomjs chapter07/recipe03.js

The script will load the SVG at the target URL and render it as a PNG. Our output should look like the following:

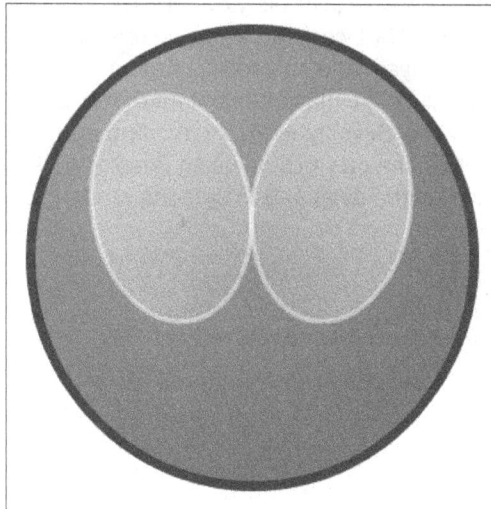

How it works...

Our example script here operates identically to the one that we used in the *Rendering images from PhantomJS* recipe earlier in this chapter. This script performs the following actions:

1. It creates a `webpage` instance and assigns it to a variable with the same name. It also assigns our target image filename to the `filename` variable.

2. It calls `webpage.open` on our target URL (`http://localhost:3000/svg/eyes.svg`) and passes it a callback function. In our callback function, it exits PhantomJS with an error status if the web page fails to load.

3. Note that our example script uses an SVG document directly as the target URL. We could just as easily have loaded a normal target URL that coincidentally contained SVG content. In fact, if we substitute `http://localhost:3000/svg-demo` for our originally cited target URL, then we will see our example work on content that brings in an SVG with an `img` element as well as an embedded `svg` element drawn to the page using JavaScript.

4. If the web page loads successfully, it makes a call to `webpage.render`, passing it the name of the file we want for the output.

5. After the call to `webpage.render` is complete, it writes a message to the console and exits from PhantomJS.

There's more...

There is no catch to rendering SVG content with PhantomJS; SVG documents are first-class citizens in PhantomJS, just like HTML. Calls to `webpage.render` will output whatever PhantomJS has drawn to its otherwise invisible viewport. This applies to SVG content just as easily as it applies to normal HTML content; we could render the contents of a `canvas` element this way as well. Once again, the only real limitation of `render` (and `renderBase64`) is that the method cannot produce an image for content that PhantomJS doesn't render—for example, plugins such as Flash or Silverlight, the `video` and `audio` elements, WebGL, and 3D CSS effects. Other than this, the only trick to using PhantomJS for effective screenshots is to be aware of any animation on the page and to time the renderings accordingly.

See also

▶ The *Rendering images from PhantomJS* recipe
▶ The *Saving images as Base64 from PhantomJS* recipe

Generating clipped screenshots from PhantomJS

This recipe introduces the `clipRect` property on `webpage` instances, and it describes its role in rendering portions of our web page content. The recipe also illustrates how to set the property dynamically (for example, to capture specific page elements).

Getting ready

To run this recipe, we will need a script that accesses a web page. We need some knowledge of the structure of the target web page so that we can define a selector to use for further targeting specific content on that web page. We also need write permissions to the filesystem in that script's working directory.

The script in this recipe is available in the downloadable code repository as `recipe04.js` under `chapter07`. If we run the provided example script, we must change to the root directory for the book's sample code.

Lastly, the script in this recipe runs against the demo site that is included with the cookbook's sample code repository. To run the demo site, we must have Node.js installed. In a separate terminal, change to the `phantomjs-sandbox` directory (in the sample code's directory), and start the app with the following command:

```
node app.js
```

How to do it...

Consider the following script:

```
var webpage  = require('webpage').create(),
    selector = require('system').args[1],
    filename;

if (!selector) {
  console.error('no selector was specified');
  phantom.exit(1);
}

filename = selector.replace(/\s/g, '-')
    .replace(/\W/g, '') + '.png';

webpage.viewportSize = { width: 1024, height: 768 };
```

```
webpage.open('http://localhost:3000/', function(status) {
  if (status === 'fail') {
    console.error('webpage did not open successfully');
    phantom.exit(1);
  }

  webpage.clipRect = webpage.evaluate(function(selector) {
    var el = document.querySelector(selector);
    return {
      top: el.offsetTop,
      left: el.offsetLeft,
      width: el.offsetWidth,
      height: el.offsetHeight
    };
  }, selector);

  webpage.render(filename);

  console.log('webpage rendered as ' + filename);

  phantom.exit();
});
```

Given the preceding script, enter the following at the command line:

```
phantomjs chapter07/recipe04.js ".jumbotron"
```

The script should print out the following:

```
webpage rendered as jumbotron.png
```

We can locate jumbotron.png in the root directory for the book's sample code; when we open the image, we should see something like the following:

How it works...

Our preceding example script performs the following actions:

1. It creates a `webpage` instance and assigns it to a variable with the same name.

2. It optimistically grabs our selector string from the system arguments and assigns it to the `selector` variable.

3. If `selector` is falsy, it exits PhantomJS with an error status. If it gets past this check, it generates our filename from the selector string, sanitizing the whitespace and non-alphanumeric characters; this is assigned to the `filename` variable. (We assign `null` to `filename` if `selector` is otherwise falsy.)

> JavaScript's notion of falsy values is partially responsible for its notorious reputation with respect to type coercion. Falsy values are those that are equivalent to `false` but are not strictly false. JavaScript's falsy values include `false`, `undefined`, `null`, `0`, and `' '` (the empty string).

4. It sets the size of the viewport on the `webpage` instance by setting its `viewportSize` property.

5. It calls `webpage.open` on our target URL (`http://localhost:3000/`) and passes it a callback function. In our callback function, it exits PhantomJS with an error status if the web page fails to load.

6. It assigns `webpage.clipRect` by evaluating `selector` on the web page and using its offset dimensions. The `selector` value is passed as an argument to the `webpage.evaluate` callback function; this callback function retrieves the first matching element with `document.querySelector`, and then matches its `offsetTop`, `offsetLeft`, `offsetWidth`, and `offsetHeight` values to the corresponding properties on the object to be returned. The returned object is assigned to `webpage.clipRect`.

7. The `clipRect` property is a contraction of "clipping rectangle", and it specifies a mask that is used when rendering the web page content, effectively creating an area of interest. Remember that calls to `webpage.render` and `renderBase64` will capture the entire web page by default; setting `clipRect` allows us to render only the selected portion.

8. With `webpage.clipRect` assigned, it makes our call to `webpage.render`, passing it the name of the file we want for the output.

9. After the call to `webpage.render` is complete, it writes a message to the console and exits from PhantomJS.

On the command line, we invoke the script in the usual fashion, but take care to enclose our `selector` argument in quotes. Enclosing the `selector` argument in quotes ensures that the selector—which can validly have spaces in it—is intact on the other side of that command-line invocation. This allows us to pass selectors such as ".jumbotron h1" into our script for better element targeting.

There's more...

As we have previously seen, the default mode for `webpage.render` in PhantomJS is to capture the entire web page—all of its contents, regardless of the specified viewport size. For novice users of PhantomJS, this can be a bit confusing. Although setting the viewport width has direct consequences on the rendered output, the height often appears to do nothing.

The `clipRect` property gives us a way to get screenshots that may be a little more aligned with our expectations. For example, if we want to get an idea of what our site looks like "above the fold", we can pass it through a variation of the preceding script, which looks something like the following:

```
var webpage  = require('webpage').create(),
    args      = require('system').args,
    width     = args[1],
    height    = args[2],
    filename = width + 'px-X-' + height + 'px.png';

if (!width || !height) {
  console.error('viewport size was not specified');
  phantom.exit(1);
}

webpage.viewportSize = { width: width, height: height };

webpage.clipRect = {
  top: 0,
  left: 0,
  width: width,
  height: height
};

webpage.open('http://localhost:3000/', function(status) {
  if (status === 'fail') {
    console.error('webpage did not open successfully');
    phantom.exit(1);
  }

  webpage.render(filename);
  phantom.exit();
});
```

Here, we pass the viewport's width and height as command-line arguments, and then set both `viewportSize` and `clipRect` based on those arguments. This allows us to get the "above the fold" screenshots in the way we expect them. For example, given that the effective apparent viewport size of Safari on iOS is 320 × 356 pixels, enter the following at the command line:

```
phantomjs chapter07/recipe04-supplement.js 320 356
```

We will get a screenshot of what our site looks like in Safari on an iOS device, as shown here:

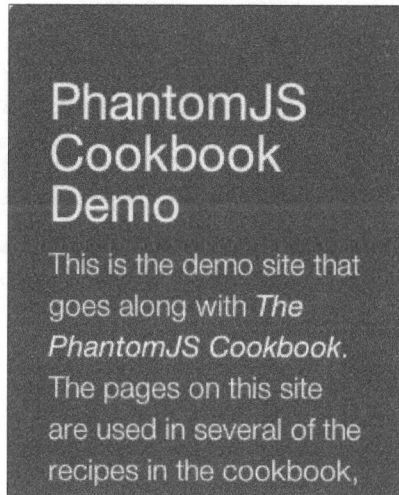

CasperJS

It's worth noting here that some of the frameworks and libraries that target PhantomJS already offer methods that do much of what we have discussed in this recipe. For example, CasperJS offers the following methods that effectively wrap combinations of `webpage.render` with `webpage.clipRect`:

- ▸ `casper.capture(filename[, clipRect, imgOptions])`: If `clipRect` is provided, the CasperJS instance (behind the scenes) will set `webpage.clipRect`, make its call to `webpage.render`, and then immediately revert the `clipRect` property.

- ▸ `casper.captureBase64(format[, area])`: This renders only the specified `area` (if provided); `area` may take the form of a CSS selector, an XPath selector, or a `clipRect` object.

- ▸ `casper.captureSelector(filename, selector[, imgOptions])`: Given a CSS selector string (`selector`), CasperJS sets `clipRect` to the offset bounds of the selector, and then writes the rendering to `filename`.

> You can find more information about CasperJS image-capturing methods in their API documentation at `http://docs.casperjs.org/en/latest/modules/casper.html`.

See also

- The *Interacting with web pages using CasperJS* recipe in *Chapter 5, Functional and End-to-end Testing with PhantomJS*
- The *Rendering images from PhantomJS* recipe

Saving a web page from PhantomJS as a PDF

This recipe goes into more detail about `webpage.render`, and it shows how to generate PDFs. We also introduce the `paperSize` property of `webpage` instances and how to control the sizes of the pages in the PDF output.

Getting ready

To run this recipe, we will need a script that accesses a web page. We also need write permissions to the filesystem in the script's working directory.

The script in this recipe is available in the downloadable code repository as `recipe05.js` under `chapter07`. If we run the provided example script, we must change to the root directory for the book's sample code.

Lastly, the script in this recipe runs against the demo site that is included with the cookbook's sample code repository. To run the demo site, we must have Node.js installed. In a separate terminal, change to the `phantomjs-sandbox` directory (in the sample code's directory), and start the app with the following command:

```
node app.js
```

How to do it...

Consider the following script:

```
var webpage = require('webpage').create(),
    filename = 'css-demo.pdf';

webpage.viewportSize = { width: 1024, height: 768 };
```

```
webpage.paperSize = {
  format:      'Letter',
  orientation: 'portrait',
  border:      '0.5in'
};

webpage.open('http://localhost:3000/css-demo', function(status) {
  if (status === 'fail') {
    console.error('webpage did not open successfully');
    phantom.exit(1);
  }

  webpage.render(filename);

  console.log('webpage rendered as ' + filename);

  phantom.exit();
});
```

Given the preceding script, enter the following at the command line:

phantomjs chapter07/recipe05.js

The script should print out the following:

webpage rendered as css-demo.pdf

We can locate `css-demo.pdf` in the root directory for the book's sample code. When we open the PDF, we should see that it has rendered the web page.

How it works...

Our preceding example script performs the following actions:

1. It creates a `webpage` instance and assigns it to a variable with the same name. It also assigns our target image filename to the `filename` variable.

> Note that, once again, we take advantage of the fact that calls to `webpage.render` to infer the file type from the file extension, hence using `.pdf` here.

2. It sets the size of the viewport on the `webpage` instance by setting its `viewportSize` property.

3. It configures the size of the target pages for the PDF output using the `paperSize` property on our `webpage` instance. It sets `format` of the paper to `Letter` (8.5" × 11"); the `orientation` is set to `portrait` (taller, not wider); it also sets `border` (or margin) to `0.5in`.

4. It calls `webpage.open` on our target URL (`http://localhost:3000/css-demo`) and passes it a callback function. In our callback function, it exits PhantomJS with an error status if the web page fails to load.

5. If the web page loads successfully, it makes a call to `webpage.render`, passing it the name of the file we want for the output.

6. After the call to `webpage.render` is complete, it writes a message to the console and exits from PhantomJS.

There's more...

As we have witnessed in this chapter's preceding recipes, the `render` method is extremely simple, and we can get a lot of mileage out of calling it with the right filename. When we break it down, all that separates this chapter's `recipe01.js` from `recipe05.js` are the following:

▸ Defining the `paperSize` property

▸ Calling `render` with a filename ending with `.pdf`

webpage.paperSize

The `paperSize` property on our `webpage` instance is what tells the PhantomJS renderer how large the pages in the PDF should be made when our content "prints". If `paperSize` is left undefined, then the web page will define those dimensions, and the resulting PDF may have an incorrect appearance. With this in mind, if we expect that our script will render to a PDF, we should provide a defined `paperSize`. The `paperSize` property is itself an object that assumes one of the following two forms:

▸ `{ width, height, border }`

▸ `{ format, orientation, border }`

In both cases, the `border` property is optional; when providing `format`, `orientation` is also optional.

Note that we can set the page dimensions explicitly as an alternative to setting `paperSize`.

width and height

The `width` and `height` properties on the `paperSize` object are mutually dependent; if you use one, you must use the other. Both properties take strings as their values, and those strings are parsed into the page dimensions. The value strings take the form of a number plus a unit; for example, `8.5in` or `1000px`. The acceptable units of measurement include the following:

- mm
- cm
- in
- px (default)

Another interesting note about the `height` and `width` properties is that they take precedence over the `format` property. For example, consider the following:

```
webpage.paperSize = {
  format: 'Letter',
  width: '5cm',
  height: '5cm'
};
```

Given the preceding code snippet, the PDF output will be 5cm × 5cm and not 8.5" × 11".

format

The `format` property gives us a way to specify one of the standard page sizes; these string values are shorthand for their heights and widths.

format value	dimensions
A3	420mm × 297mm
A4	297mm × 210mm
A5	210mm × 148mm
Legal	14" × 8.5"
Letter	11" × 8.5"
Tabloid	17" × 11"

orientation

When paired with the `format` property, `orientation` tells the PhantomJS renderer how to orient the pages within the rendered PDF. The two legal values are `portrait` and `landscape` (tall and wide, respectively); `portrait` is the default if neither value is supplied.

border

The `border` property can be used with either the `height`/`width` or the `format`/`orientation` combination—this is also optional under both scenarios. The `border` property allows us to specify the margin between the edges of the page and rendered content. We can specify the value for `border` in one of two forms.

The first form is similar to how we specify `height` and `width`, and it consists of a number and unit of measurement; the specified `border` is translated as the margin for all four edges of the page, for example:

```
webpage.paperSize = { border: '1in' };
```

This will set a one-inch margin around all four edges of our rendered PDF.

The second form is to specify an object with each margin defined individually, again using the "number plus unit" syntax, for example:

```
webpage.paperSize = {
  border: {
    top: '1in',
    right: '0.5in',
    bottom: '1in',
    left: '0.5in'
  }
};
```

This will set a one-inch margin for the top and bottom, but a one-half-inch margin for the left and right sides.

See also

- The *Rendering images from PhantomJS* recipe
- The *Applying custom headers and footers to PDFs generated from PhantomJS* recipe

Applying custom headers and footers to PDFs generated from PhantomJS

In this recipe, we expand on the discussion of the `paperSize` property, and illustrate how to use it to set up custom headers and footers in the PDF output. This can be useful for applying titles, page numbers, or time/date stamps to the PDF renderings.

Getting ready

To run this recipe, we will need a script that accesses a web page. We also need write permissions to the filesystem in that script's working directory.

The script in this recipe is available in the downloadable code repository as `recipe06.js` under `chapter07`. If we run the provided example script, we must change to the root directory for the book's sample code.

Lastly, the script in this recipe runs against the demo site that is included with the cookbook's sample code repository. To run the demo site, we must have Node.js installed. In a separate terminal, change to the `phantomjs-sandbox` directory (in the sample code's directory), and start the app with the following command:

```
node app.js
```

How to do it...

Consider the following script:

```
var webpage  = require('webpage').create(),
    filename = 'css-demo.pdf',
    datetime = new Date().toString(),
    title;

webpage.viewportSize = { width: 1024, height: 768 };

webpage.open('http://localhost:3000/css-demo', function(status) {
  if (status === 'fail') {
    console.error('webpage did not open successfully');
    phantom.exit(1);
  }

  title = webpage.evaluate(function() {
    return document.querySelector('title').innerText;
  });

  webpage.paperSize = {
    format:      'Letter',
    orientation: 'portrait',
    border: '0.5in',
    header: {
      height: '0.5in',
      contents: phantom.callback(function() {
        return '<h1 style="border-bottom:' +
            '1px #333 solid;color:#333;">' +
            title + '</h1>';
      })
    },
    footer: {
      height: '0.5in',
      contents: phantom.callback(function(pageNum, numPages) {
        return '<div style="border-top:1px #333 solid;color:#333;">' +
            '<div style="float:left;">Rendered: ' + datetime +
            '</div><div style="float:right;">Pages: ' +
            pageNum + '/' + numPages + '</div></div>';
```

```
        })
      }
    };

    webpage.render(filename);

    console.log('webpage rendered as ' + filename);

    phantom.exit();
  });
```

Given the preceding script, enter the following at the command line:

phantomjs chapter07/recipe06.js

The script should print out the following:

webpage rendered as css-demo.pdf

We can locate `css-demo.pdf` in the root directory for the book's sample code. When we open the PDF, we should see that it has rendered the web page and applied the specified headers and footers.

How it works...

Our preceding example script performs the following actions:

1. It creates a `webpage` instance and assigns it to a variable with the same name. It assigns our target image filename to the `filename` variable, gets the current date and time, and assigns it to the `datetime` variable. It also declares a `title` variable that we will use later.

2. It sets the size of the viewport on the `webpage` instance by setting its `viewportSize` property.

3. It calls `webpage.open` on our target URL (`http://localhost:3000/css-demo`) and passes it a callback function. In our callback function, it exits PhantomJS with an error status if the web page fails to load.

4. If the web page loads successfully, it calls `webpage.evaluate` to extract the page title (from the `title` element) and assigns the returned text to the `title` variable.

5. It configures the size of the target pages for the PDF output using the `paperSize` property on our `webpage` instance. It sets `format` of the paper to `Letter` (8.5" × 11"); `orientation` is set to `portrait` (taller, not wider); and it sets `border` (or margin) to `0.5in`.

6. In our `webpage.paperSize` object, it configures our `header` property; this property has `height` that we specify as `0.5in` and a `contents` block where it defines the callback function that returns the content for the header region. For our header, it outputs an `h1` (with inline styles to define the bottom border) and the page title.

7. Next, in our `webpage.paperSize` object, it configures our `footer` property; this property also has a `height` value (specified as `0.5in`) and a `contents` block where we define the callback function that returns the content for the footer region. The callback function will be called with two arguments (`pageNum` for the current page number and `numPages` for the total number of pages). The function outputs `div` (with inline styles to define the top border) with two floated inner divs: one that contains the `datetime` value and the other with the page information.

8. With `webpage.paperSize` now defined, it makes our call to `webpage.render`, passing it the name of the file we want for the output.

9. After the call to `webpage.render` is complete, it writes a message to the console and exits from PhantomJS.

There's more...

The use cases for the `header` and `footer` properties on `webpage.paperSize` are fairly self-evident; we can use this space to record metadata, such as the date or time when it was generated, the originating URL, or the page title, about the rendered page. Both these properties take the same form, and they have the similar properties of `height` and `contents`.

height

The `height` property of a `header` or `footer` object is a way for us to specify the height of the header or footer region in the rendered PDF. We specify this height using the same number-and-unit format as we do for the `height`, `width`, and `border` properties of `webpage.paperSize`; once again, the value is specified as a string, and the accepted units are `mm`, `cm`, `in`, and `px`. It is worth pointing out that the height is in addition to any top or bottom border region set, and the header or footer is between the border region and the actual content.

```
{
    format: 'Letter',
    orientaton: 'portrait',
    border: '1in',
    header: {
        height: '1in',
        contents: {}
    },
    footer: {
        height: '1in',
        contents: {}
    }
}
```

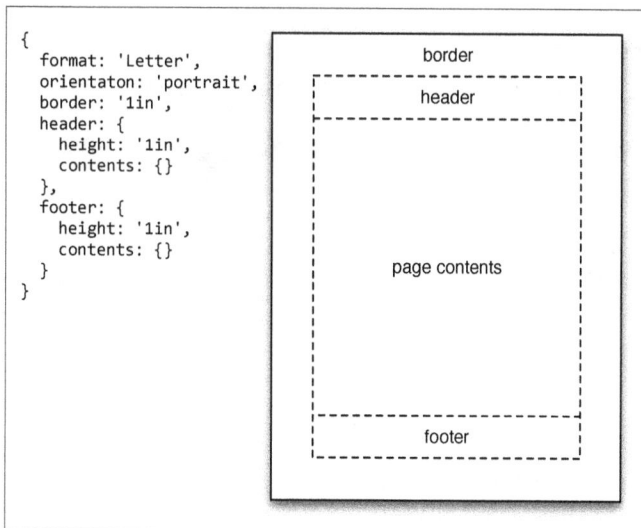

contents

The `contents` property of a `header` or `footer` object is where we can generate the content that will be applied to the header and footer regions of the rendered PDF. The value of the property takes a special PhantomJS callback object that is generated by the `phantom.callback` method (undocumented); fortunately, from a user perspective, we can think of this as simply providing the appropriate decorator on top of the callback function that we have otherwise defined and passed as the argument to `phantom.callback`.

The `contents` callback accepts two arguments: `pageNum` (holding the value of the current page number) and `numPages` (holding the total number of pages). The function should return a string that may contain HTML to format it or control the layout.

As these callback functions are "just JavaScript", we are free to perform any transformation or logic that we need inside these functions. Furthermore, they run as closures inside the PhantomJS script context (not the `webpage` context), and as such, they have access to all variables and functions we may have defined in that context. This is how we are able to print our `datetime` and `title` variables as part of the `footer` and `header`, respectively.

Lastly, the header and footer regions in the rendered PDF are effectively sandboxed portions of the layout. In other words, they do not inherit any of the styles from the target web page, and content in the header and footer regions cannot appear outside of the specified dimensions. This means that we cannot use CSS positioning in combination with these regions to produce watermarks; but it also means that we cannot accidentally overflow the header or footer.

See also

▶ The *Inspecting page content from a PhantomJS script* recipe in *Chapter 3, Working with webpage Objects*

▶ The *Rendering images from PhantomJS* recipe

▶ The *Saving a web page from PhantomJS as a PDF* recipe

Testing responsive designs with PhantomJS

This recipe provides a strategy for automatically loading a web page at different viewport sizes, capturing screenshots at each size, and thus testing our responsive design's breakpoints.

Getting ready

To run this recipe, we will need a script that accesses a web page; the target URL will need to be a responsive design with several breakpoints or viewport targets that we want to test. We also need write permissions to the filesystem in the script's working directory.

The script in this recipe is available in the downloadable code repository as `recipe07.js` under `chapter07`. If we run the provided example script, we must change to the root directory for the book's sample code.

Lastly, the script in this recipe runs against the demo site that is included with the cookbook's sample code repository. To run the demo site, we must have Node.js installed. In a separate terminal, change to the `phantomjs-sandbox` directory (in the sample code's directory), and start the app with the following command:

node app.js

How to do it...

Consider the following script:

```
var webpage    = require('webpage').create(),
    args       = require('system').args,
    viewports = args.slice(1).map(function(v) {
      return v.split(/x/i);
    }),
    filename;

function screenshot(vps) {
  var vp = vps.pop();
  webpage.viewportSize = { width: vp[0], height: vp[1] || 600 };

  setTimeout(function() {
    filename = vp.join('x') + '.png';

    webpage.render(filename);
    console.log('webpage rendered as ' + filename);

    vps.length > 0 ? screenshot(vps) : phantom.exit();
  }, 50);
}

webpage.open('http://localhost:3000/responsive-demo',
    function(status) {
      if (status === 'fail') {
        console.error('webpage did not open successfully');
        phantom.exit(1);
      }

      screenshot(viewports);
    }
);
```

Given the preceding script, enter the following at the command line:

```
phantomjs chapter07/recipe07.js 1680x1050 1280x1024 1024x768 768x1280
   640x960 320x480
```

The script should print out the following:

```
webpage rendered as 320x480.png

webpage rendered as 640x960.png

webpage rendered as 768x1280.png

webpage rendered as 1024x768.png

webpage rendered as 1280x1024.png

webpage rendered as 1680x1050.png
```

We can locate each of these screenshots in the root directory for the book's sample code. If we open each to inspect them, we should see that PhantomJS has rendered the web page content at each of the supplied breakpoints.

How it works...

Our preceding example script performs the following actions:

1. It creates a `webpage` instance and assigns it to a variable with the same name; it also assigns the script's command-line arguments to the `args` variable.

2. It plucks our target viewports from `args` and processes them, assigning them to the `viewports` variable. This breaks down as follows:

    1. Knowing that `args` is an array, and that the first element in the array is always the script name, we can get the remaining arguments by calling `args.slice(1)`.

    2. We call `map` on the sliced `args` array to generate the new array that will be assigned to `viewports`.

    3. Our `map` function takes the current command-line argument (as `v`) and calls `split` on it with the regular expression `/x/i` (splitting on either X or x). We return an array (to `viewports`) that contains the width and height (`1680x1050` becomes `['1680', '1050']`).

3. It declares a `filename` variable that we will use later.

4. It sets up our `screenshot` function that we will use to iterate through the viewports and render to disk as follows:

    1. The `screenshot` function expects one argument (`vps`) that is an array of the viewports.

2. We use `pop` to obtain the last viewport off of the `vps` array and assign it to the local `vp` variable.

3. We set `webpage.viewportSize`, using the first item in `vp` as `width` and the second item as `height`; if `height` is not provided, we default to 600 pixels.

> Recall the mapping function we used when we declared and assigned the `viewports` variable called `split` internally; this ensured that each element in the `viewports` array would itself be an array, even if it only had one element. This allows us to safely specify only widths on the command line (if we were so inclined) while still safely assigning `webpage.viewportSize`.

4. We set up our call to `render` inside `setTimeout` with a delay of 50 milliseconds.

> It is tempting to use a more straightforward iterator here (for example, `forEach` or a classic `for` loop), but that would ignore the fact that PhantomJS still needs those milliseconds to re-layout the content and reflow everything. If we used one of those more straightforward iterators, we will find that PhantomJS cannot reflow the page in its UI thread as quickly as `webpage.render` can be called in the script thread. A more-than-ample 50-millisecond delay and a recursive function are the most sensible options here, but fine-tuning may be necessary for more complex responsive designs.

5. Within the `setTimeout` callback, we assign our `filename` variable by joining the width and height with an `x` and appending the file extension `.png`.

6. We call `webpage.render` with `filename` and print a message to the console.

7. We check the length of the `vps` array. If it contains any more elements, we call `screenshot` again with `vps`; otherwise, we exit PhantomJS.

5. It calls `webpage.open` on our target URL (`http://localhost:3000/responsive-demo`) and passes it a callback function. In our callback function, it exits PhantomJS with an error status if the web page fails to load.

6. It kicks off the rendering by calling `screenshot` with `viewports` as its argument.

We then invoke the script on the command line in the usual way, but we also provide our list of target breakpoints (or viewports of interest) as additional command-line arguments. Each breakpoint is specified as width and height, separated by an X or x character. As described before, this list of breakpoints can be extracted from the command-line arguments and formed into an array of arrays that we can recurse through for our screenshots.

There's more...

In our preceding example, we provided a list of breakpoints on the command line, recursed through the breakpoints, and took screenshots of each. The breakpoints in our example are simply a subset conveniently pilfered from the Window Resizer Chrome Extension, and they should in no way be considered a canonical list of breakpoints; each project and responsive design is different, and each team needs to decide which breakpoints they want to use for testing. The viewports to target for testing is a complex question and warrants careful consideration.

Once again, we are caught by that quirk of how PhantomJS treats the configured viewport size for rendering the web page contents. Recall that `webpage.render` will output an image with the entire web page contents, and not just the viewport size that we specified. If we are truly concerned about just what shows up in the viewport, we can rewrite our `screenshot` function to take advantage of `clipRect` as well as `viewportSize`, for example:

```
function screenshot(vps) {
  var vp = vps.pop();
  webpage.viewportSize = { width: vp[0], height: vp[1] || 600 };
  webpage.clipRect = {
    left: 0, width:  vp[0],
    top:  0, height: vp[1] || 600
  };

  setTimeout(function() {
    // callback remains the same
  }, 50);
}
```

> The preceding modified version of this recipe's example script appears in the sample code repository as `recipe07-cliprect.js` under `chapter07`.

Once again, the team needs to decide: do we want a screenshot of just the viewport, or do we want screenshots of how the whole web page renders at that width?

Lastly, CasperJS provides a way of responding to the viewport size change through its API, either as a callback function passed as the third argument to `viewport` or as the callback function given to a `then` call after a call to `viewport`. For example, using Casper 1.1 or greater, we can achieve feature parity with this recipe's example, using the following script:

```
var casper    = require('casper').create(),
    viewports = casper.cli.args.map(function(v) {
      return v.split(/x/i).map(Number);
    }),
```

```
    filename;

function screenshot(vps) {
  var vp = vps.pop();

  casper.viewport(vp[0], vp[1] || 600, function() {
    filename = vp.join('x') + '.png';

    this.capture(filename);
    this.echo('webpage rendered as ' + filename);

    if(vps.length) screenshot(vps);
  });
}

casper.start('http://localhost:3000/responsive-demo', function() {
  screenshot(viewports);
}).run();
```

> The CasperJS version of this recipe's example script appears in the sample code repository as `recipe07-casper.js` under `chapter07`. Also, the instructions for how to install CasperJS appear in the *Installing CasperJS* recipe in *Chapter 5, Functional and End-to-end Testing with PhantomJS*.

See also

- ▸ The *Inspecting command-line arguments* recipe in *Chapter 2, PhantomJS Core Modules*
- ▸ The *Interacting with web pages using CasperJS* recipe in *Chapter 5, Functional and End-to-end Testing with PhantomJS*
- ▸ The *Rendering images from PhantomJS* recipe
- ▸ The *Generating clipped screenshots from PhantomJS* recipe

8
Continuous Integration with PhantomJS

In this chapter, we will cover:

- ► Setting up PhantomJS in a CI environment
- ► Generating JUnit reports
- ► Generating TAP reports
- ► Setting up a fully covered project in CI with PhantomJS

Introduction

Of all the places where PhantomJS has emerged as a compelling solution, the most powerful is perhaps in the realm of continuous integration. Since PhantomJS is a completely headless browser, it is extremely simple to install and operate on most systems—there is no fussing with **X virtual framebuffer** (**Xvfb**) and no need for binding to virtual machines. The PhantomJS binary is simply available on the host, and instances can be launched on demand from whatever jobs request them.

In this chapter, we will learn how to use PhantomJS as part of our **continuous integration** (**CI**) strategy. The chapter will survey ways of reporting test failures in CI systems as well as how to fail builds when front-end tests don't pass.

Setting up PhantomJS in a CI environment

This recipe demonstrates how to install PhantomJS in a continuous integration environment and how to expose it to the CI software.

Getting ready

We need a continuous integration server set up, where we can configure jobs that will use PhantomJS. The example that follows will use the open source Jenkins CI server.

> Jenkins CI is too large a subject to introduce here, and this recipe assumes only a shallow working knowledge of it. For information about Jenkins CI, including basic installation and usage instructions, or to obtain a copy for your platform, visit the project website at `http://jenkins-ci.org/`. Our recipe uses version 1.552.

> Although our example uses Jenkins CI to illustrate its key points, PhantomJS can be integrated with or called from any CI server platform. The example here aims to provide a clear illustration of how to configure PhantomJS, which we can adapt for any CI environment.

To run this recipe, we will need the PhantomJS binary installed and on `PATH` for the continuous integration server, which may not necessarily share the same permissions or `PATH` as our system user.

> The easiest way to find out whether PhantomJS is on `PATH` for the Jenkins CI system user is to navigate to the `/systemInfo` page on the Jenkins CI server and look for the `PATH` variable in the table under the **Environment Variables** heading. If the `PATH` value contains the path to the `phantomjs` binary, then it is available to Jenkins CI with no additional configuration.

This recipe also requires the Git plugin for Jenkins CI in order to integrate with the Git source control management software and download the sample code repository in an automated fashion.

> There are several plugins for Jenkins CI to help integrate Git into our CI workflow. The plugin we will use here is simply called Git plugin; we can find out more about it at the plugin repository site at `https://wiki.jenkins-ci.org/display/JENKINS/Git+Plugin`.

We need a project under version control with the Git source control management software.

> We can use the book's example code repository for this recipe. The public URL that we will use for this recipe is `https://github.com/founddrama/phantomjs-cookbook.git`.

This project must also contain components that expect to be run and/or tested in a web browser and the tests for those components. For the sake of simplicity, we will use a simple HTML page with JavaScript and its associated tests on the page. The web page in this recipe is available in the downloadable code repository as `recipe01-runner.html` under `chapter08`. The tests in this recipe are written using the Jasmine unit testing library, which we introduced in *Chapter 4, Unit Testing with PhantomJS*. To execute the tests headlessly in Jenkins, we will use the `JUnitXmlReporter` and `TerminalReporter` objects, and then bootstrap the testing environment using the `phantomjs-testrunner.js` script, all of which come from the `jasmine-reporters` library; these were also introduced in *Chapter 4, Unit Testing with PhantomJS*.

How to do it...

Assuming that we already have a Jenkins CI server installed and running, here is how we install PhantomJS and configure jobs to use it:

1. Perform the PhantomJS installation for that platform. Given the platform on which our Jenkins CI instance is running, we follow the PhantomJS installation instructions that are applicable to us. In most cases, a pre-built binary is already available.

> A thorough discussion of installing PhantomJS on the major platforms appears in the *Installing PhantomJS* recipe in *Chapter 1, Getting Started with PhantomJS*.

2. Expose the PhantomJS executable to the CI system user. The Jenkins CI software runs on the system as some user (for example, `jenkins`) and this user may not have the same `PATH`, permissions, and privileges as the user we otherwise use on that system. To expose PhantomJS to Jenkins CI, it must be on `PATH` for its user; to do this, perform the following steps:

    1. Click on **Manage Jenkins** in the left-side navigation.

    2. On the **Manage Jenkins** page, click on **Configure System** from the main menu.

3. On the **Configure System** page, find the section labeled **Global properties** and check the box labeled **Environment variables**.

Global properties

☑ Environment variables

List of key-value pairs

name `PATH`

value `/path/to/phantomjs/bin:${PATH}`

Delete

Add

4. Click on the **Add** button to create a new name/value pair. Enter `PATH` in the **name** field; in the **value** field, apply the path to the PhantomJS binary to the `PATH` variable like we would normally, for example, `/path/to/phantomjs/bin:${PATH}`.

5. Click on the **Save** button at the bottom of the **Configure System** page.

3. Add a job to Jenkins that will use PhantomJS. With PhantomJS now exposed to Jenkins CI, we can configure a build job to execute our front-end tests as follows:

1. Click on **New Item** in the left-side navigation.

2. Enter a name for the job in the field labeled **Item name**, for example, `PhantomJS Cookbook - Chapter 8 - Recipe 1`.

3. Select **Build a free-style software project**, and click on the **OK** button.

4. Under the **Source Code Management** block, select **Git** and enter the repository's URL (`https://github.com/founddrama/phantomjs-cookbook.git`) in the field labeled **Repository URL**.

> If the repository is private, we must configure **Credentials**. The other fields are optional, but we should configure a specific branch for the build.

Jenkins

Jenkins › PhantomJS Cookbook - Chapter 8 - Recipe 1 › configuration

- Back to Dashboard
- Status
- Changes
- Workspace
- Build Now
- Delete Project
- Configure

Build History (trend) ⊟

- #17 May 14, 2014 8:49:06 PM
- #15 Mar 23, 2014 9:51:29 PM
- #14 Mar 23, 2014 9:49:16 PM
- #13 Mar 23, 2014 9:17:13 PM
- #12 Mar 21, 2014 9:09:46 PM
- #11 Mar 21, 2014 9:05:30 PM

RSS for all RSS for failures

Project name: PhantomJS Cookbook - Chapter 8 - Recipe 1

Description:

[Escaped HTML] Preview

- Discard Old Builds
- This build is parameterized
- Prepare an environment for the run
- Disable Build (No new builds will be executed until the project is re-enabled.)
- Execute concurrent builds if necessary

Advanced Project Options

Advanced...

Source Code Management

- CVS
- CVS Projectset
- ⦿ Git

Repositories

Repository URL: https://github.com/founddrama/phantomjs-cookbook.git

Save   Apply

5. Under the **Build** block, click on **Add build step** and the **Execute shell** item. In the new **Execute shell** field, enter the commands necessary for running the front-end tests, for example:

```
phantomjs lib/jasmine-reporters/phantomjs-testrunner.js
    "$(pwd)/chapter08/recipe01-runner.html"
```

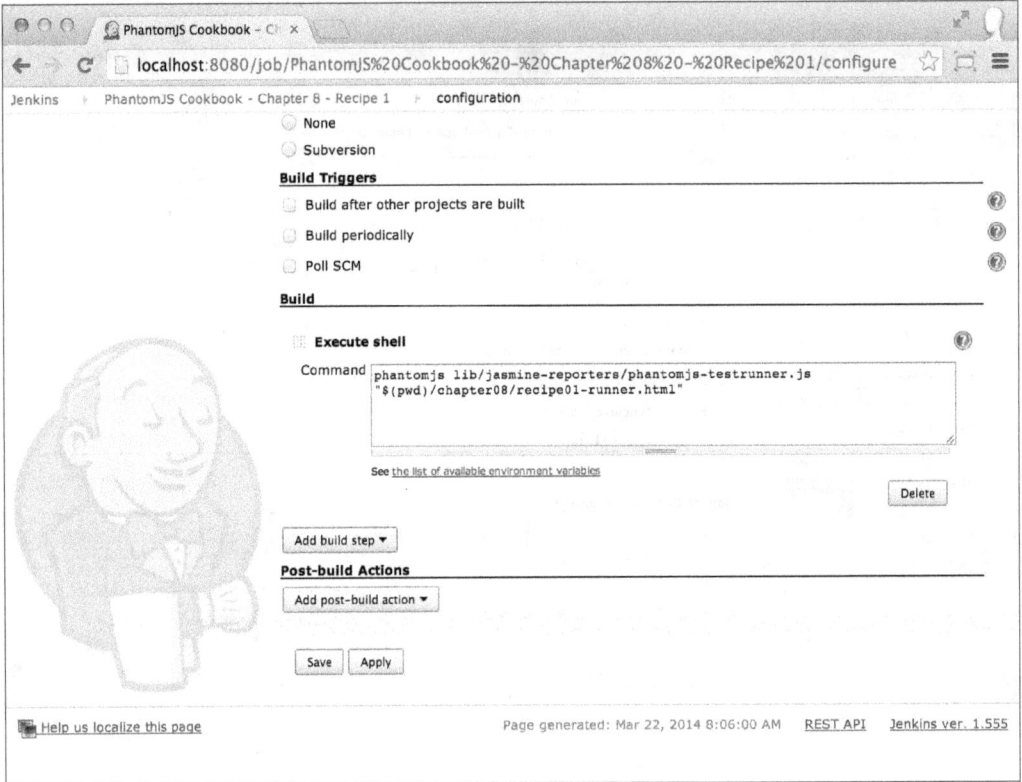

6. Click on the **Apply** (or **Save**) button at the bottom of the job's configuration page.

> The Jenkins CI project wiki has a good introduction to adding and administering software builds at `https://wiki.jenkins-ci.org/display/JENKINS/Building+a+software+project`.

4. Run the job to execute the tests. After we have added our build job, we can run it so that we can see the tests execute as follows:

1. From the Jenkins CI home page, select your job from the list in the main menu.

2. On the build job's landing page, click on the **Build Now** link in the left-side navigation.

3. The build will appear in the **Build History** panel in the left-side navigation. Clicking on the link in the panel for that specific build will take us to its page.

> If we are fast enough (or the build is slow enough), we can click on the progress bar that appears in the **Build History** panel under the currently executing build. This will bring us to the **Console Output** page for that build, and we can watch as the build executes.

4. On the build's page, we click on the **Console Output** link in the left-side navigation. This brings us to a page that lists the console output that was captured by Jenkins while running our build.

5. In the console output, we can see that our tests ran. We can also see which of our tests failed, consequently failing the build.

5. Iterate! With our build jobs running and our tests executing successfully, we can now go about the business of fixing our code, refactoring, retesting, and so forth.

How it works...

From start to finish, every step in this recipe is a fairly standard operation. The process of PhantomJS installation here is the same as was followed in *Chapter 1, Getting Started with PhantomJS*. We exposed PhantomJS to Jenkins CI by using the server's built-in tools to add the binary to PATH. We added a job to execute our tests—again using built-in tools. Finally, we ran those tests as part of our build.

The first step was covered in detail in the *Installing PhantomJS* recipe. The second and third steps are more functions of Jenkins CI than they are of PhantomJS. However, the fourth step, when we run the job, is where we need to pay the most attention.

In the *Using TerminalReporter for unit testing in PhantomJS* recipe in *Chapter 4, Unit Testing with PhantomJS*, we launched our tests using the `phantomjs.runner.sh` shell script from the `jasmine-reporters` library. This script may not function reliably when run from Jenkins CI; as such, our **Execute Shell** field does what that script would normally do, it calls the PhantomJS binary and passes it the `phantomjs-testrunner.js` script and the target URL. Our tests will execute as we expect them to, and because our test runner (`recipe01-runner.html`) uses `TerminalReporter`, we will get easy-to-read output in the console. As a result of the collection of reporters we have used in our test runner, the `phantomjs-testrunner.js` script can correctly interpret the unit test results and cause the PhantomJS process to exit with a non-zero status, thus breaking the build.

There's more...

Though our recipe uses Jenkins CI, this is primarily for demonstration purposes. There is nothing stopping us from integrating PhantomJS into a build stack that is otherwise based around Bamboo, CruiseControl, TeamCity, Travis CI, or another CI server.

The critical thing to remember when integrating PhantomJS into our build infrastructure is that we need to ensure that the PhantomJS binary is exposed through PATH to the CI server. In some cases, we might get this "for free"; depending on where we install PhantomJS, it may be available to the CI system user without the need for any special or additional configuration. Alternatively, we could manage PATH using more traditional tools at the system level by changing `/etc/profile`. Lastly, if we require more fine-grained control, we can use something such as the Environment Injector plugin for Jenkins CI to add PhantomJS on a per-job basis.

This recipe is also equally applicable to other executables built on top of PhantomJS. For example, if our job requires CasperJS to run end-to-end tests, we can follow along as before, making sure to expose the CasperJS binary on PATH in addition to (or instead of) PhantomJS.

- The *Installing PhantomJS* recipe in *Chapter 1, Getting Started with PhantomJS*
- The *Running Jasmine unit tests with PhantomJS* recipe in *Chapter 4, Unit Testing with PhantomJS*
- The *Using TerminalReporter for unit testing in PhantomJS* recipe in *Chapter 4, Unit Testing with PhantomJS*
- The *Creating a Jasmine test runner for PhantomJS and every other browser* recipe in *Chapter 4, Unit Testing with PhantomJS*

Generating JUnit reports

In this recipe, we will demonstrate how to fail builds by generating JUnit reports from tests run via PhantomJS. As in the previous recipe, our demonstration will use Jenkins CI for the sake of example.

Getting ready

We must have the PhantomJS binary exposed to the CI server, which may not necessarily share the same permissions or PATH as our user.

We need a continuous integration server set up where we can configure jobs that will use PhantomJS. Our example that follows will use the open source Jenkins CI server.

> See the previous recipe (*Setting up PhantomJS in a CI environment*) for more information on Jenkins CI and recommended plugins.

We need a project under version control with the Git source control management software. See the *Setting up PhantomJS in a CI environment* recipe, earlier in this chapter, for the Git repository URL of this book's sample code.

This project must also contain components that expect to be run and/or tested in a web browser and the tests for those components. For the sake of simplicity, we will use a simple HTML page with JavaScript and all its associated tests on that page. The web page in this recipe is available in the downloadable code repository as `recipe02-runner.html` under `chapter08`. The tests in this recipe were written using the Jasmine unit-testing library, which we introduced in *Chapter 4, Unit Testing with PhantomJS*. To execute the tests headlessly in Jenkins, we will use the `JUnitXmlReporter` object, and we will then bootstrap the testing environment using the `phantomjs-testrunner.js` script, both of which come from the `jasmine-reporters` library; these were also introduced in *Chapter 4, Unit Testing with PhantomJS*.

How to do it...

Assuming that we already have a Jenkins CI server installed and running, here is how we can fail builds and publish test reports using JUnit:

1. Configure tests to use `JUnitXmlReporter`. Most unit test suites based on Jasmine can be configured to export the JUnit-style XML reports by adding `JUnitXmlReporter` that is contained in the `jasmine-reporters` library. After including this in the test runner page with a `script` tag, we can initialize and add one of these reporters to the Jasmine environment. For example, here is what we do in `chapter08/recipe02-runner.html`:

```
var env = jasmine.getEnv();

env.addReporter(new jasmine.HtmlReporter());
env.addReporter(new jasmine.JUnitXmlReporter('test-reports/',
false));

env.execute();
```

2. Add our job in Jenkins CI and configure it to publish the JUnit reports. We can add our job by following the steps used in the previous recipe (*Setting up PhantomJS in a CI environment*; more specifically, refer to step 3 under the *How to do it...* section). However, there is one important additional step here: after applying the commands in the **Execute shell** field, we must tell Jenkins CI to publish the JUnit reports.

> When creating a new job in Jenkins CI, one of the options is **Copy existing Item**. Use this option to create the job for our second recipe more quickly, tweaking only the specific parts that need to be changed (for example, the job's name and which test runner it refers to). To copy a job, click on **New Item** from the main navigation, as usual, and type the name of the job in the **Item name** field. Then, click on the **Copy existing Item** option and type the name of the job we want to copy in the field labeled **Copy from** (Jenkins CI will automatically suggest matching names.) Lastly, click on the **OK** button.

> Note that the body of our **Execute shell** field will contain this command:
> ```
> phantomjs lib/jasmine-reporters/phantomjs-testrunner.js
>     "$(pwd)/chapter08/recipe02-runner.html"
> ```
> This corresponds with step 3.5 from the *How to do it...* section of this chapter's first recipe.

To apply these commands, perform the following steps:

1. In the job's configuration screen, click on the **Add post-build action** button and select the **Publish JUnit test result report** item.

2. In the **Publish JUnit test result report** section, find the **Test report XMLs** field and enter a pattern to match the generated XML reports, for example, `test-reports/*.xml`. Make sure that the pattern does not match any files that are not test reports.

3. Click on the **Save** button at the bottom of the job's configuration page.

3. Run the job and view the test results. We can execute tests by clicking on a specific job in Jenkins CI and then clicking on **Build Now** on the left-side navigation, as shown in the previous recipe. Again, we can click on specific completed jobs (in the **Build History** panel) and examine their outcomes, including the console output as seen in the following image:

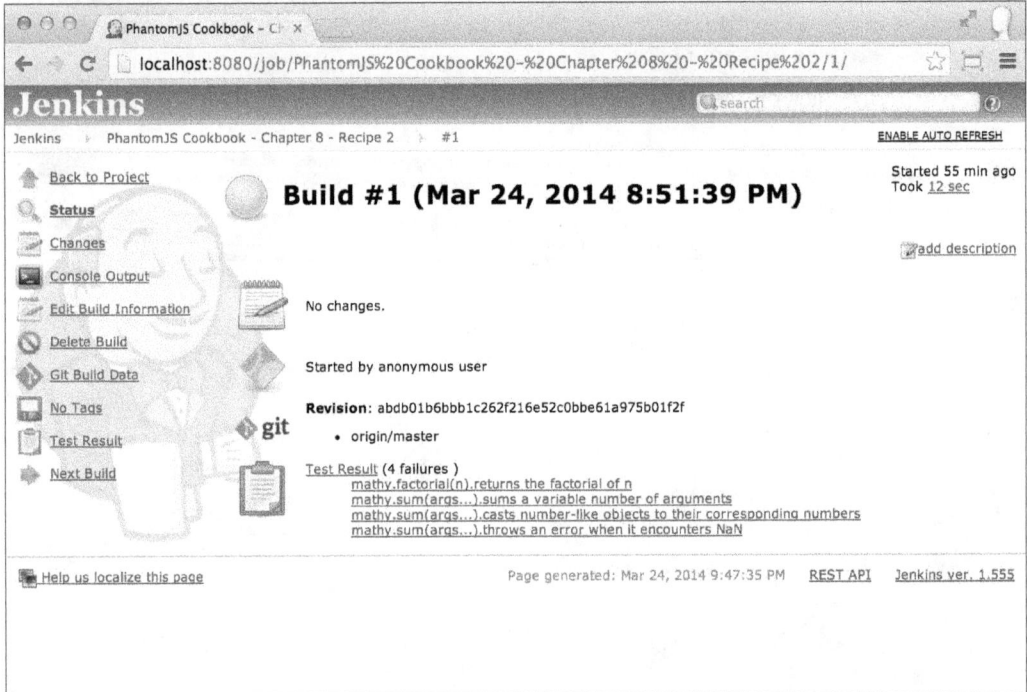

Note that Jenkins CI marks the build as **UNSTABLE** and not as **FAILURE**. This indicates that the scripts run by the job exited with a success status, but that the post-processing of the JUnit reports revealed test failures.

4. Examine the test results and iterate. As previously mentioned, we can click on individual builds and explore the test results that each job publishes. When we configured the job to publish the JUnit reports, we also exposed two more navigation items: **Test Result** and **History**. The **Test Result** page shows us the test outcomes for that specific run of the job; **History** shows us a graph of the test performance over time. We can use the data to identify defects in our code and fix issues before publishing them to production. The **Test Result** page for the first run of our job shows that four out of six tests fail, as shown in the following screenshot:

5. The history page for our job shows the test results after five runs, as seen in the following screenshot:

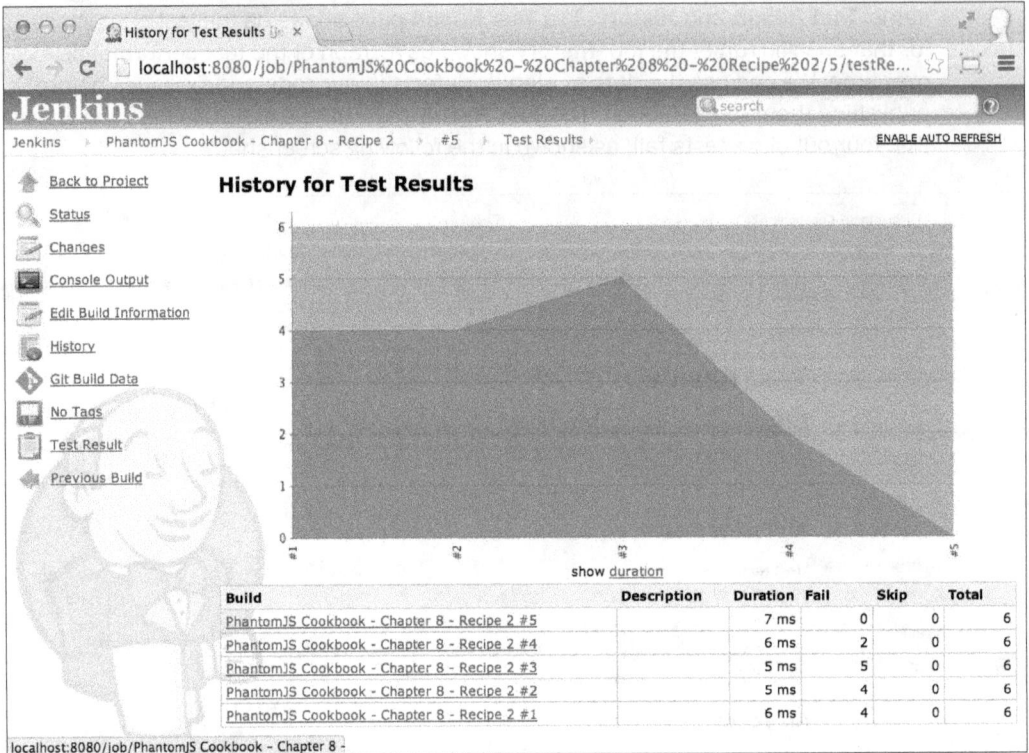

How it works...

This recipe follows the same underlying mechanisms as in the previous recipe, *Setting up PhantomJS in a CI environment*. We have our tests, we set up a job in Jenkins CI to run them, and we watch for the test results reported for each build by the CI server. In this case, we enhance Jenkins CI's ability to interpret the test results by using `JUnitXmlReporter` in our Jasmine tests. This reporter generates an XML file that contains the test results, and this file adheres to the format prescribed by JUnit, a unit-testing framework for Java that falls in the xUnit family.

Our first step is to add `JUnitXmlReporter` to our test runner. As noted before, this should be a simple matter of including the library, creating an instance of the reporter, and adding it to the Jasmine environment. The `JUnitXmlReporter` constructor function accepts three arguments:

▶ `savePath`: This indicates the directory where the XML reports should be written

> PhantomJS will create the directory if it does not already exist.

▶ `consolidate`: This indicates whether to save nested describe blocks within the same XML file as their parent (default value is `true`)
▶ `useDotNotation`: This indicates whether to separate suite names with dots instead of spaces (default value is `true`)

With the proper reporter added to our test runner, we can configure a Jenkins CI job to build the project and run the tests. Most of the job's configuration is identical to the one from the previous recipe; however, as noted before, the important difference is the addition of the Publish JUnit test result report post-build action.

It is interesting to note here that even if the tests fail, the job will be marked as a success without the post-build action. Why? In our particular example, this is because the specific combination of reporters (such as `HtmlReporter` and `JUnitXmlReporter`) does not produce markup that the `phantomjs-testrunner.js` script interprets as a failure. Thus, it does not pass a non-zero exit code to the underlying PhantomJS process, which then exits as though everything was successful. However, Jenkins CI can speak JUnit, and when we have this post-build action properly configured, it will read those XML test reports and appropriately mark the build as unstable or failed.

Lastly, Jenkins CI can produce historical reports for us about the test performance over time. This can help us to get a sense of how often we break the build, whether our test coverage grows along with our code base, and any hot spots that may benefit from refactoring.

There's more...

Our example focused on Jasmine unit tests executed in an HTML-based test runner so that we can introduce and illustrate some of the important components. However, just like we can integrate PhantomJS into most continuous integration stacks, so can we integrate most of our testing tools, for example:

▶ If we run our tests with the Karma test runner, we can install the `karma-junit-reporter` plugin, add `junit` to the `reporters` array in our configuration file, and collect our test results that way.

- If we use CasperJS for end-to-end tests, we can apply the `--xunit` argument in our call to the binary, and it will produce a JUnit-compatible XML report.

- If we choose Mocha for our tests, we can install `mocha-jenkins-reporter` using `npm`, apply the `--reporter mocha-jenkins-reporter` argument in our call to the binary, and it will produce a JUnit-compatible XML report.

When adapting this solution, the important things to remember are:

- We need a CI server that consumes JUnit-compatible XML reports

- We need a reporter for our chosen unit-testing framework, which can generate the XML

See also

- The *Running Jasmine unit tests with PhantomJS* recipe in *Chapter 4, Unit Testing with PhantomJS*

- The *Using TerminalReporter for unit testing in PhantomJS* recipe in *Chapter 4, Unit Testing with PhantomJS*

- The *Running Jasmine unit tests with the Karma test runner* recipe in *Chapter 4, Unit Testing with PhantomJS*

- The *Running Mocha unit tests with PhantomJS* recipe in *Chapter 4, Unit Testing with PhantomJS*

- The *End-to-end testing with CasperJS* recipe in *Chapter 5, Functional and End-to-end Testing with PhantomJS*

- The *Exporting test results from CasperJS in the XUnit format* recipe in *Chapter 5, Functional and End-to-end Testing with PhantomJS*

- The *Setting up PhantomJS in a CI environment* recipe

Generating TAP reports

This recipe demonstrates how to fail builds by generating TAP reports from the tests run via PhantomJS. As in the previous recipe, our demonstration will use Jenkins CI for the sake of example.

Getting ready

We must have the PhantomJS binary exposed to the CI server, which may not necessarily share the same permissions or PATH as our user.

We need a continuous integration server set up where we can configure jobs that will use PhantomJS. Our example that follows will use the open source Jenkins CI server.

> See the *Setting up PhantomJS in a CI environment* recipe (earlier in this chapter) for more information about Jenkins CI and recommended plugins.

On Jenkins CI, we need the TAP plugin installed so that we can take advantage of the TAP reports. We can install the TAP plugin in the customary fashion, using the Plugin Manager in Jenkins CI.

> For more information on the TAP plugin for Jenkins CI, visit the project page at https://wiki.jenkins-ci.org/display/JENKINS/TAP+Plugin.

We need a project under version control with the Git source control management software (see the *Setting up PhantomJS in a CI environment* recipe, earlier in this chapter, for the Git repository URL of this book's sample code).

This project must also contain components that expect to be run and/or tested in a web browser and the tests for those components. For the sake of simplicity, we will use a simple HTML page with JavaScript and all its associated tests on that page. The web page in this recipe is available in the downloadable code repository as recipe03-runner.html under chapter08. The tests in this recipe were written using the Jasmine unit-testing library, which we introduced in *Chapter 4, Unit Testing with PhantomJS*. To execute the tests headlessly in Jenkins, we will use the TapReporter object, and then bootstrap the testing environment using the phantomjs-testrunner.js script, both of which come from the jasmine-reporters library; these were also introduced in *Chapter 4, Unit Testing with PhantomJS*.

How to do it...

Assuming that we already have a Jenkins CI server installed and running, here is how we can fail builds and publish TAP reports:

1. Configure tests to use `JUnitXmlReporter`. Most unit test suites based on Jasmine can be configured to export TAP style reports by adding `TapReporter`, which is contained in the `jasmine-reporters` library. After including this in the test runner page with a `script` tag, we can initialize and add one of these reporters to the Jasmine environment. For example, here is what we do in `chapter08/recipe03-runner.html`:

```
var env = jasmine.getEnv();

env.addReporter(/PhantomJS/.test(navigator.userAgent) ?
    new jasmine.TrivialReporter() :
    new jasmine.HtmlReporter());

env.addReporter(new jasmine.TapReporter());

env.execute();
```

2. Add our job in Jenkins CI and configure it to publish the TAP reports. We can add our job by following the steps we used in this chapter's first recipe, *Setting up PhantomJS in a CI environment* (more specifically, refer to step 3 under the *How to do it...* section). However, there are a couple of important differences we need to account for in the job's configuration, which are as follows:

   1. Under the **Build** block, click on **Add build step** and the **Execute shell** item. In the new **Execute shell** field, enter the commands necessary to create the target directory for the reports, and then run the front-end tests, for example:

```
mkdir -p test-reports && phantomjs
  lib/jasmine-reporters/phantomjs-testrunner.js
  "$(pwd)/chapter08/recipe03-runner.html" >
  test-reports/recipe03.tap
```

2. Click on the **Add post-build action** button and select the **Publish TAP Results** item. In the **Publish TAP Results** section that appears, enter a value (for example, `test-reports/recipe03.tap`) in the field labeled **Test results**. Then, click on the **Advanced...** button and enable the option labeled **Failed tests mark build as failure**.

3. Click on the **Save** button at the bottom of the job's configuration page, as shown in the following screenshot:

3. Run our job and view the test results. We can execute tests as we did in the previous recipes, by clicking on the specific job, and then clicking on **Build Now** from the left-side navigation. Again, we can click on specific completed jobs (in the **Build History** panel) and examine their outcomes, including the console output.

4. Examine the test results and iterate. As mentioned before, we can click on individual builds and explore the test results that each job publishes. When we configure a job to publish the TAP reports, we also expose two more navigation items: **TAP Test Results** and **TAP Extended Test Results**. Both these views show summaries of the test results. We can use the data to identify defects in our code and fix issues before publishing them to production. Observe the TAP test results in the following screenshot:

The TAP Test Results page

Also, observe the TAP Extended test results in the following screenshot:

The TAP Extended Test Results page

How it works...

This recipe follows much the same pattern as our previous recipe, *Generating JUnit reports*. We have our tests, we set up a job in Jenkins CI to run them, and we watch for the test results reported for each build by the CI server. In this case, we are enhancing Jenkins CI's ability to interpret the test results by using `TapReporter` in our Jasmine tests and then configuring our build job to take advantage of the TAP plugin.

Our first step is to add `TapReporter` to our test runner. As we noted before, this should be a simple matter of including the library, creating an instance of the reporter, and adding it to the Jasmine environment. Unlike `JUnitXmlReporter`, the `TapReporter` constructor takes no arguments. Also, unlike `JUnitXmlReporter`, `TapReporter` writes its results to the PhantomJS console, and not the filesystem; this means that we will need to capture the TAP output.

Once we have the reporter added to our test runner, we can configure a Jenkins CI job to build the project and run the tests. Most of the job's configuration is identical to the one from this chapter's first recipe; however, as noted before, we have a couple of important differences.

The first important difference is in the Execute Shell block. The first thing that we need to do differently here is to ensure that we have created the `test-reports` directory; we do this using `mkdir`.

> If we use a Linux or OS X system, we want to make sure to use the `-p` argument to `mkdir` to ensure that our directory is created properly; if we are on Windows, we can omit this argument.

The second important difference is that we redirect the output from PhantomJS (from the `phantomjs-testrunner.js` script as it handles our target file/URL) to the filesystem. We do this because `TapReporter` does not write its output to disk of its own accord.

The next important difference is our use of the TAP plugin and the Publish TAP Results post-build action. By enabling and configuring this option, Jenkins CI is able to read the TAP report from the location we specify, parse its contents, produce the report, and then mark the build as failed if any of the tests do not pass.

See also

- The *Running Jasmine unit tests with PhantomJS* recipe in *Chapter 4, Unit Testing with PhantomJS*
- The *Automating performance analysis with YSlow and PhantomJS* recipe in *Chapter 6, Network Monitoring and Performance Analysis*
- The *Setting up PhantomJS in a CI environment* recipe
- The *Generating JUnit reports* recipe

Setting up a fully covered project in CI with PhantomJS

This recipe puts together many of the preceding lessons and illustrates how to set up a build that will use PhantomJS for automated unit, end-to-end, and performance tests, ultimately failing the build if any test fails. Our demonstration will use Jenkins CI.

Getting ready

We must have the PhantomJS binary exposed to the CI server, which may not necessarily share the same permissions or PATH as our user.

Similarly, we need CasperJS installed and exposed to the continuous integration server.

> We covered how to install CasperJS in the *Installing CasperJS* recipe in *Chapter 5, Functional and End-to-end Testing with PhantomJS*. As with the PhantomJS binary, we must take care to ensure that CasperJS is on PATH for the continuous integration server's system user; this follows the same principles that we applied in the *Setting up PhantomJS in a CI environment* recipe (earlier in this chapter).

We need a continuous integration server set up where we can configure jobs that will use PhantomJS. Our example that follows will use the open source Jenkins CI server.

> See the *Setting up PhantomJS in a CI environment* recipe (earlier in this chapter) for more information on Jenkins CI and recommended plugins.

We need a project under version control with the Git source control management software (see the *Setting up PhantomJS in a CI environment* recipe, earlier in this chapter, for the Git repository URL of this book's sample code).

This project must also contain components that expect to be run and/or tested in a web browser and the tests for those components. The tests in this recipe will run against the /form-demo URL in the phantomjs-sandbox application that is included with the cookbook's sample code repository. All the tests in question appear under the phantomjs-sandbox/tests/ directory.

The unit tests were written using the Jasmine unit testing library, which we introduced in *Chapter 4, Unit Testing with PhantomJS*. To execute the tests headlessly in Jenkins, we will use the `JUnitXmlReporter` object, and then bootstrap the testing environment using the `phantomjs-testrunner.js` script, both of which come from the `jasmine-reporters` library; these were also introduced in *Chapter 4, Unit Testing with PhantomJS*. The unit test files include `unit/form-demo-validators-spec.js` and its test runner, `unit/form-demo-validators-runner.html`.

The end-to-end tests were written using CasperJS and its testing DSL, which we introduced in the *End-to-end testing with CasperJS* recipe in *Chapter 5, Functional and End-to-end Testing with PhantomJS*. The end-to-end test file is `chapter08-recipe05-spec.js` under e2e.

The performance test will be run with the YSlow library, which we introduced in the *Executing a detailed performance analysis* recipe in *Chapter 6, Network Monitoring and Performance Analysis*. YSlow is included in the `lib` directory of the cookbook's sample code repository and will be referenced in our build job.

Both the end-to-end and performance tests run against the demo site that is included with the cookbook's sample code repository. To run the demo site, we must have Node.js installed. In order to run the demo site during the continuous integration build properly, we need a wrapper script to launch the site, run the end-to-end and performance tests, collect their results, and kill the Node.js process. This wrapper script is included in the repository as `test-wrapper.sh` under `phantomjs-sandbox/tests`.

How to do it...

Assuming that we already have a Jenkins CI server installed and running, here is how we can configure and run a build with unit, end-to-end, and performance tests, publishing test reports using JUnit, and failing the build should any of these tests fail:

1. Configure unit tests to use `JUnitXmlReporter`. The first step is to ensure that the Jasmine-based unit tests can write their test results as JUnit-style XML reports. For this, we need to add `JUnitXmlReporter` from the `jasmine-reporters` library to our test runner.

> We discussed how to add `JUnitXmlReporter` in the *Generating JUnit reports* recipe earlier in this chapter.

2. Create a wrapper script to run the end-to-end and performance tests. As mentioned in the *Getting ready* section of this recipe, our CI job will need a wrapper script to run the demo app, execute the end-to-end and performance tests, and then shut down the app. The cookbook's sample code repository includes an example of such a script at `phantomjs-sandbox/tests/test-wrapper.sh` as shown:

```
#!/bin/bash
cd phantomjs-sandbox
node app.js > /dev/null 2>&1 &
NODE_PID=$!

cd ..

casperjs test --xunit="test-reports/TEST-casperjs-e2e.xml"
  --no-colors
    phantomjs-sandbox/tests/e2e/chapter08-recipe05-spec.js
E2E_STATUS=$?

echo "Running performance test with YSlow..."
phantomjs lib/yslow.js -i grade -f junit http://localhost:3000/
form-demo >
  test-reports/TEST-form-demo-yslow.xml
PERF_STATUS=$?
echo "Performance test results stored in
  test-reports/TEST-form-demo-yslow.xml"

kill $NODE_PID

[ $E2E_STATUS = 0 -a $PERF_STATUS = 0 ]; exit $?
```

3. Add our job to Jenkins CI and configure it to execute our tests and publish their reports. We can add our job by following the steps that were used in this chapter's first and second recipes (*Setting up PhantomJS in a CI environment* and *Generating JUnit reports*, respectively). The steps that follow here refer to adding the runner for the wrapper script that executes the end-to-end and performance tests:

   1. In the job's configuration screen, click on the **Add build step** button and select the **Execute shell** item to add a second **Execute shell** block.

   2. In the second **Execute shell** block, add the following command to run your wrapper script:

      `./phantomjs-sandbox/tests/test-wrapper.sh`

   3. Click on the **Save** button at the bottom of the job's configuration page.

> It may be helpful to "clean" the `test-reports/` directory in the Jenkins CI workspace before each run. The simplest way to do this is to add another **Execute shell** block that deletes the directory, using the following command:
>
> `rm -rf test-reports/`
>
> Make sure to reorder the **Execute shell** blocks so that they run before all the tests.

4. Run our job and view the test results. We can run our comprehensive test suite here, which is similar to the suites in our previous recipes that featured Jenkins CI, by clicking on a specific job, and then clicking on **Build Now** from the left-side navigation. Again, we can click on specific completed jobs (in the **Build History** panel) and examine their outcome, including the console output.

5. Examine the test results and iterate. As mentioned in previous recipes, we can click on individual builds and explore the test results that each job publishes. Of particular interest to us is the **Test Result** page where we find a summary of all the test failures. As we expect, the post-build action that publishes the JUnit test reports aggregates the test results from all of our test phases—unit, end-to-end, and performance—and not only displays them as a single report but also marks the build as a failure if any of these test phases produces a failure. With this knowledge, we can fix or improve our code before taking it to production.

How it works...

This recipe demonstrates that it is possible, and with relatively minimal effort, to set up a comprehensive automated test suite as part of our front-end build process. Our job can execute our unit tests, run an instance of our application, execute end-to-end and performance tests against it, and collect the test results. This recipe does not even illustrate the other types of work that we may want in our continuous integration job, such as linting, minification, or concatenation of JavaScript assets.

Our first step is to add `JUnitXmlReporter` to our unit tests. This is an essential step in making our unit tests first-class citizens of the continuous integration build. As we noted in previous recipes, most unit test runners need no special modifications—we can simply drop in the reporter, add it to the Jasmine environment, and the tests will produce the XML.

Secondly, we need a wrapper script for our end-to-end and performance tests so that we can ensure that our specimen application is started properly and remains running for the duration of the tests. This wrapper script will perform the following actions:

1. Start the Node.js demo app, forward its console output to `/dev/null`, and capture its process ID.

2. Run the CasperJS end-to-end tests, specifying the `--no-colors` argument (to make the Jenkins CI console output easier to read) and the `--xunit` argument (with the path of the file where it will write its reports).

3. Run the YSlow performance test, indicating grade-level information and JUnit-style output.

4. Kill the Node.js demo app using the process ID we captured earlier.

5. Exit the script with the appropriate status code.

With our unit tests ready and the wrapper script in place for our end-to-end and performance tests, we can add the job in Jenkins CI. We have already discussed at length how to add and run these jobs in previous recipes. The main thing that sets this recipe apart from the others in this chapter is that it aggregates the test results after the build has completed. This allows us to fail a build if any of our established tests fail, regardless of whether those tests are at the unit, the functional, or the performance level.

See also

▶ The *Running Jasmine unit tests with PhantomJS* recipe in *Chapter 4, Unit Testing with PhantomJS*

▶ The *Installing CasperJS* recipe in *Chapter 5, Functional and End-to-end Testing with PhantomJS*

▶ The *End-to-end testing with CasperJS* recipe in *Chapter 5, Functional and End-to-end Testing with PhantomJS*

▶ The *Executing a detailed performance analysis* recipe in *Chapter 6, Network Monitoring and Performance Analysis*

▶ The *Setting up PhantomJS in a CI environment* recipe

▶ The *Generating JUnit reports* recipe

Index

Q

QImage class 224
Qt 9
QUnit 143
QUnit tests
  running, with PhantomJS 142-145

R

Read-Evaluate-Print Loop (REPL) 7, 11
readLine method 59
read method 59
remote-debugger-autorun argument 25, 32
remote-debugger-port argument 25, 31
renderBase64 method 227, 228
render method
  about 222-225
  output formats 224
reporters 119
reporters, Jasmine
  ConsoleReporter 123
  JUnitXmlReporter 123
  TapReporter 123
  TeamcityReporter 123
requestData object
  properties 103
require method
  about 60
  versus injectJs method 41
resourceError object
  properties 107
responsive designs
  testing, with PhantomJS 244-248
Ruby 160
RubyGems
  URL, for downloading 160
run-jasmine.js script 120
runtime
  version, inspecting at 34

S

Scalable Vector Graphics. *See* SVGs
scrolling
  simulating 92-95

seek method 59
Selenium 152
Selenium client
  Webdriver, using as 156-159
Selenium Standalone Server JAR
  URL, for downloading 156
Selenium tests
  running, with GhostDriver 152-155
  running, with PhantomJS 152-155
sendEvent method
  about 87
  button argument 87
  mouse events 87
simple performance analysis
  configuration options 194
  executing 192-194
Source
  PhantomJS, installing from 10
sourceURL property 44
specifications 117
stream methods
  flush 59
  read 59
  seek 59
  write 59
  writeLine 59
stream object 58
suites 117
SVGs
  rasterizing, from PhantomJS 228-230
  rendering, from PhantomJS 228-230
system environment variables
  inspecting 50-52
system module 51

T

TAP format
  using 216-218
TapReporter 123
TAP reports
  generating 267-273
TeamcityReporter 123
TerminalReporter
  using, for unit testing 121-123
TerminalReporter constructor 123
Test Anything Protocol. *See* TAP format

[PACKT] PUBLISHING | open source*
community experience distilled

Thank you for buying
PhantomJS Cookbook

About Packt Publishing

Packt, pronounced 'packed', published its first book "*Mastering phpMyAdmin for Effective MySQL Management*" in April 2004 and subsequently continued to specialize in publishing highly focused books on specific technologies and solutions.

Our books and publications share the experiences of your fellow IT professionals in adapting and customizing today's systems, applications, and frameworks. Our solution based books give you the knowledge and power to customize the software and technologies you're using to get the job done. Packt books are more specific and less general than the IT books you have seen in the past. Our unique business model allows us to bring you more focused information, giving you more of what you need to know, and less of what you don't.

Packt is a modern, yet unique publishing company, which focuses on producing quality, cutting-edge books for communities of developers, administrators, and newbies alike. For more information, please visit our website: www.packtpub.com.

About Packt Open Source

In 2010, Packt launched two new brands, Packt Open Source and Packt Enterprise, in order to continue its focus on specialization. This book is part of the Packt Open Source brand, home to books published on software built around Open Source licenses, and offering information to anybody from advanced developers to budding web designers. The Open Source brand also runs Packt's Open Source Royalty Scheme, by which Packt gives a royalty to each Open Source project about whose software a book is sold.

Writing for Packt

We welcome all inquiries from people who are interested in authoring. Book proposals should be sent to author@packtpub.com. If your book idea is still at an early stage and you would like to discuss it first before writing a formal book proposal, contact us; one of our commissioning editors will get in touch with you.

We're not just looking for published authors; if you have strong technical skills but no writing experience, our experienced editors can help you develop a writing career, or simply get some additional reward for your expertise.

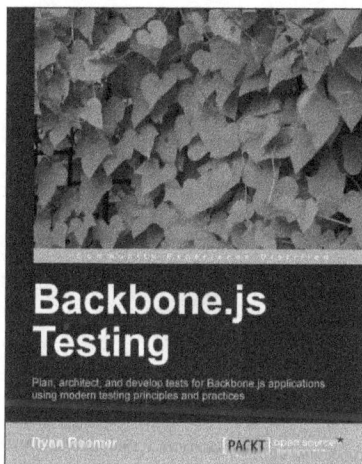

Backbone.js Testing

ISBN: 978-1-78216-524-8   Paperback: 168 pages

Plan, architect, and develop tests for Backbone.js applications using modern testing principles and practices

1. Create comprehensive test infrastructures.

2. Understand and utilize modern frontend testing techniques and libraries.

3. Use mocks, spies, and fakes to effortlessly test and observe complex Backbone.js application behavior.

4. Automate tests to run from the command line, shell, or practically anywhere.

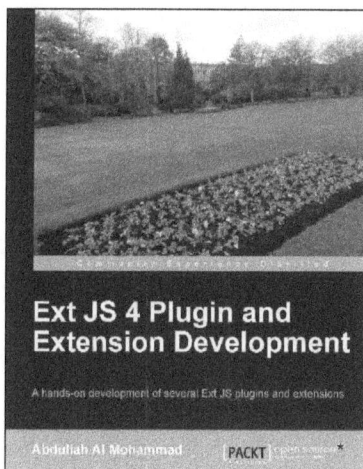

Ext JS 4 Plugin and Extension Development

ISBN: 978-1-78216-372-5   Paperback: 116 pages

A hands-on development of several Ext JS plugins and extensions

1. Easy-to-follow examples on Ext JS plugins and extensions.

2. Step-by-step instructions on developing Ext JS plugins and extensions.

3. Provides a walkthrough of several useful Ext JS libraries and communities.

Please check **www.PacktPub.com** for information on our titles

* 9 7 8 1 7 8 3 9 8 1 9 2 2 *